I L♥VE
MONDAYS

I LVE MONDAYS

and Other Confessions
from Devoted Working Moms

MICHELLE COVE

SEAL

I LOVE MONDAYS
and Other Confessions from Devoted Working Moms

Copyright © 2012 Michelle Cove

Published by
SEAL PRESS
A Member of the Perseus Books Group
1700 Fourth Street
Berkeley, California

Library of Congress Cataloging-in-Publication Data

Cove, Michelle.
  I love Mondays : and other confessions from devoted working moms /
Michelle Cove.
      p. cm.
  Includes bibliographical references.
  ISBN 978-1-58005-435-5
  1. Working mothers. 2. Work and family. 3. Parenting. 4. Mother and
child. I. Title.
  HQ759.48.C67 2012
  306.874--dc23
                          2012032851

10 9 8 7 6 5 4 3 2 1

Cover and interior design by Kate Basart
Printed in the United States of America
Distributed by Publishers Group West

For Ezra and Risa Cove, my safe harbor

CONTENTS

INTRODUCTION

My daughter, Risa, was three years old when I started my first documentary. I was thirty-eight . . . and a little scared. I'd never even made a home video before! Plus, I knew nothing about filmmaking, but as a writer, I knew how to tell stories, so I figured I'd learn as I went—cheaper than film school, if not a little more chaotic. I sent out a request to family and friends who worked in creative industries, asking if they knew anyone in the film business that I could speak with for inspiration or practical tips. It turned out that my brother knew a successful documentary editor living in Los Angeles who would speak to me. Gold! This guy (I'll call him "J") was a twentysomething editor with true Hollywood street cred, and he graciously agreed to answer my questions by phone, with one stipulation: it had to be *that day* at 2:00 PM because he was leaving the next day for Japan and wouldn't be back for several weeks. So I said "no problem" and prayed my daughter would be napping at that time, according to schedule. (Yes, you are rolling your eyes right now because you know that kids don't *ever* follow schedules when we need them to, and they certainly don't fall asleep at a specified time. But you have to understand, I felt desperate.)

Before the editor's call, I paced around the house, rehearsing the questions in my head, counting down the minutes, trying to remember everything I wanted to know. I put Risa down for her nap a few minutes before 2 PM. Not a hint of resistance; I closed the door quietly and breathed a sigh of relief. The editor called right on time, I gave him the project background, and just as we were getting to the good stuff (the tips I needed), I heard my daughter yelling from upstairs: "Mamaaaa!" I tried to ignore it, but her calls got louder. "MAMA!" *Damn it. She's fine, leave her*, I thought, trying to focus on what J was saying. *What if there is something wrong?* I suddenly thought. Then tried to squelch *that* thought too: *What could happen to her if she's contained in a crib with a soft blanket? Then again, you hear horror stories about kids strangling on curtain cords!* That was it. I tiptoed to her room with the phone cradled to my ear and opened the door as quietly as I could, trying to focus on the phone conversation. Just behind the door, my girl stood clad in diaper only, covered head to toe in diaper cream. Within the span of fifteen minutes, she'd apparently climbed out of her crib, found the cream, disrobed, removed the cap, and painted her face and body with the thick white paste. She looked like Casper the Friendly Ghost and seemed delighted with herself. At another time, any other time, this might have been funny.

I assessed the situation the best I could: There was no apparent damage; however, it would take just a few finger smears to the face to get that cream directly in her eye or mouth. (*Could she go blind? Was it poisonous?!*) *Argh!* The editor was now waiting for me to respond to something he'd said, and I had to make a quick decision. I looked around her room, grabbed a set of crayons and paper, and threw them (oh, yes, *threw them*) on the floor by her feet, closed the door, went to the stairwell, and finished the call. In the end, my daughter took the bait and distracted herself by making artwork. She lived to see another day, and I received helpful information on how to get started with my documentary. I can't say I'm proud of my actions, but it was the best I could think to do in the moment.

I'm sure you've been there yourself. After all, more than 70 percent of women with a child over age one work outside the home, according to the International Association of Working Mothers.[1] What do we all have in common? Guilt. In fact, if you Google "hardest part of being a working mom," you'll find pages upon pages of blog entries from moms around the U.S. worrying they are not giving enough of themselves to their kids. While some wish they could afford to stay home with their child, many of us *want* to be working and understand that if we were home making sock puppets or painting egg cartons with our kids on weekday afternoons, we'd end up sniffing too much Elmer's glue. If you're like me, you crave—no *need*—intellectual stimulation and an office of your own. We love being "Mommy" but also cherish our work title that connects us to the outside world and makes us feel needed in ways beyond parenting.

I learned over the past few years that we're all sick of pointless and pressure-inducing mantras like "find the balance" and "you can have it all." Please! We are big girls who know that juggling a career and family is messy and complicated. It was freeing to hear Anne-Marie Slaughter--a professor of politics and international affairs at Princeton University, and the mother of two teenage boys--say in her Atlantic Magazine cover story "Why Women Still Can't Have it All" last July, "I'd been telling young women at my lectures that you can have it all . . . I'd been part, albeit unwittingly, of making millions of women feel that they are to blame if they cannot . . . rise up the ladder as fast as men and also have a family and an active home life . . ."[2]

Yes, let's stop striving to "have it all," and put our attention, as Slaughter suggests, on where it belongs: creating more flexibility in the work place so women (and men) can attend to both their career and their family—and not get penalized in the future for making a "lateral" move professionally for the sake of the family. We can also open up to each other about how and when we're struggling with the work-parent juggle so we know we're not alone in navigating this rocky terrain. Says Gina Robison-Billups, president of the International Association of Working Mothers, "When we share our guilt and that terrible feeling that we're not giving enough of ourselves to our kids, we realize that other moms feel the same way—it's incredibly liberating."[3] In fact, if you ever want to bond with another working mom, just ask her: "What was the moment when you almost lost your mind trying to balance career and family?" We all have at least one of these bad-mommy stories, and sharing these confessions is like offering one another gifts that say "Hey, we're all struggling with this, and that doesn't mean it's not worth it." Even though we *choose* this path, it's hard, and we're all making it up as we go.

Back to my "bad mommy" tale (and not my only one, mind you). After Risa's body-painting session, I decided not to tell my husband—or anyone else for that matter. I felt awful about the whole thing and feared people would look at me with disdain or horror. But the next week, I had a change of heart and decided to tell several of my working-mom friends. Far from criticizing me, they gasped, laughed, sighed, and groaned. Each one shared her own bad-mommy stories—those special times they were certain that the Department of Social Services would come remove their child because mommy had gone *too far*. In all of these stories, there were no right answers or wrong answers (no one was talking about physical or mental child abuse, just less-than-stellar judgment calls), and we didn't judge each other—we all understood how easy it was to stumble in panicky moments of juggling parenting and career. One thing is for sure, we all felt better after sharing our humbling stories. Plus, barrier broken, we started to truly open up to one another and ask, "What would you do in this situation?" or "What can I do if this happens?"

What a relief! Why hadn't we gone here before?

My friends and I had compared dating horror stories and wedding fiascoes and pregnancy scares. We lived for sharing our new-mom confessions, snorting at what we'd done in our various states of mental and physical exhaustion: leaving the telephone in the freezer, more than once (that was me); driving around several times a week with wallets and coffee cups on top of our cars; weeping in front of the UPS man; falling asleep at high-level company meetings. Sharing our tales of embarrassment and woe deepened our connections and made us feel . . . well, less nuts. So why hadn't we done this when dealing with our working-mom horror stories? What's so different about *this* stress that made it untouchable?

Working-mom guilt is just different. It's one thing to make bad choices because we are exhausted from giving *so much* to our children. But it's quite another when we are possibly putting our own needs before our child's. It starts when maternity leave is over and it is time to reenter the work world, which usually comes with a wave of anxiety and, let's get real, for many of us, a wash of relief to be back in the company of actual grown-ups. Even while we feel pangs of separation from our child, we are enthralled with the idea of peeing alone and not having to figure out where to leave the baby. Many of us practically skipped back to the office (even with our doubts), and our worlds then split definitively into family and career. Now taking time away for work meant robbing the family and vice versa. Suddenly, our brains would be engaged in a constant state of tug-of-war.

When we open up about this burden, we *help* relieve our stress while bringing down our guilt. I know this from personal experience and from hearing it over and over from working moms around the country. That's why we need to get over our embarrassment at not handling the juggle well—and our shame when we botch it—and talk to one another, so we don't have to carry the weight of this alone. In addition to offering empathy and a listening ear, we often have *sound advice* to offer each other (or warn against) based on real life experiences. There's no reason we each have to reinvent the wheel—at least not alone.

That's what this book is all about: a way to open the conversation, help working moms see we're all in this together, and offer strategies that have already been tested by moms as well as experts. Let's not discount the fact that good advice from an expert can change our lives immediately if we are willing to hear it and put it into effect. In researching and writing this book, I talked with numerous child psychologists, women's life coaches, pediatricians, daycare providers, teachers, business consultants, therapists, social workers, executive coaches, and others, and you'll find the very best of their advice woven throughout this book. I know I'm already parenting differently and with more confidence having heard their wise words, and I'm excited to share them with you.

What's Different About This Book . . .

- -

There are so many self-help books on the market telling women not to feel guilty about being a working mom, and assuring them they are entitled to their happiness. That's nice, but it's not really helpful when your daughter is clinging to your thigh as you're trying to get out the door to make the flight to your work conference; or your son is furious because you're missing his soccer tournament due to a mandatory company-wide talk; or your coworkers are pissed off because you have to leave early to pick up your child for early dismissal while they pick up the slack; or your child has strep throat and you are due in a funder's meeting in twenty minutes. Sure, you're entitled to happiness. So what? You need a plan, not a platitude.

With so many moms in the workplace right now, I often wondered why there weren't dozens of books like this out there already. Maybe it's because only now is it starting to become socially acceptable for women to admit that they even *like* their jobs and prefer *not* to stay home with their children all day long. In a 2009 blog post on "Working Moms" (www.circleofmoms.com), a mother in one forum asked, "Am I the only working mom who doesn't feel guilty about working?" Over 980 moms commented, the majority saying that they too like their work and would go stir-crazy if they were stay-at-home parents.[4] In a 2009 blog entry in *The Washington Post* titled "What About Moms Who Want to Work?"—for which guest blogger Stephanie Himel-Nelson wrote about being a mother who loves her full-time job—hundreds of women wrote comments congratulating the author and thanking her for expressing how she felt. It's a relief for women to hear publicly that it is not only *acceptable* to work if you're a mom, but it's alright to go ahead and enjoy it.[5]

The Moms I Connected With . . .

I started this book by creating a survey for working moms, asking what they enjoy most about their career and what their biggest parenting worries are. I also asked them to describe a particularly difficult emotional challenge, and the one piece of advice they would tell other working moms when it came to dealing with the juggle. I received over one hundred emails from moms who live in small towns, cities, and 'burbs all over the country, with kids ranging in age from infancy to late teens (with most under age twelve), and who represented a wide array of professions. I heard from marketers, filmmakers, organization directors, entrepreneurs, doctors, editors, teachers, managers, artists, and so on.

It was interesting to me that so few of the women said the paycheck is the "best part" of working, although clearly this is an enormous and often necessary benefit. Instead, they said the greatest reward is the sense of *meaning* and *fulfillment* their work provides them. They enjoy being stimulated intellectually by the work; by problem solving, engaging with bright adults, and feeling like they're accomplishing something important. They love the feeling of adding something—an idea or product or service—to the world and the pride that stems from doing so. Some cherish the freedom of working for themselves with a flexible schedule while others enjoy being part of a large team and all the benefits that come from that. Other responses to the joys of working included "It's so nice and quiet at the office," "I can calmly read emails while drinking coffee," "People listen when I talk!" and "I feel like me."

The "hardest part" of working, most moms said, was the guilt they felt, and it came in two varieties: guilt over not being there enough for their children, and guilt for not doing enough at work because they were caring for their kids. Women also spoke of ongoing daily concerns, such as, "The worst part of my day is the hour commute from home to work when I can't switch gears," and "I can't even remember going on a date with my husband"; or more specific concerns, such as, "I worry my one-year-old will feel less loved if I drop him off at daycare a few minutes early so I can get a coffee for my commute," and "My son's asthma and teething issues joined forces on the same night that I had to create an important questionnaire for work."

I talked to dozens of working moms on the phone to dig more deeply into the survey results. The mothers I spoke with, I should point out, had little or no interest in being "supermoms," a term used over the last several years by the media to describe mothers striving to be perfect and "do it all." The moms I talked with have clearly tossed aside the goal of being perfect for enjoying their careers while raising well-adjusted kids. They don't feel the need to bake brownies from scratch for the bake sale or make organic play dough for their children. In fact, this hardcore mommying seemed downright laughable to many of them. They want to know how to handle their supervisor's wrath when they must leave early to pick up their child at school early during a work crunch. Or how to explain to their child that Mommy can't come to the school picnic because she has to meet an important client or she might lose her account. They want to feel successful at working and parenting; they aren't looking to be exemplary.

What You Can Expect from This Book . . .

I looked over all the interviews and surveys and divided them into the eleven most common worries, or "confessions" for working moms (I admit "top 10" is catchier but what can I tell you? There are eleven). I've given each particular confession its own chapter. Within that chapter you'll hear from working moms who share their biggest worries, where they stem from, and how to combat them. In addition to reassurance, you'll find specific, hands-on steps to creating limits and boundaries that minimize guilt and maximize confidence in your ability to juggle work and family. The strategies come from parenting experts, the moms I spoke with, and my own personal experiences.

Know in advance that this book validates, even celebrates, your desire to work. As for how to use it, you can read this book cover to cover, or skip ahead to the issues you find tough *right now*. As all of us know, the concerns we experience keep changing. Once you handle one, another pops up like an amusement park game of Whack-a-Mole. The idea is not to get to a place where there are no issues (oh, wouldn't that be swell?) but to get a clearer understanding of what strategies make life easier for you and your family. This will give you more energy and strengthen your reserves, while boosting your confidence at work and at home. Why is this good? As the old saying goes, "If Mama is happy, everybody is happy."

Chapter 1

THE SORRY LOOP

Confession: "I'm tired of apologizing when I can't please everyone."

T he morning begins with you rolling out of bed, trying to get everyone, including yourself, dressed and fed—and apologizing to your child about something. It may be that you don't have time to play hide-and-seek, help with his math homework (which happens to be due today), or search for the library books gone missing again. You don't have time, you explain for the umpteenth time, because you have to get to work. You are late. Your child stares at you blankly or possibly emotionally unravels while you zip up your jacket and try to remain calm. You can sense the situation is about to devolve into a full-on explosion, and to defuse the situation, you offer an apology: "I'm sorry, sweetie, but Mommy really has to go to the office." This leads to tears of frustration from your child (perhaps your own are forming), and even more zealous rounds of "I'm really sorry."

On top of that, maybe you're also apologizing to caretakers, teachers, supervisors, or coworkers on a fairly regular basis. After entering your child's classroom, for instance, the teacher asks if you can stay for a few minutes because she has to tell you about a new development in your child's behavior. Of course you want to hear it (although, oh please, let it be a good development), but you also have to haul your butt out of here because there is a work meeting starting in thirty minutes that you'll just make if you leave this second. You head to work feeling horrible about bailing on your child's teacher; or you can stay put, be late for work, and have to apologize profusely to your boss or coworkers. Someone is going to be ticked off—and *you* are going to be the bad guy.

In all of these situations, everyone will recover—hey, they always do—but at what and whose expense? What does it say if you keep making empty apologies to your child or coworkers? At what point will your apologies actually start to lose meaning? How does asking forgiveness so routinely affect your basic sense of worth? What you'd also really like to know is, given how hard you're trying to make everyone happy, shouldn't someone be acknowledging your efforts and accomplishments?

QUIZ: ARE YOU A BROKEN RECORD OF APOLOGIES?

1. **Your child was expecting to go out for ice cream with you tonight but you just found out you have to stay late at the office due to an unexpected deadline. You:**
   a. panic because your child is going to be an emotional wreck. He was counting on this, and you hate being the villain.
   b. decide, "Deadline be damned!" and when your boss is distracted, you sneak out of the office and back to your home.
   c. explain to your child that you have to stay late at work unexpectedly, apologize sincerely, and pick a new date for your outing.

2. **Your child is clinging to your thigh as you try to make your way out the door to get to the office. You're already ten minutes late, so you:**
   a. spiral into an athletic reverse turn so your child loses his grip, and then you make a mad dash for the car.
   b. give your child a hug, let him know you can't wait to be together later, and head out the door.
   c. take off your coat and try not to cry as you explain (just as you did yesterday and the day before) why Mommy has to work and when you will be home.

3. **Your daughter asks you to make her an intricate French braid before play rehearsal, but you are supposed to be on a conference call in five minutes. You:**
   a. tell her you can't right now but will do it happily for the next rehearsal if she wants.
   b. make her the French braid; you'll tell everyone on the conference call that your cell phone died.
   c. distract her by telling her there are cookies on the counter if she wants to have one right now!

Answers: If you answered "c" for number 1, give yourself one point. If you answered "b" for number 2, give yourself one point. If you answered "a" for number 3, give yourself one point. If you received at least two points, you're on the right track for not over-apologizing. If you received less, pay extra attention to the steps in this chapter because—sorry to say—you're going to need them.

Reality Check
- - - - - - - - - - - - -

You've established a meaningful career that helps you maintain a sense of identity beyond "Mama" while allowing you to bring home the bacon to pay family bills. You're a loving mom who wants to be there for her children, and while the two sometimes clash, that doesn't mean you've done anything to apologize for.

Providing your child with a model of what it looks like to have a career *and* a loving family is something to be *proud* of. That's easy to forget in the midst of trying to juggle the two—a messy and underappreciated job in itself. But reaping the rewards of work and family is a model we clearly believe in, which is why we deal with the hassles and occasional heartbreaks. We want our children to grow up to also find this balance, and to retain a strong sense of individual identity that's not limited to their role as parent (and, hey, if their jobs happen to pay so handsomely that they can purchase us ocean-front property when we retire, that'd be fine too). It's not our job to make this model look easy (which would be false advertising, at best). Rather, it should illustrate to our child that it's worthwhile to experience both domains, in spite of the complications. Apologize for showing our kid *this*? No way.

I love what Sara, a foundation program director from Rhode Island, had to say about trying to balance her job with producing a film and parenting her one-year-old son, Oscar: "All working moms, no matter who they are or what they do, constantly hear a nagging voice of doubt echoing in their own brains. For me, in making a film in addition to my 9-to-5 job, it's doubt and guilt multiplied. In that echo chamber, I hear myself asking: 'Am I selling the film short? Selling Oscar short? Neglecting my husband? Performing well enough at work?' But when I am able to push through this self-interrogation, I know that being a mom has given me a new sense of bravery. After years of supporting the artistic practice of others, it is only now as a mother that I have taken on a project with producing a film that I can truly call my own. I'm doing it for myself, yes, and for the greater good I think this story will bring to bear, but I'm also doing it for Oscar. I want my son to see his mother working hard to pursue her own dreams. For me, it's important, for both his freedom and mine, to understand that we can be a close and loving family who supports each other in life's adventures, wherever they may take us."

Nor should working moms have to say we're sorry at work so often for taking care of our child, as long as we're meeting expectations and achieving goals. It's all too easy to get wrapped up in apologizing for having to run out early or show up ten minutes late, and not be able to join our colleagues for post-work social outings. But caring for our child and making sure she is thriving comes first, every working mom I interviewed told me, and that's not something we need to ask forgiveness for. We can't control what our coworkers and/or boss think of us putting family first at these times; we *can* decide how we respond to any comments or accusations made about us when we've missed the occasional meeting or obligation to be there for our child. Reining in our apologies is the first step in the right direction, along with using them only when it is truly appropriate. Says Bonnie Marcus, a motivational speaker and president of Women's Success Coaching: "Women tend to over-apologize because we are always trying to make everyone happy. If an apology is necessary because we made a *mistake*, we should apologize. We lose our integrity and power when we over-apologize. It may make us feel better in the short term because of our desire to have everyone like us. However, we pay the consequences in the long term when we lose the respect of our children and boss by taking a subservient position when it is unnecessary."

So let's talk about how to break the nasty habit of overdoing the apologies once and for all.

Step 1: *Check your inner apologize-o-meter.*

Linda, thirty-five, is an accountant with two boys under age seven who discovered one day just how much of an over-apologizer she was. "The two months leading up to the tax deadline are nuts, and I barely have time to breathe. I find myself apologizing all the time without even thinking about it—to clients if it takes me a few extra hours to get them my questions, to my family members because I'm sometimes absentminded during this time. One afternoon, I was hoping to get to the grocery store during this crazy period to buy the special grape popsicles my sons love as a surprise, but I ran out of time and couldn't get there. I apologized to them both the second I got home for not being able to get the popsicles, and they just looked at me blank-faced because they didn't know I was planning to do this. It was a strange moment, and I kind of realized I had been apologizing all day long. So it just fell out of my mouth."

The first step to reducing needless apologies is realizing how much we are doing it. If you're not sure, but suspect that you might be on the extreme side, follow the advice of clinical psychologist Janet L. Wolfe, PhD, who recommends keeping a log for one week.[1] Record each time an "I'm sorry" pops out of your mouth, what happened just before the habit (in this case, apologizing without good reason), and how you were feeling at the time. The next step, Wolfe says, is to analyze the data and look at what your triggers are. Do you apologize when you're feeling guilty or sad about upsetting your child or boss? Do you do it because you can't think of anything else to say on the spot? All this tracking is not to make us feel bad about our behavior (heck, the last thing we need is more guilt) but to help us *notice* the pattern so we can tweak or change our behavior if necessary.

Plenty of women whom I talked with already had suspicions, or at least a hunch, that they were tipping the apologize-o-meter, such as one mom who admitted, "If I counted how many mornings start with me saying, 'I'm really sorry, but I have to go *right now*,' I would tape my mouth closed." Another confessed, "I say 'I'm sorry' like some people say 'hello,'" and yet another mom said, "When my boss sees me heading toward him after 3:30 PM, he says, 'I know, you're sorry; you have to get your kid. See you tomorrow . . .'"

Maybe this is the case for you, or maybe you'll be surprised, even shocked, to learn how frequently you dole out an apology in a given week. If this is the case, don't be alarmed or embarrassed. You are not alone. In fact, a friend of mine volunteered to try counting "sorrys" and told me, "I honestly didn't realize how many times a week I apologize to my child for going to work until I kept the journal. It's awful. What the heck am I even apologizing so much *for*?"

Don't despair—the good news is that this is a habit you can break fairly quickly once you recognize the problem, and life is going to become a lot more pleasant as a result.

Step 2: *Change your default settings.*

- -

When it comes to breaking *any* habit, a person needs to have not only a desire to change it, but also sheer determination (and if you're a working mom, you've already got the latter in spades). Suggests parenting expert and therapist Carl Pickhardt, PhD, "The habit of automatic apologizing can be broken when you commit to catching yourself and immediately self-correcting." When you realize you're on the verge of saying "I'm sorry," stop and take a deep breath (inhale until that breath reaches your heart before you exhale). Then, take a moment to consider whether you are doing anything *wrong* and whether apologizing is *appropriate* for the situation. For instance, is it really that *wrong* to feed your family Pop Tarts for breakfast every now and again because you have to be in the office extra-early for a meeting? Or hightailing it out of work early to pick up your child who broke out in some kind of bizarre hives at day camp? Most of us would agree these are *stressful* situations, but there's no need to ask for forgiveness from our children or boss in either case.

So why exactly do we do it? Many of us use apologies as a default to make other people feel better quickly. Says Susanne Gaddis, PhD, an executive coach known as "The Communications Doctor": "We are indoctrinated as children to pacify adults with apologies to get them off our backs. We quickly learn that 'I'm sorry' ends the uncomfortable situation, making us free to move on to other things. Because this behavior works, we carry it into adulthood." So what *can* we say in these uncomfortable situations, if not "I'm sorry"?

Pickhardt suggests that if you do blurt out an unnecessary apology to your child ("I'm sorry that I didn't have time to play another two rounds of Connect Four"), you can withdraw it, saying, "On second thought, I retract my apology, since I actually did nothing to be sorry for." Then, we should express compassion for our child without holding ourselves accountable for doing something *wrong*.

It's important that our children feel free to express their emotions, knowing that we can handle hearing even the difficult ones, says Dr. Victoria Samuel, a clinical psychologist who established The Parent Support Service in England: "Careful listening shows that you respect your child's feelings . . . Being listened to can cause difficult feelings to evaporate . . . cue less moaning, less tantrums, less tears. Most importantly, if you listen to your child, she is more likely to listen to you."[2]

I would just add that while we want our children to feel heard, we do not want them to think they have the power to make us alter the course of our workday by turning on the waterworks. Because most of us have seen that happen more than a few times.

In fact, children don't even *want* the power really to make you miss your work event, because it means Mommy is not in charge. And if you're not in charge, that means he or she *is*, and that is one wicked-scary idea for a kid. We have to remember that we are the parent here, and our children are looking to us to set the rules even when they're no fun to hear. Says Gaddis, "Although our children may put up a fight or try to manipulate us by whining and complaining, ultimately they are best served by having us stand our ground. Rather than saying, 'I'm sorry!' acknowledge their feelings by saying, 'I know that you're unhappy with me right now. And that's okay. But Mommy has to work.'"

> **Try This:**
>
> Rather than apologizing to my child when she's bummed-out that I'm leaving for an evening or weekend afternoon work engagement, here's what I found works (which I discovered by trial and error, really): Get down to your child's eye level (by squatting, sitting, whatever you need to do to get down there) and acknowledge the sadness. Look your child straight in the eye and say, "I see you're upset and that you will miss me." Then give her a big hug (not one of those half-assed pats that says, "I'm partway out the door already"). You can add, "I'm going to miss you too and will peek in on you when I get home." You say all of this while looking at your child directly (and not glancing at your watch or the door behind you), and then you leave, ladies. Saying the same thing over and over dilutes the message.

Step 3: *Set boundaries* before *the crisis.*

Many of us toss around apologies because we haven't made it clear to our supervisor or staff members under what conditions we'll put family matters ahead of work ones (i.e., "Maybe if I apologize profusely to my boss for missing the Christmas party to be at my child's holiday concert, she will be less peeved when I tell her about it the day before"). The reason we don't alert our supervisor ahead of time is usually that we had no idea what choice we would make until the last minute, and we haven't figured out which family situations trump work obligations. Will we finish a meeting we're leading before going to get our sick child at a friend's house? If our child's recital falls on the same day as a client meeting, which will we attend? Who knows? So we wait and wait, hoping for a bolt of clarity-lightning to strike. Then when it doesn't, we make a last-minute choice and feel awful for not giving our boss or coworker a proper heads-up.

To avoid this situation, devise basic action plans *ahead of time* for how you'll react for certain work/family situations that repeat themselves (the nurse calling to say come get your child, a client requesting an unplanned meeting during your child's big event, a vacation getting interrupted with a call from the boss). Granted, much of parenting involves making up the rules as we go, and we can't possibly prepare for every possible scenario (I mean, honestly, who is going to anticipate a game plan for what to do if our toddler shoves a peanut in his nose at daycare and no staff member can get it out?). But we can start to get a feel for what kind of parenting responsibilities will always take precedence over work so our coworkers will be more prepared. Establishing these limits when we're clearheaded will also help us feel calmer when the situation rears its ugly head again, and that means we will be less likely to apologize.

K, a New Jersey mom with a daughter in high school, told me, "I have made it clear to my coworkers that when my daughter is competing in a big volleyball game, I'll be going and sitting in the stands. I was an athlete when I was a kid and my mom missed almost all of my games, which I hated. So it's my priority to be at most of them, and I've let my coworkers know that I'll come in early or late on the days before to make sure they don't get stuck with all the work. I never feel bad about it, and it's as clear as can be."

Make sure you stay consistent with the limits. The only way limits will be respected, says Ronald L. Pitzer, family sociologist at University of Minnesota, is if they are "consistently applied and enforced." That way, when your colleague asserts, "I know you have to leave to pick up your child, but could you just . . . ," we can respond calmly, "I need to leave now. As we discussed, I pick up my daughter this week at 4:00 PM." It also works the other way around. If your child says, "Can't you just give me and my friends a ride to the mall this one time after school?" you can reply, "No, you know that every Wednesday I stay late at the office." End of story, no long-winded explanation or apology needed.

> **Try This:**
>
> Make a list of situations from the past several months where you had to tell your boss or client that you couldn't deliver something or be somewhere on time because you had an important family obligation. (Obviously, if your child has to go to the ER, no one is going to quibble with you missing work.) What parenting situations can you actually predict will arise again? Once you know these scenarios, make them clear to your supervisor or client with a solution for staying on top of your work. Pitzer advises focusing on the positive in these situations, and what is possible. In an article he wrote about setting limits for kids, called "Setting Limits for Responsive Discipline," he says to tell your child, "Play in the yard, not in the street," instead of just saying, "Don't go in the street."[3] When applying this principle to coworkers, say something like, "During my son's karate demonstrations, I'll need to leave early—and I will make sure the work is handed in the day before so you meet your deadlines."

Step 4: *Don't ignore "bad mommy" feelings.*

Jacquie, a forty-year-old physical therapist from Florida, and mom of a six- and a four-year-old, confesses, "The hardest part of the tug-of-war between working and parenting for me is feeling responsible to my patients, who go without treatments if I cancel appointments . . . and also feeling like I shouldn't even hesitate to get home to my kids if they need me because they should unquestionably be my first priority." Making it even more challenging, says Jacquie, is that "I make my own schedule so I have no one to blame but myself." While labeling frustration or guilt doesn't make the situation stress-free, it allows her to move through the feelings rather than letting them fester.

Unfortunately, there will be no end to the moments when we feel we've let down our children or coworkers because the two are so often and infuriatingly pitted against each other in our calendars. But we can control our response to these upsetting feelings once we acknowledge them. I'm talking about those moments when we feel like the worst mommy *ever* for not seeing our own son in his last school debate so we could balance the budget that is way overdue, or letting down our coworker because we *did* go to the debate and didn't get the budget done for the company on time. It's normal in these moments to feel sadness, resentment, and even grief—and it's essential that we label the feelings that arise instead of trying to bury them. In a *Psychology Today* article titled "The Wise Open Mind," Ronald Alexander, PhD, the director of the OpenMind Training Institute, warns, "The longer you avoid your pain and attempt to push it away, the more difficult it will be to break out of your paralysis."[4]

The key for all of us is to take note of these moments ("I feel anxious and upset . . ." or "I'm worried how this pace is affecting the family") rather than distracting ourselves by racing on to the next task. Alexander advises "simply noticing your grief or sorrow and experiencing compassion for yourself," allowing the assortment of feelings to surface while taking deep breaths.[5] Additionally, I believe in calling a good friend who can soothe our spirits or make us laugh while we weep about our latest maternal failing and assure us that many a mom has done worse. Lastly, soak in what Tobi Spino advised in her 2010 Urban Suburban posting in RivertownsPatch.com called "The Joys—I Mean Guilt, Wait, No, I Mean Joys—of Motherhood": "Your kids love you for being *you*. And that means they love the working you, the stay-at-home you, the you that takes them to class, and the you that lets their favorite babysitter take them to class. They love every version of you—except perhaps the time-out-giving you."[6]

Step 5: *KISS (Keep it simple, sister).*

- -

Susan, a Chicago freelance writer and mom to a three-year-old, says, "My kindergartner will sometimes ask why I can't pick her up from school like the other kids' moms. It kills me. The answer is that I have to be at work, but she doesn't care about that or understand what that means. What can I do except apologize?"

Just because children don't always like that we're working (until, of course, our paycheck allows them to get that cool new charm bracelet, remote-control race car, or iPod they've been eyeing), that doesn't mean we have to apologize for the fact that we do work. Think of it like this: Our kids don't like that we won't give them brownies for breakfast either, but we hardly feel compelled to apologize for giving them something with actual nutrients. We can acknowledge their feelings in the same way we do for ourselves (see Step 4).

If your child does have more questions about why you work, keep up with the simple explanations for little ones. For instance, if your five-year-old daughter asks *why* you have to work, tell her, "I like that at work I can think and learn like you do at school." Personally, I'm a fan of saying something like this as opposed to "Mommy *has* to work," which sends the message that there's no joy in having a job but we have to do it anyway. You can also add, "I get paid to work, and I like being able to help buy things for our family." If this leads into a bigger discussion about how meaningful you find work or what you do there or why you enjoy being with coworkers because your child is curious about what you do, then fantastic!

Try This:

When your child is bummed-out that you're going to work or staying late, psychologist Veola Vasquez, PhD, suggests you help him articulate how he is feeling if he is too young to put it into words himself. "Make your best guess as to why your child feels as he does," she says ("I hear you are sad because you wish I could pick you up after school like some of the other mommies").[7] That's it. If your child goes on to ask, "Why can't you?" don't get defensive and ramble about how hard it is to go to work sometimes. Instead, respond by saying, "I have to be at work." Don't apologize or go into a long drawn-out explanation of what you are doing all day long, and that if you leave early, it's not fair to others and blah, blah, blah. It's too much information when, generally, the child is just expressing a moment of frustration and simply wants a hug.

Step 6: *Put faith in your child's resilience.*

Fern, a fifty-three-year-old RN consultant and mother of two from Pennsylvania, says that while she loves the diversity of the work she does and the opportunity to stay current on medical and nursing information, she often "battles with the guilt of not being home when I know the family is waiting for me!"

Kiki, thirty-four, is a marketing and sales director for a small company in Oregon and mom of a fifteen-month-old. She sometimes wonders, "Am I going to create an emotional scar if I need to answer an email real fast when I'm at home with my child. Or, if I drop [my son] off a few minutes early so I can get a coffee for my commute, will he feel less loved?"

We don't want our children to hurt *ever*—and heaven forbid we are the direct cause of it. It is one thing to deal with our upset child after a bully torments her, or someone says something to our child that crushes her spirits (like, "Are you a boy or a girl?"). These moments feel harrowing enough; but it is a whole other deal when our child is looking at us with a tear-stained face, begging us not to leave the house, or calling us at work pleading for us to come home. Now we're the cause of the pain, dagger to the heart delivered.

When my daughter was five, I had to travel cross-country for a meeting on the day of her ballet recital. I must have said I was sorry to her at least a half-dozen times. I felt awful and worried that my absence would mar her childhood and she would think I didn't love her enough. The final time I apologized, she looked at me with pure exasperation and said, "I know! It's *okay*, Mommy!" She was already over it, and I was the one who couldn't seem to let go. It hit me that bringing so much attention to the situation over and over with my apologies was a lame attempt to let myself off the hook and wasn't something that helped her in any way. That was the last time I over-apologized at my child's expense.

The bottom line is that we are not causing emotional scars by dashing off emails, answering work calls, or stealing extra minutes for ourselves to grab a cup of coffee. Says Joshua Eagle, a child psychologist who specializes in mindfulness-informed work with adolescent boys and their families, "Over the years, I've seen a lot of different kids and teens in my practice, and I think most people would be surprised at just how resilient young people are in general. I've seen kids who you wouldn't expect to thrive defy the odds to do just that—kids being raised by older sibs, kids being raised by the foster system. So, will taking the occasional ten or twenty minutes from time with your child to answer work emails or return a business call cause irreparable harm? It's unlikely."

If we stop to think about it, it's kind of insulting to our children when we assume they are too frail to handle these miniscule disruptions in life. Think about it: Is your child too unstable to handle you sending a fax during playtime or taking time for yourself to take a yoga class? Right, mine isn't either.

Step 7: *Avoid the bribery game.*

- -

Melissa, thirty-six, a Massachusetts manager and mom of a four-year-old daughter, confesses: "My husband normally does the morning routine, as I go in super early; then I pick up my daughter at day's end. One day, my daughter woke before I left for work and had a meltdown because she wanted me to get her dressed, but I was late for a meeting. I tried to explain that if I didn't get to work on time then my boss would put me in 'time out.' Her answer was . . . 'So, then go to time out!' Needless to say, I hurried to get her dressed, kissed her a million times, and promised her a treat on the way home. Yes, I resort to bribery when necessary in these situations!"

Our sweet little children know how to push our buttons better than anyone in the world. They know, for instance, that one quick way to get what they want is to get misty-eyed, appear dejected, and plead with us for the chocolate-chip cookies (right there in the cabinet) to ease the pain. Candy, toys, getting to stay up late, a new video game, later curfew . . . our kids learn quickly that leaning on our guilt button for a few extra seconds may lead to a whole array of rewards and prizes.

Bribery—which, let's face it, most of us have resorted to at some point—does ease our child's sorrows for about one moment ("Yes, I have to leave, but here's an Oreo" or "If you promise to stop crying, I'm going to let you stay up ten minutes later tonight"). But most of us have discovered the hard way that bribery gives us only short-term peace and long-term awful consequences. It teaches our kids that they can and should manipulate us, and the little smarty-pants will keep upping the ante like professional poker players in a Vegas casino. Whereas a few M&Ms are enough to stop little Jenny from crying today, tomorrow it's two pieces of chocolate and a lollypop, and by next week, it's a full-on penny-candy arsenal. Jenny is learning the fine art of negotiating by beating someone (you) down emotionally, which may help her if she becomes a trial lawyer or policewoman, but it's not a good quality as part of a happy family unit.

As tempting as bribery is as a quick fix, stick with limit setting and be clear with your limit setting. Advises Bonnie Marcus, MEd: "Rather than bribing, I think it's important to set realistic expectations with our children that there are times that mom needs to work and times that she can spend great quality time with them. There should be no reason to bribe a child if this is understood as part of the normal routine."

> **Try This:**
>
> *If your child cries or yells after you say you're leaving for an evening work event, say, "I'll miss you too and check in on you when you're sleeping." If your child keeps crying, offer a big hug and leave him to your significant other or babysitter without trying to cheer him up by offering a reward. Take a deep breath and remind yourself that this is a small deal and your child will recover quickly. If you're worrying right now, "It's too late! I'm a briber! The die is cast . . . ," hold up; you can still change the dynamic. Your child may be surprised (and pissed off) when you don't offer the consolation cookie next time and even try to get his or her way by crying harder, stomping louder, and insisting that it's not fair. Hold your ground. It's going to take several rounds of testing to make it clear to your child that the bribery days are over. Refuse to budge and the behavior will change. Meghan, a business owner I met recently, experienced this herself after getting an "I hate you!" from her second grader when he didn't get his way. Her response: "I said 'get in line' and didn't even flinch. I took the emotional charge right out of it," she said proudly, "and he stopped staying it."*

Step 8: *Go easy on yourself if you slip.*

- -

Even if you make excellent headway in minimizing your apologies, there may be times when you revert to old habits. All it takes is one brutal day (we don't get the promotion we were expecting at work, we have to fire a staff member we like, our child wakes up with a sore throat, our significant other leaves town for a business trip) to shake up your routine and send you back into an apologizing tailspin. After being oh-so-careful, there you are again yelling "Mommy is so *sorry!* If you stop crying, I will get you a cookie/stuffed animal/trip to the moon . . ." or "Please let go of my leg. Mommy is so sorry but I have to go back to the office." Now, in addition to feeling stressed, you feel like a failure for resorting to old behavior you worked so hard to eradicate.

At times like this, we all need to remember that we are human. We shouldn't punish ourselves for slipping up. Instead, we should be as gentle with ourselves as we would be with a friend who is being too hard on herself. G. Alan Marlatt, PhD, and Deborah S. Romaine suggest in their book *The Complete Idiot's Guide to Changing Old Habits for Good* that we consider "tapering off" a bad habit rather than going cold turkey. The idea is that if the habit is a hard one for you to break, doing less of it is at least better. This is most effective, they state, when you give yourself a measurable deadline over a set period of time (i.e., "In one month, I will no longer apologize when it's not necessary, and I will do less and less of it each week").[8] Whether you opt for cold turkey or tapering off, accept the slip-ups, vow to get back on track, and be good to yourself. You can do this.

Maya, a thirty-one-year-old writer from California and mom of three, confessed: "It was the worst week. I'd just found out my mom was sick and needed my help. My son was supposed to be at camp but couldn't go because he had strep throat. My husband was working late at the office to meet a deadline. I was running around yelling at everyone. I kept apologizing to my family for being grumpy, to my boss for needing to take time off, and to my mom for the delay in me getting there. It was just an endless loop of saying I was sorry to everyone and feeling like a failure. Once I got through the week and had a chance to catch my breath, I turned it around. I stopped apologizing right away and eased up on myself."

Try This:

If you feel like you've veered off course and are starting to beat up on yourself, think about what you want to model for your child in terms of getting back on track. When our children screw up by repeating old bad behaviors, do we want them to keep beating up on themselves? Or do we want our children to recognize the mistake, learn from it, and move on? I love this quote from certified yoga coach Michelle Ghilotti Mandel, in her article "How to Grow from Mistakes," on Tinybuddha.com: "Accept the idea of a failure en route to your goals. In essence, plan for some roadblocks, nod when they come (you knew they were coming), and move on as quickly as possible."[9]

Proceed with Caution If . . .

you try all the steps in this chapter and find that you still can't stop yourself from over-apologizing. If this is the case, it may be time to explore what's behind the guilt, with a therapist who can shed light on whether there is something deeper going on: unresolved issues from your past, doubts about whether you truly want to be working at your current job or at all, or exhaustion from an overfilled schedule. Be willing to do this deep emotional work for yourself and also for your child, who is learning ways to respond to stress directly from watching you.

On the Flip Side . . .

maybe you go too far the other way and stop apologizing *altogether*. You feel guilty when you do something wrong but don't say "I'm sorry" because you're afraid of resorting to old habits. But as psychologist

Annye Rothenberg, PhD, author of books such as *Mommy and Daddy Are Always Supposed to Say Yes*, points out, it's important to own up to our mistakes: "When you do something you shouldn't, make sure *you* apologize, so your child sees how automatic it is." If, for example, you have to break a promise you made to your child, say: "I am really sorry that we can't (fill in the blank) like we discussed. I know you're upset, so let's go right now to the calendar and pick a new time." Make sure you follow through and appreciate that you're teaching your child the value of saying "I'm sorry" when she makes a mistake or does something wrong.

SHOUT-OUT TO . . .

Alanna, a forty-one-year-old freelance designer in Massachusetts and mom of two, found a good way to rein in the apologies at work: "Working part-time is tricky and always has been. Generally, the rule with my husband and me is that on the days that I am working, he is responsible for staying home with sick kids or picking them up early from school. This way I can honestly bill myself as the most responsible part-time employee that my office has ever had. I come in on time, never call in sick, I don't make personal phone calls, I don't read personal email, etc. There are of course times where my husband cannot do the sick day or pickup—and on those rare occasions, I do not apologize for leaving early, simply because they are rare. But making sure they are rare is the key."

Chapter Wrap

- - - - - - - - - - - - - -

Step 1: *Check your inner apologize-o-meter.*

Tune in to how frequently you are apologizing in any given week to get a sense of whether there is an issue.

Step 2: *Change your default settings.*

Before you utter the next "I'm sorry," take a moment to determine whether it is justified.

Step 3: *Set boundaries before the crisis.*

Come up with basic guidelines around when family obligations will trump work and convey those to your boss with a solution.

Step 4: *Don't ignore "bad mommy" feelings.*

By giving ourselves room to experience our guilt or worry, we are able to move on more quickly.

Step 5: *KISS (Keep it simple, sister).*

Know when your child is looking for an explanation about why you have to work, and when she just needs a hug.

Step 6: *Put faith in your child's resilience.*

Know that your child is not going to suffer in any significant way when you take a little extra time for yourself.

Step 7: *Avoid the bribery game.*

Instead of distracting your child from being sad by offering treats and rewards, lay down clear limits and expectations.

Step 8: *Go easy on yourself if you slip.*

If you revert back to over-apologizing, accept it as part of the learning curve instead of beating yourself up.

Chapter 2

MULTITASKING MISHAPS

Confession: "I'm terrible at multitasking."

While rushing to get your child ready to leave the house in the morning ("Where are your shoes?" "Brush your teeth right now or we are going to be so late!" "Where are your SHOES?!"), you're fretting about all the tasks you have to do once you start your workday. There's the staff meeting at 9:15 AM . . . you have to meet with your intern . . . wait, did you remember to email your client about next steps before you meet again? What's the name of your intern again? It starts with an "S."

As soon as you get to work, your mind switches gears back to family. Did you accidentally pack nuts in your child's lunch (you've been instructed three times already that the classroom is nut-free and you could accidentally kill two kids if you forget!). Do your kids have their instrument, binky, homework, permission slip, or the other half-dozen items that were supposed to make it into their diaper bag or backpack? During lunch, while talking to your colleagues, you remember that—*crap!*—you forgot to take out dinner to defrost and now there is nothing to eat for dinner *again* (is it legal to serve grilled cheese every night for a week?). During dinner, while rinsing off the spatula, you can't remember if you mailed out the contacts you promised to get to the freelancer. By the time you slip into bed, you're spent—and your brain is still flipping back and forth: *work, mom, work, mom.*

It's frustrating being unable to focus on just work at the office, or just family while you are right there with them. This inability stops you from accomplishing what you've set out to do at work on any given day, and it makes you feel like a lame mom at home ("I should be enjoying my time with my child, not thinking about the work budget!" "I should not be rehearsing my talk with the boss tomorrow while tucking in the twins for bed; who DOES that?!"). Plus, you can only imagine how much more energy and resources you would have if you could shut down one portion of your brain at will. But you just can't seem to quiet your brain. Why can't you make your mind focus on one task at a time? Is your child going to remember you as the distracted lady who mumbles weird things to yourself and posts sticky notes all over the house? Is your boss or staff going to think of you as the flake that always looks checked out? Can you *learn* to multitask or is it genetic?

QUIZ: ARE YOU GOOD AT SEPARATING FAMILY AND WORK?

1. When you glance at the picture of your children on your office desk, you most likely:

   a. feel a tug of missing them and then get back to work.

   b. are so overcome with grief that you pick up the phone and call home, daycare, or afterschool to hear their voices.

   c. imagine what they're doing right now and get so swept up that you lose all track of time.

2. While baking cookies with your child on the day before your big presentation, you:

   a. rehearse your talk over and over (in your head, of course) just to make sure it's perfect.

   b. focus on being with your child and plan on rehearsing what you'll say tonight.

   c. jot down notes about the presentation while telling your child that you're making recipe adjustments.

3. During any given workday, you tend to call home to say hello to your child:

   a. rarely; you have always been able to immerse yourself in work until you call it a day.

   b. so many times that it takes you twice as long to finish the tasks you're supposed to complete.

   c. once on a typical day, maybe twice if your child is handling something out of the ordinary.

Answers: If you answered "a" for number 1, give yourself one point. If you answered "b" for number 2, give yourself one point. If you answered "a" or "c" for number 3, give yourself one point. If you received at least two points, you're probably doing pretty well staying engaged in the moment. If you received less, pay extra attention to the steps in this chapter because your focus could use some fine-tuning.

Reality Check

- - - - - - - - - - - - - -

Many of us have been duped by media "experts" into believing that women are natural multitaskers. Case in point: This exact phrase ("women are natural multitaskers") was the lead-in sentence of a 2011 CNBC article titled "Careers and Sexes: Are Men Better Than Women at Social Networking?" and it was stated in both a 2011 Huffington Post piece called "What Men and Women Really Want in Love (and How to Get It) and a Redbook.com article titled "Sex-Life Road Test."[1] And that's just a sampling! Seeing this assumption over and over *seems* to make it true—and leaves us thinking, "Oh, great, it's supposed to come *naturally*?"

Even if multitasking *did* come naturally (which, by the way, is not supported by most scientific evidence), that doesn't make it something we should prize. Senior Editor Christine Rosen of *The New Atlantis: A Journal of Technology and Society* says in her 2008 article "The Myth of Multitasking" that multitasking is "now shorthand for the human attempt to do simultaneously as many things as possible, as quickly as possible, preferably marshalling the power of as many technologies as possible."[2]

Doing as many things as quickly as possible . . . is that *good*?

Russell Poldrack, a psychology professor at the University of California, Los Angeles, doesn't think so: "We have to be aware that there is a cost to the way that our society is changing, that humans are not built to work this way. We're really built to focus. And when we sort of force ourselves to multitask, we're driving ourselves to perhaps be less efficient in the long run, even though it sometimes feels like we're being more efficient."[3]

Nor is it realistic for most women to separate our thoughts into two distinct categories so that work and family thoughts never blend. C'mon! We're not robots here. By the way, business experts and executive coaches talk about the need for compartmentalizing—separating our work lives from our family lives, depending on where we are physically at the time—you'd think every woman should be able to turn on her laser-beam focus whenever she decides to. It's challenging enough getting through the day accomplishing *half* of our work obligations while also making sure the kids are in bed before midnight. Many of us would agree it's common to find ourselves distracted by thoughts of our children at various points throughout the day, and work ideas while at home.

But truth is, it may be better for you to *avoid* compartmentalizing. As Linnette M. Beck, president and founder of Beck Natural Medicine, says, "Compartmentalization is often used as a type of denial—one of avoidance—so important issues aren't dealt with." In other words, completely denying the sadness you feel for missing your child's play because you have to present a paper is *avoidance*, not successful multitasking. So instead of obsessing about how to focus single-mindedly—while avoiding your true feelings—stop and appreciate that you're probably better off leaving room for mixed feelings. That said, there are definitely some working moms who are able to multitask and compartmentalize naturally, and that is truly wonderful for them. If you're one, I envy you—and you may want to skip ahead to the next chapter. If you aren't one of these ubertaskers, the following steps will help you navigate the multitasking landscape with less stress and expectation.

Step 1: *Know you're in good company.*

- -

Where is the message coming from that working moms are *sup-posed* to separate our feelings into tidy boxes? For one thing, we've got celebrity moms such as Katie Couric, Julia Louis-Dreyfus, Gwyneth Paltrow, and Teri Hatcher, speaking out publicly about the importance of being able to compartmentalize as a working mom. Popular blogs for working moms, including *Mamapedia* and *Working Mother,* have stated that the key to easing our stress is to compartmentalize, while numerous life coaches and career coaches for women promise to teach women the ins and outs of *how* to compartmentalize. For example, Phoenix Career Coach Krista Milne said in an Examiner.com piece: "Think of your brain as a receptacle that holds paper file folders. While at work, keep the personal issues in the appropriate folder and focus on the work tasks at hand. When issues arise that can be addressed later, put them in a 'tickler' file folder so you can address them at the appropriate time."[4]

Here's why I find that idea supremely unhelpful: I, myself, have never found it possible to tuck away my worries and sorrows when I'm overwhelmed, although it sounds terrific ("I'm just going to file away the worry *I can't believe my daughter's being bullied by the mean girls* in my tickler file and get back to filling out this work form"). So when I hear about "perfecting" my ability to compartmentalize, I feel only pressure and the belief that I'm failing miserably. I know I'm not alone on this, given numerous comments I received from working moms, including:

> *"I will be sitting at work and these visions of my kid's face will just swoosh by me like a hallucination. My*

best friend who works says the same thing happens to her. I wonder if dads ever experience this. Is this even normal?" —Tanya, thirty-nine

"I'll be baking cupcakes with my daughter and all of a sudden I figure out an idea for work and I'm dying to try it out. I need ways to just shut down my brain sometimes. No more ideas, please! Then I feel guilty about having these thoughts during my time with my daughter because I'm supposed to be focusing on her, so then I'm stressed and feeling guilty." —Jillian, thirty-one

"Yesterday, I was working at the design studio and the whole day went by and I realized I hadn't once thought about my kids—is that awful? I had wanted to call my son and check in to see how his math test went, and I completely forgot. God, I'm an awful multitasker. I can't seem to focus on more than one thing or my brain would explode. Is that bad?" —Ali, thirty-eight

So know you're in good company if you haven't gotten a handle on the whole multitasking mission. Plus, there are plenty of experts who agree with the good doctor Poldrack in believing the human brain wasn't built to function this way. Susan Newman, PhD, social psychologist and bestselling author of over one dozen parenting books, shared with me, "Life is messy, and it is near impossible to put all aspects of it into orderly form, particularly if you are a parent . . . pressures, stresses, and tasks that need attention will overlap, no matter how organized and efficient you think you are." I am also comforted by what Amy Brinn, LICSW, parenting coach and supervisor of a parenting stress-line, told me: "When work thoughts permeate at home, and home thoughts permeate at work, it can feel crazy making. We can't stop ourselves from *thinking*."

So instead of feeling guilty about our limitations in multitasking and compartmentalizing, let's put our energy into better outlets— like figuring out where to get takeout dinner tonight.

Step 2: *Make space for sadness.*

You are sitting at your desk typing when a wave of worry washes over you: *I wonder how she's coping with not being invited to the party, I hope he takes the bottle, I know how fussy he's been with teething! Why are her grades suddenly slipping; is she in some trouble?* Or perhaps you're simply *missing* your son or daughter and feeling disconnected. Then you get frustrated because feelings like this are not helpful, and they're distracting you from work. At this rate, you worry that you are never going to be able to concentrate enough to get your work done by the end of the day. If only we could shut off our feelings and focus on the work, we'd be so much better off, right?

Perhaps not . . . I love what psychotherapist F. Diane Barth, LCSW, says about this: "Feelings are how we tell ourselves what's going on in our lives. Filing them away, whether in little boxes or in the back of our heads, is one of the things therapists help us *stop* doing! Some people go to work and just focus on what they're doing there, but that's because that's how they're made! Others of us (and I'm certainly guilty as charged) find ourselves thinking sometimes about our loved ones when we're at work, and work when we're with our kids—and that's okay, definitely not bad. The trick is to find ways to focus on whatever the task is at hand, while *also* making room for thoughts and feelings (and daydreams) about the other parts of our lives."

Barth's suggestion: Note your drifting thoughts (for example, worrying about whether our kid is eating while we're supposed to be focusing on preparing an important proposal at work), *without criticizing them.* Pay attention to them for a minute, decide whether or not you need to act on them (did you forget to tell the babysitter to give your three-year-old his medicine at lunch? If so, you do need to call, don't you?), and then get back to whatever you're working on. If we can note our feelings, breathe into them, and acknowledge them without criticizing them, then we don't have to fight them; and they don't have to hang around waiting for us to pay attention! Again, feelings have meaning, and it's often helpful for us to notice them and try to understand what that meaning is, and then it's much easier to let them go.

I have definitely found Barth's tip helpful. If I just allow myself to feel the feelings instead of fighting them, it doesn't take long for them to pass. It's when I resist *(Get back to work; there's nothing you can do about it right now so just get the job done!)* that I can't seem to move forward with whatever I'm supposed to be doing. Kate, a thirty-seven-year-old masseuse with a two-year-old and an infant, told me, "I used to feel bad if thoughts of my kids drifted into my mind during a session with a client, but now I'm starting to just make room for thoughts about missing them during the massage and then tell myself I can check in with my stay-at-home husband by phone after the session is over. It's getting easier for me to notice the feeling and then move on."

Step 3: *Interrupt the spin cycle.*

- -

While it's not a problem if your feelings interrupt you for a few minutes here and there throughout the day, it's a whole other issue when you're dealing with a heavy-duty worry that needs your undivided attention and a definitive solution. Then it's not just about noting a feeling; it's about dealing with a tricky (if not messy) situation.

For instance, you think your child's tennis coach is driving the team so hard physically that it is pushing the kids' safety limits; your kid's teacher told you last night that your son is falling too far behind in math; your husband/partner has been putting too much pressure on your daughter to get top grades. In these cases, we have to gather more information, analyze the info, and figure out solutions—or at least first steps.

Work is not the time or place to do this, and trying to will likely eat up hours of our day. We still need to *acknowledge* the feeling ("I'm worried," "I'm disappointed in myself," "I'm pissed off!"). But then we need to make a conscious choice to table the problem solving until after work. Knowing that you can come back to the brainstorming later (not just berating yourself for extending your work time worrying about home issues) will make it easier to focus on getting the job done. This is a case where compartmentalizing—or separating—*is* healthy. Having a time slot reserved—whether it's on the drive home from work, after dinner, or during a morning walk—to brainstorm will help you let go and get back to work. It's no different than putting a sticky note reminder on your computer to call someone later so your brain won't send annoying reminders every ten minutes.

It also goes the other way—when your brain is spinning with work problems while you're with your family. While setting up a picnic at the park, you are obsessing about whether you're going to get the promotion tomorrow, or worrying about a coworker quitting while you're in the midst of playing a board game with your child. When you're disengaged with your family like this, you're not even *with* your family. You may as well be back at the office because you're not adding anything but stress here. As Dr. Cara Gardenswartz, spokesperson for the American Psychological Association (and mom) put it, "Quality time when you are fully present is far more important than the number of hours you log."[5]

If you're thinking, *Yeah, but it's not like my child can tell I'm secretly thinking about work stuff,* you are wrong. David Code, author of *Kids Pick Up Everything,* states, "Stress is highly contagious between parent and child, even if the parent is unaware of his or her own anxiety," while parenting expert Lori Lite, author of the *Stress Free Kids* books, says, "I do believe that children feel their parents' stress.[6] Children that do not know how to manage stress in a healthy manner will see it manifest in other areas like overeating, headaches, even anger." Not good.

It also may help to remind yourself that there is nothing you can do about the work situation right now. As we all know, agonizing about a possible outcome doesn't actually do anything remotely helpful. So make an intentional choice to be clued in to this time with your family. This is something you can do with excellent results. I like what Carole, a forty-three-year-old communications director and mom to children ages six and thirteen, had to say: "Balance is a myth. I think you have to look for moments on each front where you can give your undivided attention and be there. Kids can see you faking it. They know when you say you're listening but you're really practicing that difficult employee conversation in your head."

> **Try This:**
>
> *If you find yourself preoccupied with a worry while hanging out with your child, come back to the moment by focusing on what's right in front of you. Advises Henrik Edberg, owner of The Positivity Blog and author of The Power of Positivity, "Look at what's right in front of you right now. Listen to the sounds around you. Feel the fabric of your clothes and focus on how they feel."[7] This will help bring you back to the moment. You can even pick something specific about your child to lock onto: What is your child doing right now? Look into your child's eyes; listen to the noise he/she is making.*

Step 4: Don't leave feelings on hold.

- -

I remember getting a phone call from the school nurse fifteen minutes before I was scheduled to do a live online chat with the *Washington Post*. The nurse told me my daughter had lice (NO!), and I'd better come get her right away. Um, *when?* I asked if I could pick up Risa in forty-five minutes (*ugh,* guilt) and she said that's fine. Risa could stay with her in the nurse's room (more guilt!). I took a few deep breaths, reminded myself Risa was not bleeding to death, and then made myself focus on the task at hand. Every once in a while, while posting responses, my thoughts drifted to Ew, *LICE!* or *I'm going to have to get a comb, clean the sheets, vacuum the house . . . and* EW! but then I'd reprimand myself, thinking, *Focus! Type!* By the time I finished, picked up my daughter, and bought all the medical supplies, I wanted to curl up into a ball and weep.

Jackie, a thirty-one-year-old California mom to a one-year-old and pregnant with her second child, recalls a grueling night as chief of staff for her boss, who was running to become the state's next attorney general: "It was eighteen months of near hell for me. One night I remember particularly well. I was working on a twenty-seven-page questionnaire due to a union for endorsement purposes. I was in charge of drafting policy-heavy essay responses. Of course, toddlers do not care what is going on in their parents' lives, and my son's asthma and teething issues joined forces on the same night—the night before the questionnaire was due. I vividly remember soothing my son while jotting down notes for responses. Then I'd put him to bed, write four to five answers, and do the same thing all over again until 4:00 AM."

We've all had those days when work deadlines and family needs smash into each other without warning, leaving us in chaos without a moment to catch our breath—much less come up with a sophisticated game plan. At times when our attention is needed everywhere, we just have to keep switching gears and get the jobs *done*. Susan Newman, PhD, advises, "When life's curveballs become overwhelming, it is often less stressful to resign yourself to the problems and crises *in front of you*, and don't worry about what you can't get to until you can. Agonizing accomplishes nothing other than adding more stress to an already stressful situation."

Also, it will go better if we don't fret about parsing out equal amounts of attention to children and work. (The end goal is to get through the day without losing our marbles.) Says Amy Brinn, LICSW, "Sometimes you'll put out a little more energy for work, sometimes a little more energy for what is happening at home. If we can be less anxious about that, it will all balance out over time." I know that what also helped during the lice (*ew!*) fiasco was to keep reminding myself, *This day has an ending, this day has an ending* . . . I also learned at the end of that hateful day that it's better to process the feelings at least a little before calling it a day rather than going to sleep and trying to forget it ever happened.

Otherwise, I would just carry the stress right into the next day as soon as I woke up.

Rachel Starck, licensed counselor and life coach, put it like this: "When we bury our feelings by sweeping them under the rug, hoping they will resolve on their own, they usually do not go away. Instead they build up, fester, and can eventually contribute to episodes of major depression or anger outbursts. It is far more effective for your long-term health and balance to process feelings as they come up (perhaps not the very moment they come up, but within days at least). Empower yourself by owning your feelings, acknowledging their existence, work through them, resolve what you can, then move on!"

Try This:

Once you get through your minefield of a day, try a little Buddhist meditation practice: Find a quiet place to sit or lie down and allow all the feelings you experienced during the day to bubble up: anxiety that you wouldn't meet your deadline, fear that your child is sick, heartache that you couldn't just cuddle with your child for a long time, and whatever else comes up. Suggests wellness coach Elizabeth Scott, MS, "Think of yourself as an 'observer of your thoughts,' just noticing what the narrative voice in your head says, but not engaging it. As thoughts materialize in your mind, just let them go."

My own addition: When you feel calmer, congratulate yourself on getting through the day of combat in one piece. No one else is going to congratulate us for getting through a day alive, so we should do it for ourselves.

Step 5: *Be extra patient during major shake-ups.*

For those wondering how long it will take to adjust to these new ways of dealing with your feelings, it depends on how determined you are and what kind of support you're getting. But here's a rule of thumb you might find helpful: changing a major habit takes about two months. In a 2009 article in *European Journal of Social Psychology*, Phillippa Lally and colleagues from University College London recruited ninety-six people who wanted to form a new habit, whether it was eating a piece of fruit with lunch or going for a short run each day. According to researchers who interviewed the participants, the average amount of time it took to go from practicing a new behavior to doing it automatically was sixty-six days.[8] So there you go.

That said, it may take longer to figure out how to deal with intense and competing feelings when you're handling major life shake-ups. Tanya, forty-one, a New Haven mom who works in early education, took off a year from work as an educational consultant so she could bond with her adopted daughter, Amelie. Tanya then returned to work at reduced hours, and "I was always fantasizing about being with her and wondering what she was doing," Tanya says, and admitted that she called home all the time to find out what her little girl was up to. Tanya says she *still* struggles with bouts of sadness from missing Amelie while at work and stresses about the fact that she leaves more work unfinished at the end of the day than she did before having a child. "I love my job," she says, "and I worry sometimes that maybe I am shortchanging the people I am consulting with."

Yes, it's harder to get a handle on navigating our feelings and keeping ourselves focused when dealing with a major change at work or home, like going back to your job after having a child. The same is true of any emotional transition, whether it's a job promotion, demotion,

moving to a new house or community, dealing with your child's teething, handling a nightmare phase (whether it's your child's fear of
monsters kicking in, or your nightmares about an evil boss yelling
about your lack of priorities). When your brain is extra-full during
these transitional periods, go easy on yourself and appreciate that
you're in a different place than you were at your highest-functioning
level. Says Tanya: "I had to accept that as a new mom, I was in a different head space. Things are different, and it took me about eight
months to figure out that I can't give the same amount of attention to
my job that I did when I didn't have a child." How did she accept it?
"I'm easier on myself for not making my clients top priority every single second," she says, "and I appreciate that I'm still good at my job."

Step 6: *Chill out during your commute.*

- -

One of the biggest challenges in juggling family and work
thoughts that run amok, moms told me repeatedly, is the daily
transitions—those moments when you're not at work or at home
(a.k.a., "mommy limbo"), such as when you're driving home from
the office, taking the train in to work, or coming home from a
business trip. It's often hard being in this in-between space, with
our minds racing all over the place. You're wondering why your
son had a meltdown over waffles while you were trying to prepare for your next meeting, or you keep reliving the horror of
firing an employee before you get home (knowing your child is
expecting your full attention).

Leslie, a thirty-two-year-old community relations senior manager in New Hampshire and mom to two-and-a-half-year-old twins
and an eight-month-old, says the worst part of her day is her

one-hour commute from work to home: "I don't have it in me to switch gears from professional Leslie to fun-loving Mommy after an exhausting day of being 'on.'"

Jenny, a forty-something therapist in Massachusetts with two kids, says, "I always think I'm going to come home and there will be a huge hug from my children, who will be waiting at the door. Instead, they are always waiting to tattle on each other and throw each other under the bus. So I spend the whole commute home feeling stressed-out worrying about what's to come and also worried because I most likely didn't get my work done."

Commute time doesn't have to be treacherous. Why not make the intentional choice to use the commute as an opportunity to *unwind?* Says Kathy Caprino, MA, founder and president of Ellia Communications: "The anxiety and worry that overflows from one domain to another (work to home, and vice versa) during commute time depletes your energy, your health, and your well-being because it interferes with your ability to be your highest and best in each situation. It creates a vicious cycle that reinforces that you're not your best in *either* arena. In the end, you begin to feel you're letting down everything and everyone who matters most."

Try This:

Spend the commute time doing things that bring you more peace, relaxation, focus, and well-being, Kathy Caprino suggests, such as sleeping, journaling (write about the key things you've learned or great stuff from that day you'd like to document), or reading something engaging but non-work-related if you're on a train or bus. If you're driving, listen to calming, soothing music or uplifting, motivational audiobooks that excite you.

Step 7: *Commit, and then drop it.*

- -

Meredith, a thirty-six-year-old program coordinator from Massachusetts with a five-year-old and a seven-month-old, recalls: "I was in the throes of planning a large conference for work that meant going out of town and leaving my family for a week, and it was the night of my daughter's kindergarten graduation. There were things for work that I felt at the time needed my immediate attention, but I obviously wanted to be fully there for my daughter's celebration. . . . it was awful. I was checking my email on my phone constantly during the ceremony and could feel how wrong it was, but I couldn't seem to stop myself. I felt completely conflicted and out of control, like I knew my priorities were out of whack."

Antje, a forty-year-old brand manager from New Jersey and mom of a three-year-old, recalls having to "drop everything at 5:22 PM in order to get to daycare on time. I knew that what I needed to do would take me five minutes to finish if I kept going, or it would take me an hour the next day because I would have to think everything through all over again."

Like Meredith and Antje, we working moms can do a real number on ourselves when we make hard (no-win) decisions about whether to prioritize a work event or family event—after countless toiling—and then go on to *second-guess* ourselves. Maybe you already decided that on a particular evening you're going to prioritize going to a meeting over a family celebration (or vice versa) and then, just when the matter is settled, you begin thinking, Hmmm, *maybe I shouldn't* . . . The guilt eats away at you, further dividing your focus (*I know I told myself I will go to the swim meet today but how the heck am I going to get caught up at work?* or *I know I decided to go to the networking event but what if my children feel neglected right now? Oh, shoot. I should have stayed with them tonight.)* Back and forth, our doubts torment us in a game of emotional Ping-Pong.

Rachel Starck tells me it is very common for moms, even *the most confident* ones, to second-guess their decisions. "Waffling back and forth, and then feeling guilty after coming to a decision, is an energy drain."

It's not *just* about finalizing an answer. It's also about learning to let go of the decision-making so we can get out of our swirly brains and be in the moment. I like what Dr. Thynn Thynn, a teacher of Buddhism who won the Outstanding Women in Buddhism Award in 2005, says: "Usually the mind flitters between thoughts and feelings about the past, present, and future. Staying with the moment is just a way to train the mind to cease flitting."[9]

This is something I've been trying to do more of recently, and it's definitely helpful. For example, if I commit to going to work later so I can go watch my daughter sing in a talent show, I no longer torture myself about how I'm going to get all my work done. The way I see it, as soon as I make the decision, the die is cast. I'd rather roll down my car window during my drive to the performance, enjoy the sun on my face, and belt out songs with the radio than allow my mind to "flit" while worrying about work problems. I'm already blowing off the work. I might as well enjoy myself!

Try This:

To minimize wasting your energy, life coach Rachel Starck suggests using an exercise or ritual. "Practice breathing in and out intentionally, mindfully, and while focusing on your breath, use an affirmation such as 'let it go' with your breathing. Repeat for one or two minutes. Your mind will wander back to questioning, or doubting, but you will kindly redirect your intention back to breathing and repeating the affirmation."

Proceed with Caution If . . .

you're not able to meet the majority of your work goals because you're so consumed with missing/worrying about your child. It's appropriate to miss your children at various times throughout the day, to think about them and wonder what they're doing. But if you are dwelling on the separation most of the day, it may be time to consider whether you can afford to reduce work hours, at least temporarily. Or it may be time to evaluate whether your lack of focus has something to do with the type of work itself. Are you overwhelmed (or underwhelmed) by your job? If so, are there work responsibilities you can shift to alleviate the stress? When you find yourself drifting off into thinking about your child next time, stop and ask yourself what you were thinking about just before you started trailing off. It will likely give you some insight into whether you're in fact trying to escape something.

On the Flip Side . . .

maybe sometimes you feel guilty because you're so good at compartmentalizing that a whole workday can pass without even once thinking about your kids. Then, when you do think of them, you suddenly are flooded with shame because what kind of mother doesn't think about her kid all day long? The answer is: a mom who has no problem compartmentalizing. It certainly doesn't mean that you adore your child any less; it just means you focus on the task in front of you at any particular moment. As long as you're able to concentrate on parenting when you're home with the same focus you apply at work, there's nothing to sweat about.

SHOUT-OUT TO . . .

Robyn, twenty-nine, a New Jersey mother of four daughters under the age of seven, found a positive way of looking at the tug-of-war between work thoughts and parenting thoughts. Robyn, a book editor for years, switched gears two years ago, and is attending nursing school to become a midwife. While Robyn knows better than anyone that there is "no win in the parenting/work tug-of-war," she also knows that "the reason it's such a struggle is because these are the most important things in my life." Robyn reminds herself in highly stressful moments that "the only way it wouldn't be a struggle is if I didn't care so much about both my work and my kids. In that way, it's pretty fortunate!"

Chapter Wrap

- - - - - - - - - - - - -

Step 1: *Know you're in good company.*

Realize that most women can't build impenetrable walls between work and home—and shouldn't be asked to.

Step 2: *Make space for sadness.*

Feel your feelings fully so you can let them move through you.

Step 3: *Interrupt the spin cycle.*

Work on tuning in to the moment by noticing small details when you have trouble focusing.

Step 4: *Don't leave feelings on hold.*

If you're having a hyper-stressful day, make sure you leave time that evening to work through the feelings instead of just turning in early.

Step 5: *Be extra patient during major shake-ups.*

Lower your expectations about performance levels during big transitions that come with feeling overwhelmed.

Step 6: *Chill out during your commute.*

Make an intentional choice to turn your commute into a relaxation opportunity.

Step 7: *Commit, and then drop it.*

Once you make the decision of what gets top priority right now, let the matter go and enjoy.

Chapter 3

UNEXCUSED ABSENCES

- - - - - - - - - - - → Confession: "I hate missing my kid's big moments, but not enough to quit my job."

After a particularly brutal day of work, where perhaps you wanted to poke your eyes out after a three-hour meeting, you head to daycare to pick up your child. You are eagerly awaiting a giant hug from your little one, which promises to be the highlight of your day. When you set foot in the classroom, however, you are met by the teacher, who blurts out, "You're never going to believe it . . . your child rolled over on his belly!" Instead of feeling happy and proud, you feel absurdly jealous. No fair! You wanted to be the one to cheer for your child after a successful 180-degree turn. You paste a phony smile on your face as the teacher tells you every little detail.

Why do our child's big moments always seem to take place at the same time as a major work obligation? You can almost bank on the fact that your child's first step, recital, driving lesson, or prom night will fall on a day when everyone at work is counting on you to be present. The guilt of not being there firsthand to witness a victorious moment eats away at all of us ("I bet I was the *only* mom who wasn't there!"). You can imagine your child crying to his future therapist while accepting the unlimited prescription for Prozac because *you* didn't care enough to be there for the big important moments. What does your kid care about you earning paychecks and enjoying your meaningful career? Your child wants an all-access pass to you. End of story.

On top of the guilt, which is painful enough, you feel robbed. It is one of life's sweetest pleasures to raise your proverbial pom-poms to cheer for your child. There are so many tumbles and spills and, yes, monumental screw-ups throughout the years (both your kid's and your own), and you deserve to experience the joyous milestones, too. You love those perfect moments when your child turns to you with the look that says, *"Did you see me?!"* and you get to gush with pride. How many of these moments have been experienced by the babysitter, teacher, daycare provider, or someone else other than you? *Ugh,* you don't want to think about it. Worse, how many of these special occasions will pass before there are more moments missed than shared? Will you look back and curse your career for stealing these once-in-a-lifetime moments? Will your child feel unloved?

QUIZ: HOW DO YOU COPE WITH MISSING OUT ON MILESTONES?

1. **Your child asks whether you will go to her hockey game tomorrow, and you still haven't met your work deadline, so you:**

   a. tell her that you won't be able to make this one because of a work obligation, but you will definitely cheer at the next game.

   b. go to the game (hey, there are only so many games in a season) and then spend the whole two hours freaking out about the work piling up.

   c. attend the game, but sleep through most of it because you were up so late last night getting your work done so you could come.

2. **When your child asks you why Daddy always takes him to his doctor's appointments, you:**

   a. burst into tears right then (or later) because what kind of bad mommy doesn't go to the doctor with her own child?

   b. tell your child you'll try to go to the next one, even though there's no chance in hell, given your work schedule.

   c. say that Daddy's work schedule makes it easier for him to go, but luckily, you are able to do plenty of other things together.

3. **When your child's daycare provider tells you that your toddler ran without falling for the first time, you:**

   a. beam! You're so proud, you give your little tike a huge hug and heap on the praise.

   b. feel distraught because you hate missing all the good stuff.

   c. worry for the millionth time whether your child is going to be more connected to her teacher than to you.

Answers: If you answered "a" for number 1, give yourself one point. If you answered "c" for number 2, give yourself one point. If you answered "a" for number 3, give yourself one point. If you received at least two points, you likely have good perspective on your tremendous value as a mom, even when you miss milestones. If you received fewer points, pay extra attention to the steps in this chapter because there are numerous ways to make this easier on yourself.

Reality Check

- - - - - - - - - - - - - - -

Many of us worry that our children will be scarred emotionally when we miss one of their big experiences due to our work. On our guiltiest days, it's more than worry; it's *panic*. Is our job robbing our child of too much mommy time and creating lasting emotional damage? Here's something we should all let sink in: UC Irvine researchers combined the results of *sixty-nine different studies* on whether children are impacted negatively in their behavior and/or academic performance due to mom working. In 2010, their findings were published by the American Psychological Association, stating that with very few exceptions, children whose moms returned to work when the kids were young fared just as well as those with stay-at-home moms![1] Are we going to argue with sixty-nine studies?

Our mothering abilities are not determined by seeing firsthand every one of our child's milestones. According to Sherrie Bourg Carter, PsyD, a nationally recognized forensic psychologist and author of *High Octane Women: How Superachievers Can Avoid Burnout*, "It turns out that family features—such as the family income and educational levels, and a mother's sensitivity and psychological adjustment—are more strongly and consistently associated with healthy childhood development than whether or not a child spends time in daycare or with other relatives because the mother works." And you know what brings in more family income and psychological adjustment? You going to a stimulating job and bringing home the bacon.

It's crazy to assess our parenting based on missing a milestone here and there. I think of it like this: When we get our work performance reviews—whether it's from a supervisor, staff, or board member—it's *annual*. Our work performance is not being judged for our daily performance (who could stand up to that much analyzing?). That's how we should look at our parenting performance—over a stretch of time, and remembering that our child's feelings are based on all the hugs, kisses, laughs, and caretaking we dole out in any given month. Adds Carter: "I think it is important for moms to remember that being emotionally sensitive, and earnestly invested in their child's world when they do spend time together, and consistently role modeling strong, healthy, and positive skill sets, is what is going to last in their children's minds. That's what will guide their children's choices and actions long after they're gone—not whether mom missed their class party in Kindergarten or their first pitch at a little league baseball game."

Step 1: *Avoid projecting your sadness onto your child.*

- -

The goal of this chapter is to help provide perspective when it comes to missing milestones, not to persuade you that it's not a big deal. It stinks missing your child's victories, big or small, and there's no use pretending it doesn't. Hey, you deal(t) with the high-octane poopy diapers, endless loop of late nights, temper tantrums, and possible visits to the ER. You *get* to be peeved that you're not there for the sweet glories. But it's important to know that it is *your* sadness we're talking about here, and not necessarily your child's.

Gillian, thirty-nine, accountant and mom to a ten-year-old boy, admits, "It's a given that in the height of tax season, when all my clients need help at once, that my child has a starring role in the community theater play. I go to opening night but not the next nights, like all the other moms. The other moms tell me not to worry, they will cheer extra-loud for my son when I'm not there, but I do worry about it. Does he think I'm neglecting him? He says 'no,' but does he really? I hate this time of year because I'm so frantic and also because I know the play is coming."

While we feel bummed about missing our child's event, it's the guilt we experience *on top of that sadness* that can bring on full despair. It's at these times that we need to remind ourselves that it's bonding with our child that matters. Roseanne Tobey, a counselor and founder of Calm and Sense Therapy, echoes what Carter told me: "Never missing an event is not what makes you a good parent. Staying connected to your children in a way that helps them know your loving support is there for them is what is important. Offering guidance and support—as well as proper limits and consequences in proper balance—is what being a good parent is about." If we can remind ourselves of this at the time of missing the occasional milestone, we can feel appropriate sadness and lose the despair.

Try This:

Now that we know what to tell ourselves, what can we tell our child? Advises Jules Spotts, PhD, a child psychologist and author of You Can Say No to Your Teen: "Your approach with your child should not be, 'I am so sad that I will not be at your big event!' Moms should talk about their sad feelings with other adults who will be supportive of how bad she feels about not being there. And moms do need to talk out those feelings, especially so [those feelings] don't come up while interacting with her child. To her son or daughter, the mom should say, 'I know that you would like me to be there at the party . . . and I just can't change the commitment I have to work.' Notice that it is 'and' here, and not 'but.' By saying this, the mom is recognizing the kid's feelings and empathizing—while also stating the facts."

Step 2: *Don't rob your child of the experience.*

- -

When my daughter was seven, she had a speaking part in her grade's "community meeting" (this is the meeting for the whole grade that parents are invited to attend, thereby torturing working moms who can't attend, since it doesn't end until after 9:00 AM). I was not able to go, and my daughter was understandably nervous about saying her lines in front of the whole grade. I felt awful that I couldn't say, "Don't worry, I'll be in the room with you, and you can look right at me if that helps!" Would she be an emotional mess? I worried. Would she be able to get the lines out? Who would comfort her if she got so nervous she ran off the stage crying?

I'm not the only working mom to panic that my child might mess up because I wasn't there in person to give the encouraging smile or literal thumbs up. In our minds, it is these small mama motivations that help our child deliver the speaking part, shoot the winning basket, or nail the drum solo. Some moms of younger children told me they have kept their child from participating in events to avoid any potential sorrow.

Take Jonna, thirty-nine, an articles editor at a family magazine and mom of a two- and a three-year-old, who recalls: "At the end of my son's first year at nursery school, there was a Spring Show scheduled for a Friday, with a rain date of Monday. Friday was fine for me, but Monday I had a meeting I had to attend with a guest from out of the office. What are the odds, I figured. Naturally, it poured on Friday. My child and I both missed the show because I could not bear the thought of him being there and not seeing his mommy in the audience. My son has zero memory of this, of course, but I *still* feel bad that he missed it."

The reality is that our child is most likely going to do just fine—especially if there is another parent or close relative (like a grandparent) who will attend, says child psychologist Laurie Zelinger, PhD. How your child will fare around your absence, she states, depends on your child's age and temperament, as well as the bond she has with you, the reaction of her peers, the importance placed on the event, and your approach toward the event. "A clingy child who has anxiety or separation issues might be very upset when they see their peers being hugged and congratulated by their parents after the event," Zelinger says, "In contrast, an older child who is developmentally moving toward spending more time with peers and away from parents will be less affected by a parent's absence." So, like so many aspects of parenting, you likely know best what your child can handle.

One more thing to remember, says Zelinger: It's not such a bad thing on occasion for your child to see that she can thrive—perhaps even shine—without you cheerleading from the audience: "We would be doing our children a disservice if we robbed them of all adverse experiences. While we want to keep those disappointments to a minimum, it helps build resilience when we anticipate our children's reactions [like missing an event] and prepare them for real life events."

Try This:

To minimize your child's disappointment at your missing a particular event, get resourceful. I heard from plenty of moms who gave their child a picture of themselves to take to the event, or wrote a letter for their child to read before and after the event. For my daughter's community meeting "performance," I let her wear my special locket, which has a picture of my husband and me in it. She loved that we were "there with her," and the locket worked like a charm (literally).

Step 3: *Make friends with technology.*

- -

If possible, certainly call your child on the phone before and/or after the big event to say good luck or congrats or "go get 'em!" In this day and age of in-your-face technology, we can finally use our gadgets for connecting in many ways, not just by phone. Says Carl Pickhardt, PhD, child psychologist and author of numerous parenting books, "A parent never has to miss marking a child's important occasion with so many ways of being there now: Text, call, email, message before and/or after the event. Just because you can't be there as a physical presence doesn't mean you cannot make voice or message contact."

Lori, a thirty-eight-year-old learning and development coordinator from North Carolina, and mom to two kids ages six and three, told me, "I missed my daughter's first birthday because I was giving a presentation at a conference. It was an important milestone for my career and she was only one year old, so she won't remember. But we did have a small party via Skype and then a big party when I got home."

Gina, a forty-three-year-old nutritionist and mom to twin seven-year-old boys, also takes advantage of new technology: "I knew I was going to have to miss my son's solo at the school holiday concert—which was going to be in front of his whole grade—because I had an important work presentation I couldn't get out of. So I did rehearsal runs all week beforehand with him, listening to his song over and over until he felt comfortable. He knew how proud I was of him, and I had my husband videotape his performance with his iPhone so my son and I could watch it and celebrate that night."

If you're away on a business trip when your daughter starts crawling—and you're desperate to see it—ask your partner or caretaker to

Skype with you so you can sneak a peek and yell hurray through the phone or computer. If your son is playing lacrosse in the semifinals— and you're at the office on deadline—have your partner or a friend videotape the game. Later, you can watch the event with your child, and let him give you a play-by-play. Unlike during the actual game, you'll be able to make comments and ask your child in-the-moment questions like: "Look at you! How did you feel when that happened?" or "Did you know you were going to take that amazing shot?" or "How were you able to do that with all the pressure?" Frankly, it may even be a *better* bonding moment because you're sharing the experience, not watching it from the crowd.

Try This:

Make a plan with your child before the event to connect so he or she can be excited about it too. Tell your son or daughter: "I'm not going to be able to watch your [fill-in-the-blank] because of a work obligation, and I want to find a way to experience it with you. Would it be okay if I have Dad video-tape it so we can watch it together this weekend?" If your child doesn't get into the spirit, suggest you throw in popcorn during the viewing and make a family celebration out of it. If your child says, "But it's not the same as you being there," don't lie and say that it is. I've found honesty is the only way to go: "It's not the same, you're right. I wish I could be there. But I would love to watch the video replay with you if you are up for it." As I'm sure you've experienced, giving your child the power to say yes or no helps.

Step 4: *Recognize your fingerprints.*

- -

When you stop to think about it, there is no specific *moment* when children accomplish most major developmental milestones. There is a process that gets kids from point A to point B, and it's usually pretty involved. Think of children learning to stand, for instance: They don't go from crawling to standing in one day, high-fiving everyone as they make the rounds. First there is pulling up to a standing position using furniture, human legs, or the family dog. Then there is the falling (oh, the falling!), tears of infuriation, more determined attempts at standing, a bite from the dog who didn't appreciate his fur being grabbed, and standing with wobbling (getting closer). Then finally, FINALLY, one day there is standing.

The process can go on for days, weeks, or longer. Same holds true for walking. Children don't just go from standing to ambling through the hallways one day—having never done it—while you're at work. They take a first step, plop to the ground, scream, get up, try another step, spend countless hours conquering the Frankenstein walk, arms stretched in front for balance, crashing into walls, moaning with disappointment, and then shrieking with joy as they cover a little distance. Nor do children suddenly win an award or play in the finals; just getting to that position takes a whole lot of sustained effort over time.

It's a *journey* every time your child reaches a milestone, and you, mama, are the cheerleader during this process. You provide hugs of encouragement, dole out the Band-Aids, and wipe away the tears. It's you who explains that the dog wasn't trying to be mean when he bit; he was just protecting his fur. You are the one to insist "you can do it" or "try again" or "you'll get it—I know you will!" So whether you catch the exact moment of your child doing the task executed perfectly for the first time is not the point (a treat, but not the point). So instead of berating yourself for your absence, appreciate that you helped get your child to the victory in the first place. Your fingerprints are all over this achievement.

Here's something else to consider: Even if you *did* quit your job so you could be home for all those "first" moments, you'd *still* miss a whole bunch of them. Ask any stay-at-home mom. You go to answer the phone and miss your child's first step. Your child loses her first tooth while sleeping at her grandma's. You can't go to your child's first debate because you have to visit a sick family member. Unless your eyes are trained on your child at every given moment (and Lord knows, if that's happening, you have far more serious problems than a missed milestone), you're going to miss plenty of "firsts." So just continue doing everything you're doing to help boost your child's confidence, and enjoy the sweet moments of the whole journey rather than flipping out over missing the finish line.

Step 5: *Instill a "mum's the word" policy.*

- -

This would all be easier, you may be thinking, if your childcare provider would stop poking the emotional wound of missing out by exclaiming, "You're never going to believe it—your little girl spoke her first word today!" or "Guess what? Your son scored the winning point today!" As the provider goes into the detailed play-by-play, you want to yell, "Okay, okay . . . zip it, lady!" If you can't be experiencing these moments firsthand, you certainly don't want that fact rubbed in your face. Unsure how to handle it (clearly throwing a punch at a caregiver is inappropriate), you nod robotically and mutter, "That's wonderful," while trying to stop the tears from flowing.

"I started crying when my child's nanny told me that my son went to the potty for the first time while I was at work," a mom friend told me once. "She told me how it happened and how they celebrated over sundaes at the local ice cream shop, and I just burst into tears—so embarrassing. Then she felt horrible, which made me feel even worse. Finally, I just told her that it's hard for me to hear about the milestones that I missed and would prefer to discover them on my own."

News flash: You don't have to fake happiness or even *listen* to these play-by-plays. While you may not be able to control the timing of a milestone, you can certainly control how you find out about it. Ask your childcare provider to spare you the details. *I can't do THAT,* you may be thinking. Of course you can. In fact, it is often even *par for the course* at daycare centers. Allegra Inganni, school-age program director at the Child Educational Center in California, told me, "At our center, we don't specifically have a written policy about not sharing milestones with families, but it is an unofficial practice that the teachers do not share any significant milestones that occur during the day. There are so many complex emotional components that go into a parent leaving the child (especially an infant) in daycare, that it is routine practice here to not share a milestone and let the family discover it for themselves."

You'll see the big moment when you see it, and it will be special for you and your child because you're experiencing it together. Your cheerleading is sweeter for your child than his daycare provider's could ever be. You're *mom*.

Try This:

Inganni encourages parents to "think about what your preference is—being told about milestones or not—and let that preference be known at the center early on." Tell your childcare provider calmly, "I just want to let you know that it's hard for me to hear about when I miss my child's special moments, and I would prefer discovering them on my own." Or, if you do want to know about your child's milestone, let the provider know the level of detail you'd like. Once this weight is lifted, you can simply bask in the glory of your child's accomplishment. If you have a stay-at-home husband or partner, let him know what works for you, realizing that it may also change over time. Some months you might crave email updates about your little one's latest milestone, along with all the sweet details; other months, it may just be too hard to hear about them. Instead of taking out your resentment on the caregiver for not being able to read your mind, make it clear how you would like the updates handled and be up-front about your feelings. Nichole Smith, founder of The Guilty Parent website (www.theguiltyparent.com), said she made this mum's-the-word agreement with her husband and never looked back: "It was our way of honoring and respecting one another's feelings and not missing out on these great moments in our children's lives."[2]

Step 6: *Stay rooted in one place.*

Liz, forty-two, an Internet strategist in Massachusetts and mom to a four-year-old, admitted: "In the process of building a website, there were many late nights and some weekend work. At the same time, my son was starting his first soccer season and there was push and pull in my heart about where I should be spending my time. Work needed me, but this was my child who needed me too."

It's tough to be faced with these choices, and frankly, sometimes the choice simply isn't ours, and no amount of gnashing our teeth or obsessing over what could have been will change it. That happened to Darcy, a thirty-six-year-old analyst in Colorado and mom to two boys ages nine and six, when her birthday dinner clashed with a work deadline. "I was working for a particularly difficult boss during one of my birthdays," she recalls, "and my family had to go to dinner *without me* because I had to stay late to work on a project that ended up getting shelved anyway. They were disappointed that they didn't get to take me out."

If you're *not* regularly wishing you could be at two places at one time, you're probably not a working mom. We're just about always in two places *mentally*, processing work tasks while hanging out with our kid and vice versa. Mostly, it's a way to torment ourselves since we're certainly not doubling production in any way.

Given that we can't clone ourselves *yet*, make the conscious choice to focus on whatever environment you're in *right now*, and stay present in that space. Hey, you might as well because there is nothing at all you can do except be wherever you are. I like how Maria, a forty-five-year-old international trade specialist from Virginia and mom of three, put it: "Take a deep breath, know it's a marathon, and you'll always have another chance to go to a school play or write the perfect briefing paper. Enjoy what you're doing right *now* rather than thinking of the next thing you have to do."

Try This:

When you find your thoughts (or heart) racing, do what the Zen-Buddhists do: Bring yourself back to the moment by zooming in on what's happening all around you—the sights, smells, sounds, tastes. I found it helps to practice staying in the moment during days that aren't overly stressful: I focus, for example, on what it feels like to brush my teeth without letting my mind wander, or listening to the sound of the water in the shower without worrying about what's to come during my day. I'm not always successful, but I think practicing it and trying to make it a habit helps me do it on the days when I really need it.

Step 7: *Consider the path untaken—with a clear lens.*

Crissi, thirty-four, an online content producer in California and mom to an eleven-year-old son, a fourteen-year-old daughter, and a sixteen-year-old stepson, admits that come summer, she "can't even begin to tell you how guilty I feel that I'm not there to take them to the beach, or let them have friends over, keep them off the video games or away from the TV." Simultaneously, she says, "I *like* working. When I take time off work for a simple 'staycation,' I am bored out of my mind. And more often than not, I go back to work feeling like I accomplished nothing—as if there wasn't enough time to relax, create family time, or do all those things I fantasize about doing whenever the weekend seems just too far away. Knowing that I am a poor manager of my time, I am well aware that being a stay-at-home mom would not be a good choice for me."

Just because we experience guilt and disappointment for not being home sometimes does not mean we've made a bad decision for ourselves in having a career. I sometimes picture what it would *really* be like if I were home for days on end without the mental stimulation of my work. I think I'd last a week before getting bored and cranky, and I know that my family would suffer the unpleasant consequences of that. I crave and need the satisfaction I get from working, and need has nothing to do with how much I love my daughter. So on the days when I found myself wishing I was home to catch my child's victories and milestones, I tried to play out the whole fantasy . . . would I truly be happier without my career? Would those brief moments of witnessing my child's accomplishment be enough to sustain me for the rest of the day? Nope.

Most of the women I interviewed told me the reason they work in the first place is for the overall satisfaction and meaning that come from doing work they care about. If you've picked up this book, chances are you feel the same.

> **Try This:**
>
> Katherine Reynolds Lewis, an award-winning journalist who writes regularly about parenting and business, suggests working moms jot down the reasons we work: "Write down your motivations. Once you've reassured yourself that you're doing what you need to do, then simply let go of the guilt. Trust yourself and the choices you've made for your family."[3] And keep the list, she advises, for those moments when guilt arises again.

Step 8: Let your child have a say—even if she's angry.
- -

Don't wait until the last minute to let your child know you won't be attending her event. Assuming your child is old enough to understand, tell her weeks ahead of time, and express your sorrow over missing the event. Again, I'm not talking about dumping your guilt on your kid so she has to cheer *you* up. Let your child know you wish you could be there, listen to how she is feeling, and see if you can come up with a plan together for how to honor the occasion.

Jill, a thirty-nine-year-old mom from Boston who has a sixteen-year-old son, told me, "I really wanted to be there during his driving test, which I knew was like the biggest and best thing in the world for him. But I couldn't get out of a work commitment. So I told him, 'Hey, I know you're going to do great and I'm excited for you. I'm also disappointed that I can't be there because I know what a big deal this is. Is there a way that would feel good to you to celebrate?' He suggested that when he got his license, he should get to drive me to his favorite restaurant to celebrate—my treat, of course—and I agreed. That's what we did. He passed, and I let him drive me to dinner—white knuckles clutching the dashboard, of course."

Your child wants to know you're disappointed (even your tween or teen who may give you the infuriating "whatever" shrug). It counts when you say, "I am so proud of all the work you've done to get to this place, and I sure wish I could be there in person to see it," or "Wow, you must feel great about this achievement. I know that I do!" But it's quite possible your child will respond with something like, "If you really cared, you'd come." This is the line that brings most mothers to their knees, and it's important not to flip out or give some long-winded testimony about how much you do care. Child psychologist Jules Spotts, PhD, advises: "What you want to avoid is becoming defensive, trying to justify and prove you're caring, or getting insulted that you have been accused of such a deep insult. Nor should you change your plans to prove that you care by going to the event."

Advises Spotts, "Say, 'Honey, over here (gesturing with your left hand to one side) is caring for you and loving you. That is a forever thing that never changes, and we both know that. Over here (gesture with other hand to the right side) is that I am just not able to come to this very important event, and I am aware that it is sad for you that I can't be there. This is a sad event (motion to right side), this is the caring and love for you that is always there (motion to left side).' That should be the whole deal, which might be a minute or so, and not an extended monologue, which would contradict the idea of this being one event *only*."

Proceed with Caution If . . .

you're missing so many milestones that your child is expressing resentment and hurt feelings. It's not going to scar your children if you miss some of their "Hey, look at me!" moments. But if you are missing many or most of them—and your children are clearly feeling neglected—it's time to adjust your schedule. When you hear about the next big event in one or more of your children's lives, give your boss a heads-up way in advance and mark it on any shared calendars you use. Then, figure out how you can get work coverage if need be. Don't put it off in the hope that things will somehow resolve themselves; you need to handle this right away. Assuming the work event is set in stone, can a staff member you work with attend the work event for you if you agree to take the next one? If there is a deadline you'll have to meet, can you work your butt off beforehand to meet the deadline earlier? It may mean spending a day working over the weekend, in advance, to get everything prepared. But the payoff is clearly worthwhile.

On the Flip Side . . .

maybe, when you feel guilty, you sometimes become so hell-bent on attending every one of your child's milestones that your boss and/or colleagues resent all your time away from the office because they have to cover for you. If this is the case, it's not going to fly in the office for long, and you have to admit they have a point in how unfair it is to expect them to cover for you each time. It's in your best interest to pick and choose which milestones or events you will attend and which to forgo. It's about balance here and making your decisions with intention. Your son or daughter will not resent you if you don't make it to every single event of theirs—and there will be an endless number of them over the years—so pace yourself.

SHOUT-OUT TO . . .

Anique, thirty-one, a molecular cellular biology PhD student in Massachusetts and mom of a two-year-old son. "I went back to the lab—doing experiments, writing academic papers, and preparing presentations—when my son, Isaac, was barely nine weeks old. I sometimes feel sad knowing the little moments my son experiences go by without me. When I feel like too many of these moments are happening, I'll stop the mental gymnastics and try to really focus on enjoying the mornings and evenings when I'm home with him— staying present with the bedtime story I'm reading him or the bath he's splashing in. If those sad moments come up while I'm at work, I try to satisfy my Isaac-craving with a quick look at a family picture or online video of him, and then plan something fun and small I can do once I see my little guy."

Chapter Wrap

- - - - - - - - - - - - - -

Step 1: *Avoid projecting your sadness onto your child.*

Harping on your absence after your child has moved on is unfair to you and your child.

Step 2: *Don't rob your child of the experience.*

Encourage your child to fully participate, even if you can't be there.

Step 3: *Make friends with technology.*

Have someone record the big event so you can relive it with your child later.

Step 4: *Recognize your fingerprints.*

Remember that your child's milestone was the result of an entire journey you *did* attend.

Step 5: *Instill a "mum's the word" policy.*

Let your child's provider know if you want to experience milestones on your own and not hear play-by-play reports.

Step 6: *Stay rooted in one place.*

Once you choose whether you'll be at work or your child's event, commit to fully engaging in that place.

Step 7: *Consider the path untaken—with a clear lens.*

Remind yourself that even though it's hard to miss the big moments, being a working mom is the path that best works for you.

Step 8: *Let your child have a say—even if she's angry.*

If your child is old enough, let her choose a way that the two of you can celebrate a victory together.

Chapter 4

ON THE ROAD AGAIN

Confession: "When I travel for business, I feel guilty for leaving the family but happy to get away."

Picture this: You're trying desperately to button your coat while reaching for your purse so you can get out of the house and make your flight. As you reach for the front door, your child hurls her little body in front of the door, shrieking, "NOOOO, don't *goooo!*" If you don't leave this second, you're likely to miss your flight, but you hesitate because your heart is breaking seeing your daughter lose it like this. What are you supposed to do? There are no words to make this situation better; you know that because you've tried every one of them. Will your child suffer permanent emotional damage if you gently push her aside to get out that door?

With every business trip, there's also a nagging feeling that all your best-laid plans will unravel when you go—in spite of all the plans you laid out for your partner or caretaker. You're consumed with doubt: Will your husband or partner forget to give your child her medication, despite the reminder sticky note you left? Will your child be sent to school with her lunch tote, and will there actually be *lunch* in it? What if the carpool's official "space-cadet mom" forgets she is on soccer duty and leaves your child stranded after practice again? In spite of the endless logistics you've handled (whether you're off for two days or two weeks), you can't imagine things can go off without a hitch. And then guess who's going to get blamed? That's right . . . *you are.* Bad mommy strikes again.

QUIZ: DO YOU "CARRY ON" GUILT (ALONG WITH LUGGAGE) DURING BUSINESS TRAVEL?

1. **After hunting down your airplane seat, cramming your luggage into the carry-on bin, and sinking into your seat, you think:**

   a. Nirvana! I can read my novel, do the crossword puzzle, or check out all the films I missed this year with the in-flight entertainment.

   b. I wonder if my child has calmed down by now. I'd better check in at home as soon as the plane touches down.

   c. Oh, no, I totally forgot to make a list of my daughter's favorite snacks!

2. **During your work conference, you get an unexpected free hour to do what you wish. You spend that time:**

   a. calling home to check in. When no one picks up, you immediately begin imagining worst-case scenarios that include trips to the ER.

   b. worrying about whether your child is feeling neglected and hurt.

   c. checking out the neighborhood near your hotel; it feels good to explore again.

3. **Before heading home, you make one last stop at:**

   a. the exercise room in the hotel. Who knows when you can sneak in another workout?

   b. the airport gift shop. To make up for your absence, you're going to bring home dozens of goodies for your children.

   c. the local coffee shop where you can get clear phone reception; you need to hear your child's voice right this very moment!

Answers: If you answered "a" for number 1, give yourself one point. If you answered "c" for number 2, give yourself one point. If you answered "a" for number 3, give yourself one point. If your sum total is two points or more, you're probably doing just fine but there's always room to grow; if your total was less than two, use this chapter to learn how to travel with less emotional baggage during your next getaway.

Reality Check

- - - - - - - - - - - - -

Work trips don't translate to abandoning your children. Abandoning your children means leaving and not coming back. This has very little to do with going away for a specified amount of time for business travel, making sure that your child is safe and cared for while you're gone, and staying connected to the family while you are away. So when it comes to managing your stress (and your guilt), remember this and do your best not to confuse the two.

Fortunately, there are plenty of actions you can take right now to bring the tension level waaaaay down for you and your family. One of the most important things is realizing that not only will your children be *okay* after you leave, but they will bounce back after your departure a lot faster than you probably will. You're on your plane or train thinking, "Man, I hope she has stopped sobbing, poor baby!" and she's playing Connect Four with her babysitter or gone off to go grocery shopping with Dad and is pleading for the chocolate-covered Oreo cookies. "It's the same as when we drop them off in nursery school and we're so frightened worrying about how they're going to manage without us—and, of course, some children cry," says family therapist and school consultant Meri Wallace. "But if we call the school within the hour, we find out they're playing and having fun."

As one mom shared with me, "After my husband dropped me off at the airport for a work trip, I turned around to wave to my child in the backseat. Big mistake! She was waving slowly and tears were streaming down her face. I felt like I was going to die, it was so awful! I spent the flight with a sinking feeling in my stomach, and only found out that night when I talked to my husband that my daughter cheered up the second they got out of the airport. She was singing along with the radio all the way to school. Man, I wish I'd known that! It would have saved me some major agony."

That said, even knowing our children will probably rebound quickly doesn't eliminate the worry and guilt that tend to accompany us all the way to our destination. Business travel doesn't always have to be this emotionally loaded. Luckily, there *are* things you can do to take the stress level down a few notches. This chapter is full of them so let's get started.

Step 1: *Appreciate the value of business trips.*

When I asked working moms about the hardest part of business travel, the answers ranged from "The logistics of what has to be handled beforehand are staggering!" to "I know it's absurd, but I worry my baby won't remember me when I get home" to "I always seem to get sick by the time I get home." But the most frequent answer—by a landslide—is worrying that our kids and their routines will fall apart while we're away.

Thankfully, this is rarely true (well, routines may unravel, but kids who are not experiencing extreme anxiety of some kind typically do just fine). Says Wallace, "It's okay that our kids are sad and maybe even a little angry when we leave—it's appropriate and means that they're attached to us. Moms have this mythical ideal in our heads that we're supposed to be with our kids 24 hours a day. We're not! One of the prime goals of childhood is to separate from the parent and become independent. If our kids are by our side the whole time, they're not able to!"

I've definitely also found that business trips got easier as my child started getting older and we could talk about them and find strategies to deal with missing one another that work for us. I love calling home from a trip and hearing my seven-year-old share the tiny details of her day; it was not quite so rewarding when she was a year old and trying to shove the entire phone into her mouth!

It should be said here that if you're taking frequent extended business trips and noticing that your child is no longer thriving, it is time to try to negotiate with your boss about reducing the length and/or frequency of your trips (I'm not suggesting you put your job at risk in these tough economic times, but rather seeing if there is room for flexibility). Signs that children are not thriving, says Wallace, include regression (like sucking their thumb after having given it up), crying at the drop of a hat, creating reasons to be oppositional with you on everything when you get back from a trip ("Why are you wearing your hair like *that*?"). If this sounds familiar, ask your boss about flying to and from the meeting on the same day, so you're back to say goodnight to your child. Or perhaps you can use Skype or videoconferencing to attend an off-site meeting without ever leaving town at all. Do let your child know, Wallace says, that you see he is having a hard time and you want to be home more, too, so you are doing your best to try to travel less.

It's also helpful to appreciate that it is often *important,* professionally, for us to go on our business trips. Says Edward Chalmers, a contributor to Askmen.com's "Power and Money" section: "No matter what type of industry you're in, business travel will usually be necessary as you climb the corporate ladder. Even if you detest traveling, it's a career-limiting move to refuse without a very strong and compelling reason."[1]

Working moms also tell me that trips often offer new inspiration pertaining to work, can be necessary for finishing certain projects, allow them to network with others in their field, and bring new insights into how they think about their profession.

One more built-in bonus of these trips: reconnecting with your identity. As one filmmaker mom of two told me, "The dirty little secret is that it feels good to just focus on myself for a few days and remember who I am outside of being a mom!" Stepping away for a short time from your role as "mommy"—and remembering spontaneity and independence—is revitalizing. More than a few moms confessed that they have come to *love* business travel because it's one of the few times they can focus on their own needs. Really, it can be quite wonderful getting a small break from our children yelling *"Mommm!"* from the other side of the house, tripping over the toys and backpacks littering the floor, and screaming "Turn that music down!"

Step 2: *Be aware of your delivery.*

- -

Marilyn, a thirty-seven-year-old filmmaker in New York, recalls all too well the stress of seeing her older son (now ten) unravel emotionally when she would announce she would be taking a one-week business trip. "He, like me, can get anxious quickly," admits Marilyn, "and one day he said 'I hate it when you leave!'" Then he threw the emotional grenade: "Mom, don't you know that as we get older, we *need* you here more?"

The worst! Most of us are already worrying about what it will mean for our kids and their daily routine when we take off for a business trip. So having our child push hard on that guilt button can spiral us into a full-on tailspin. *My child thinks I don't care about her! What if she thinks I'm never coming home? What if my business travel sends my child down the slippery slope to full-on abandonment issues?* Before we know it, we may be considering canceling our trip, weighing the financial and professional repercussions of doing so against our inflated concerns.

Know that how you communicate the news of your departure—as well as your tone when you call from the road—makes an enormous difference in your child's reaction to your traveling. If I sound calm and confident when I tell my daughter I'm leaving for a trip, she handles it well. She might pout and say, "No I don't want you to go," but if I respond, "I will miss you too" in a steady voice and give her a big hug, that's usually the end of it. Whereas if I wailed, "I know, these business trips are so hard for both of us!" or "I hate being away from you, too!" I can guarantee you there would be a mini-meltdown. It's equally important that I remain calm when I call home.

Suggests Amy Kossoff Smith, founder of Momtinilounge.com, which offers tips and tools for "the business of motherhood": "Tell your child when you call home, 'I miss you—and I'm also having an adventure. I bet you are too. What's been going on?' That way, we set a much more positive tone." She adds, "If we call home and say, 'I miss you *so so much*' in a whimpering voice, our kids are going to get upset too."

Marilyn learned how much delivery mattered after witnessing her son become so distraught about her departures that she worried he would spiral into a depression after she left. She took him to see a therapist, who assured Marilyn that her son was not suffering any kind of crisis. "Basically, he just missed me when I was away," says Marilyn, "and the therapist assured me this was okay, and that I shouldn't skip business travel. My son would be just fine." What was amazing, she adds, is that the psychologist's feedback made *her* feel less stressed, and her son's anxiety went way down as a result. Marilyn says she is now able to leave more room for her son to express his sadness when she's traveling, without *her* feeling keyed up. Her son feels "appropriate" sadness, she says, and Marilyn has gained confidence that they can both handle her trips now.

Step 3: *Make it easier for your partner.*

- -

Just when you're starting to get a handle on all the logistics of your departure, your husband or partner may invariably drop some kind of guilt bomb, such as "I don't know how I'm going to get all my work done this week while watching the kids," or "So *how* long are you going to be gone?" or "Man, you are so lucky you're going to have your own hotel room. I'd kill for that!" Perhaps even more tormenting is "You owe me big-time." Now on top of guilt, there is an owing? Hey, you're not going to Vegas with the girls for a week; it's a *business* trip. The response we'd love to receive instead? "We'll miss you, but this is a great work opportunity, so go do your thing!" (A pretty high bar to set, I know.)

Pam, an assistant professor of forest ecology and mother of two children under five, knows these moments of travel guilt well. On top of the stress of leaving her kids, Pam confesses that she sometimes feels like she's using up her "travel credits" when she takes business trips. "There is all this guilt because I have to travel so much for my job," she says, "and my husband doesn't." In some ways, it would be better, she admits, if he would take business trips too, "just so it would feel more even."

Whether or not we receive our partner's well wishes, we can have conversations and planning sessions to make sure our time away goes as smoothly as possible for him. Discuss ahead of time, for example, whether it works better for him if you call home in the morning or evening, and every day or every other day. For the record, Phaedra Cucina, author of *My Mommy's on a Business Trip,* suggests calling early in the day rather than later: "So often it's hard to catch the kids in the evening, with our own meetings running late. They are often asleep before you can call. Instead, phone when the kids are getting up. That's when they're in that lovey, snuggly mindset and you can start their day off with a smile."[2] That said, your partner may be running around scrambling to get your kid to school, so make sure it works on his side.

Give your husband plenty of leeway to do things *his own way* while you're gone. This is not the time to micromanage. Advises Susan Bartell, nationally recognized parenting psychologist and author of *The Top 50 Questions Kids Ask*, "Moms who micromanage while they're away need to recognize that this is *their* issue—that it's because you feel guilty that you're not there. If you felt comfortable enough leaving your child with this person in charge, then you have to trust that this person is going to take care of your child. Say to yourself, 'They're managing without me,' and be glad that you can have the independence to take care of what you need to and things aren't going to fall apart."[3] That's what Lisa, a forty-seven-year-old law professor and mom of three, tries to do: "Whenever I travel, I leave a detailed itinerary that I send to my husband, our nanny, everyone I carpool with, and their nannies. However, I'm satisfied if everyone gets where they need to be, survives in one piece, and some homework gets done."

Try This:

Follow the advice of career coach Jill Frank. In her article "3 Simple Ways to Take the Pain out of Business Travel," she writes: "One of the biggest frustrations of travel is being out of the loop ... Kids are constantly bringing home important notices from school ... If you aren't there to ... handle these notices, what happens to them? Establishing organization and communication systems will keep you sane and ensure that nothing falls through the cracks."[4]

Make it easy for your husband by setting out a basket or folder that he can drop important notices into so you can read them when you get home. (Obviously he should follow through on any tasks with deadlines that take place before you get home.)

Step 4: Walk your child through the game plan.

- -

"When my daughter was four, I made the mistake of telling her about my business trip three weeks ahead of time—bad call," one mom admitted to me. "Every day for three weeks she would wake up asking whether this was the day I was leaving. It didn't matter how many times I told her the number of days or showed her the calendar; she had no grasp of what three weeks looked like. Basically, my gaff caused her undue stress and left me feeling awful. Well, now I know better."

Yes, when to tell your child about the trip depends on the age of the child. According to Bartell, it depends on whether your child is able to understand the concept of time. If your child is between ages three to seven and can "X" off days on the calendar, give the child a week's notice. If your child can't do this yet, give him a few days' notice. If he's older than seven, it depends on the child's needs and wishes. "One of my clients is a working mom who travels a lot," says Bartell, "and her daughter in fourth grade likes to know her mom's travel schedule for about three months in advance. It's good for her and makes her feel like she has some control over scheduling. You have to ask your child what works for them."[5]

Next, let children know what their time at home without you is going to look like. As award-winning parenting consultant Barbara Meltz put it, "Children are all about predictability and egocentricity. What they want to know is, 'What about me?' Children need to know that while you are gone, their routines will stay the same."[6] Let them know that their day will still look exactly the same as always: Wake up at 7:00 AM, breakfast, go to school . . . go to sleep at their regular time. Hearing you tick off all the routine tasks of their day will be comforting and reassuring. Your child may even ask, "Do I still have to go to bed at the same time?" or "Do I have to do my chores while you're gone?" The answer is "Yes. Your day will look the same."

Your child will also like hearing you describe what the day will look like when you return home. You might say, "Next Tuesday, you and Daddy will come to the airport and I will meet you as soon as I get off the plane, and I will run to you and give you a huuuge hug!" or "I will get home on Monday night past your bedtime, so I'm going to peek in on you the second I walk through the door. When you wake up on Tuesday, I'll be waiting to give you a smooch."

Spelling out the details of your reunion, says Vivian Friedman, PhD, a professor in the division of child and adolescent psychiatry at the University of Alabama at Birmingham, reassures your child how much you look forward to being with him again. Your child may, in fact, ask you many times when you're coming home, because the answer makes him feel secure.[7]

Try This:

While you're discussing the game plan, schedule with your child a time(s) for phone calls or Skyping. Have your child mark those times on a calendar so it's right there to be viewed if she has a wave of missing you while you're gone. A calendar is concrete; it allows children to see, quite literally, when you're coming home and when they'll get to talk to you. If you aren't sure how many times you'll be able to call because your work schedule is full, tell your child the minimum number of times you'll be calling; you don't want to overpromise and not deliver. It's better to surprise her with a couple of extra calls that you didn't know you'd have time for than disappoint her when you don't call.

Step 5: *Take the pampering plunge.*

My daughter was still a baby the first time I took a business trip that involved flying across the country to San Francisco. I felt guilty about leaving my husband at home to deal with all of the early morning wake-ups and worried about how my daughter would fare without me. The idea of being so far away for more than a day literally made my heart hurt. That said, the moment I walked into my boutique hotel room and lay down on the bed, I felt my whole body relax. It was so peaceful. Nobody needed me at that moment. There was a clean bathtub with my name on it, and I knew I would get a full night's sleep before work the next day. It was heaven.

For moms who don't feel comfortable indulging themselves during work trips, it's time to reconsider. These business trips usually involve a lot of work. Whether it's talking on panels, schmoozing, sitting through an all-day conference, walking around trade shows, attending long meetings . . . it can be seriously draining. Says mom and businesswoman Amy Kossoff Smith: "Often, it's hard to even find time to *do* something decadent during business trips because they're so jam-packed. But it's important to take care of ourselves. Take a walk on the beach for thirty minutes or explore a new area where you're staying. You don't want to come back from your trip burnt-out, which is not good for your child either, because they're going to want your attention after the trip."

As Smith suggests, pampering yourself doesn't have to mean spending heaps of money, if that's the concern. Sure, it's nice to book a rejuvenating two-hour facial, full-body massage, or dine out at a restaurant that doesn't hand out crayons and children's menus, but many moms I spoke to said the little pleasures felt just as indulgent: eating a giant Snickers from the minibar in the hotel bed while watching an On Demand movie, soaking in a hot bath until their skin turned pruney (maybe even while eating that Snickers bar), or skipping one of the networking dinners to curl up with a good book. One mom said her guilty pleasure is ordering a pancake breakfast from room service while watching the morning TV shows in her pajamas at least once before returning home.

Here are some of the other simple pleasures women said they treat themselves to while on the road for work:

> *"Taking a nap in between work events—it's heaven!"*

> *"Calling friends on the phone and having the luxury to really listen and talk with them because I'm usually so rushed."*

> *"I like to sit in the hotel lobby with a glass of wine and just watch people coming and going, imagining their life stories, like who's having an affair!"*

> *"I bring takeout dinner to my room and eat it in my bathrobe."*

> *"Going to a restaurant by myself. I wouldn't want to do it all the time, but it's really nice once in a while!"*

Why feel guilty about these sweet moments? We spend countless hours taking care of our family's needs, as well as those of our boss or colleagues, friends and parents, not to mention the menagerie of fish, lizards, hermit crabs, and rescue mutts that finagle their way into our homes. Hey, we working moms are entitled to a little self-indulgence. In fact, it's heartening to hear that in November 2009 a poll of 4,000 women conducted by *Working Mother* and Country Inns & Suites by Carlson found that 62 percent said the amount of travel was just right for them, and 57 percent said what they like most about business travel is the personal time.[8] So go ahead and enjoy, because before you know it, the chocolate mint on your hotel pillow will be replaced by tiny chocolate fingerprints on your own pillow at home.

Step 6: *Don't rush home after one bad phone call.*

- -

It's quite possible that at least once during your trip when you call home, your husband, partner, or caregiver may plant a seed of doubt about your being away, or even send you into full-fledged panic. For the sake of example, let's say it's your husband. He might tell you, "Oh by the way, Mikey is fine now, but he threw up twice last night after dinner," or "Lucy is freaking out because her best friend said she is no longer invited to her birthday party."

Ack! screams your maternal brain. *DISASTER! Must get home! Somebody book me a flight!*

Anne, thirty-nine, an insurance underwriter from Rhode Island, knows a thing or two about these stressful calls. She has three kids, ages five, three, and one, and travels four or five days a month for work. She recalls making one business trip after her second child was born, and her husband, who was watching the kids, called when he was "at the end of his rope." According to Anne, her husband was frustrated because he couldn't get their son to sleep, a task that Anne usually handled. Anne admits that she felt so worried that she cut her trip short and went home. While she says it was the right decision for her at the time, she also "felt embarrassed, professionally, about this because I work almost exclusively with men, who didn't understand why I had to leave."

There are certainly no-brainer situations in which you'd cut the trip short, namely anything involving the words "emergency room" (unless it's not life-threatening, and you and your husband agree that he's got it all under control). But most of the calls coming to you in fits of frustration probably don't require that you jump ship and head home. So before you start flinging all your clothes into your Samsonite, take a deep breath. Okay, now ask yourself whether this is really something that requires your presence. Is there truly an urgency to get home today (like your son just swallowed a handful of Ambien thinking they were Tic Tacs?) or can the situation be contained, even fixed, by your partner? If he's soothed your child a thousand times already, then you *know* that he can likely handle this one. If not, this might be a good time for him to figure it out.

Plenty of women I interviewed spoke proudly of their husband's commitment and involvement on the parenting front. That said, many also said they are used to running the show at home for the most part. If this is true for you, think of your husband or partner as the understudy that has to go on stage after the star of the show (you!) announces she can't perform. He will rise to the occasion if you are not there to fix it. Says Carin Goldstein, licensed marriage and family therapist, "As mothers, we are the masters of keeping the ship's engine running smoothly and effectively, all while multitasking till we're blue in the face. Hence, it is our innate ability to spring into action when a child is in need. However, we shoot ourselves in the foot when we displace that innate impulse onto our husbands, who call in a panic because little Johnny threw up all over himself. Ladies, I have three words for you: Stop enabling him. It's one thing if he's calling you because the house is on fire (literally), but it's another thing when he needs to call 'mommy' to rescue him from being the other parent." He really will figure it out.

Lisa, a thirty-nine-year-old attorney, remembers the day when her husband, Scott, sent their daughter off to school for a field trip without packing her a lunch. "It didn't say on the permission slip that parents should pack a lunch," Lisa says. "I only knew because I'd volunteered on a field trip before, so I should have told him." Was it a catastrophe? No, their daughter, Hannah, made do with snacks and contributions from her friends ("everyone had to lend me pieces of their *own* food," Hannah complained), and Lisa and her husband both felt terrible. "But you can bet it won't happen again," Lisa says, "and now we look back at that day and laugh." It simply exemplifies one of the fall-through-the-crack moments of parenting we've all experienced a dozen times.

When you get home, thank your partner again for taking over parenting duty while you were away. He may want to share some of his frustrating hurdles (read: moan and groan to get some sympathy; hey, who among us hasn't done that?). If it sounds like he handled the problems well enough—everyone has their limbs intact and no one is in trauma therapy—tell him "nice job!" Remember, you want him to feel confident in parenting, and most especially when you're on the road. If you list all the things he did "wrong," you're basically announcing that it's better for the family if you never travel. Many of us like to think that we are so central to nurturing our kids, whether it's their bodies or feelings that need healing, that life will fall apart if we aren't home to soothe them. There's a lot to be said for being the *main* source of comfort in our kids' lives, but not the *only* source.

> **Try This:**
>
> Here's a quick lifesaver for your partner, if he's struggling, that several moms told me they do before hitting the road. Record yourself reading a short story or leave a message for your child (your partner can even probably record it on his cell phone, or you can leave it on your answering machine). It can just say, "I love you so much and can't wait to talk to you tomorrow!" That way, if your child is experiencing a wave of missing you, your partner can play this at any time, including when your child is having a hard time falling asleep.

Step 7: *Skip the souvenirs—or at least go small.*

- -

One midwestern mom of two kids confessed, "I always brought gifts home to my kids when I went away. In fact, I'd load up my suitcase (like Santa Claus) and come home to very excited children. But one time I was running late and had no time to grab any gifts before coming home, and the kids threw total tantrums. I thought they'd understand, but I was obviously delusional. I'd set the precedent that my departure always means gifts for them, thereby creating little monsters."

Another mom confessed, "I bought gifts for my daughter while I was away on business trips until the last time. I walked in the door to her saying, 'What'd you get me? What'd you get?' I handed over this cute stuffed animal wearing a T-shirt with the name of the city I was visiting—which took me about forty-five minutes to find, mind you—and I expected her to be jumping up and down. Instead she said, 'That's cute! Did you get me anything else?'" That was the last time this mom bought her daughter a gift while she was away. "Now I think that my coming home is the gift," she says, "and that's what my daughter can look forward to!"

Stocking up on souvenirs is a common strategy, with a belief that the better the gift, the less guilt moms feel about leaving home. Heck, it even makes phoning home easier because moms can announce, *"Oooh,* I got you something good!" or "Wait until you see what Mommy bought you!" The problem, as moms find out all the time, is that you are seriously screwed the one time you don't come home with something (or a gift that's not good enough), because you've locked yourself into that expectation. It is fine to bring home a little something special for your child *sometimes,* but making gifts mandatory is pretty much a setup for disaster. Advises Kathleen Barton, life coach and author of *The Balancing Act: Managing Work & Life,* "I don't suggest going out and buying a gift for your kids on each trip, because they'll soon expect it! . . . Instead, bring home a small memento from your business event or hotel. When I attend trade shows, I always pick up 'giveaways' from the booths."[9]

> **Try This:**
>
> Here's another idea, if you like the souvenir route: Start a small collection of something you can add to. One mom told me she picks up a magnet from whatever city she is traveling to for her child; another told me she always takes at least one photo while she's away, wearing the bead necklace her daughter made her; another brings home a nice-smelling soap from the hotel she stays in (okay, that's me). All of these ideas are easily packable, don't take heaps of time to track down, and show "Mom was thinking about you while away."

Step 8: *Celebrate if the kids don't miss you desperately.*

Kim, thirty-seven, is the mom of two boys, ages six and eight, and the executive director of a national nonprofit organization in Washington, D.C., that advocates for hemophiliacs (people with bleeding disorders). She loves helping give a voice to people with the disorder, especially since one of her sons suffers from hemophilia. Her work, she says, could not be any more meaningful to her. The problem is that Kim lives in Wisconsin, so her job involves traveling back and forth to headquarters on the East Coast. This means the constant hassles of logistics—mapping out a weekly calendar, getting carpools lined up for her kids, making sure her son is getting his medication, and all sorts of other tasks. Kim says she also struggles with connecting to the boys while she's away because "When I call them on the phone they don't want to talk. They just say 'hi, love you, bye!' and I have to find out how they're really doing from their dad or whichever parent picked them up during carpool." Kim says she has basically trained them to say, "I miss you too," but she continues to crave declarations of love.

Those who experience this emotional disconnect, like Kim, know how easy it is to believe that your children's reactions reflect apathy toward you, since your departure apparently doesn't even register as a blip on their emotional radars! Before you weep into your hotel pillow, consider that your children are simply getting caught up in day-to-day life. Yes, they miss you, but at the moment you happened to call, they were engaged in something else, and that's *good*. Because even though it may feel frustrating (Where's my "I love you, Mom!" or "Come home!"), it means that your children are adapting just fine while you're away. "Take it as a sign that your kids are thriving because you've provided them with good care and given them enough confidence that they can separate from you," says Meri Wallace. This is a reason to celebrate, not to pine over.

Then there's the challenging transition back home to contend with. You are on your way home, dreaming of the giant hugs you're going to give your children the moment you see their adorable faces. The taxi can't get to your house fast enough! You rush to the door, throw it open, and your children look at you and declare, "I got a C on my test today!" or "Hi Mama! Can I have a playdate with Mandy tomorrow?" *Seriously?*

Or maybe you will have the reverse problem—a constant clinginess upon returning home, especially from a toddler-age child. Sure, it was adorable the first night home, and it was not so bad the next day or two, but now you're starting to wonder if it's ever going to stop. It's nice to be cherished, but you are starting to feel caught in a death grip. How long is this new attachment-to-the-hip going to last? Child psychologist Kenneth N. Condrell, PhD, reminds us that toddlers have no concept of time and don't understand when you're coming back.[10] So your daughter or son is likely ecstatic that you really did return, and will ease up on the grip as soon as her or his routine—with you—gets back to normal.

> **Try This:**
>
> To offset the travel blues you or your children might be experiencing, plan a special day with them when you get back. Suggests Tracy Porpora, journalist and author of The Complete Guide to Baby Sign Language: 101 Tips and Tricks Every Parent Needs to Know, "Schedule a fun day or trip for the following weekend when you return where you and your children enjoy a day in the park or a trip to the local zoo. Whatever you plan, make the focus all about the kids and enjoying family time together."[11]

Proceed with Caution If . . .

you're thinking that "winging it" is okay and that the caretaker will figure things out intuitively. Whether the caretaker is your partner, friend, babysitter, or neighbor, this person needs information spelled out in an organized way. Leave a typed-up document with your cell phone number, hotel and flight information, your child's cell phone number (if appropriate), contact information for doctors and dentists, as well as neighbors or emergency backups. If you have a house alarm, leave the name of the alarm company. Also leave notes on what a typical day looks like for your child, including times for homework, meals, snacks, afterschool activities, etc. Make sure the refrigerator is packed ahead of time and the laundry done to minimize hassles for the caregiver.

On the Flip Side . . .

maybe the caregiver ends up not needing your notes and reports that things went so swimmingly when you were away that you wonder if this person is the far better parent. Why didn't your children give him a hassle about cleaning up or doing homework?! Why don't they make it so easy on *you?* You don't want to feel in competition here, but when he says the week watching the children was "no problem," your draw drops open. *No problem?* Take a deep breath. "What this means is that you have a healthy child," says Dr. Bartell, "and the fact that they are able to turn to someone else for nurturing doesn't minimize your role as the most important caregiver. It tells you that your child is able to successfully turn to other people for help and can nurture themselves. This means you're raising an emotionally healthy child!"[12]

SHOUT-OUT TO . . .

the smart mama (who emailed anonymously) with this awesome idea. "I travel quite a bit for business and found a way to make my departure much easier on my six-year-old girl and myself. I have her pack something small in my suitcase that I promise not to look at until I arrive at the hotel. It could be a small stuffed animal or a note she writes or a smiley face pin. The little treasure assures her I'll be thinking about her while I'm away, and it's always a wonderful discovery for me when I unpack. Plus, she's excited to talk about my finding it when I call home for the first time."

Chapter Wrap

- - - - - - - - - - - - - -

Step 1: *Appreciate the value of business trips.*

Occasional business trips show your children that they can thrive without you for a short period while moving you forward professionally.

Step 2: *Be aware of your delivery.*

Reduce your child's worries about your trip by using a calm, positive tone when you announce your departure and when you call home.

Step 3: *Make it easier for your partner.*

Express your appreciation if he or she is single parenting while you're away—and put the kibosh on passive/aggressive comments.

Step 4: *Walk your child through the game plan.*

Your child will be much calmer about you leaving if he knows what to expect while you're gone.

Step 5: *Take the pampering plunge.*

Give yourself permission to indulge yourself a little during this time when you don't have to take care of anyone else.

Step 6: *Don't rush home after one bad phone call.*

It's one thing to cut the trip short if there is an emergency, but sad feelings—which are appropriate—don't count as an emergency.

Step 7: *Skip the souvenirs—or at least go small.*

Buying your child decadent gifts to assuage your guilt ends up putting more expectations on you and hiking up stress levels.

Step 8: *Celebrate if the kids don't miss you desperately.*

If your children don't fall apart while you're gone, it means they felt safe and secure—not that you're unloved.

Chapter 5

THE SCHOOL DROP-AND-DASH

Confession: "I want to volunteer at my kid's school but feel overwhelmed by the endless requests."

You race into school at breakneck speed, dragging your child behind you by the hand. Is this *really* the fastest your kid can move, you wonder, and make a mental note to quit buying high-carb snacks. You finally reach the classroom, wearing a smile of false calm for the unhurried moms chatting in the hall, then give your kid a quick hug, a smooch, and wishes for a great day. If nobody says a word to you—no teacher with a reminder to bring snow boots tomorrow, no PTA mom with a reminder about the coat drive, no class parent approaching you with a look of intent—you may just get to your meeting on time. You avoid all eye contact, turn, and walk briskly out the door, promising yourself you'll leave more time tomorrow for a saner drop-off. As you get into your car, you breathe a sigh of relief because it seems you might just make it to work without having to sprint again. (Now imagine if you have *more* than one child!)

That's just the school drop-off. There is a whole *world* of school tasks, expectations, and responsibilities you are having trouble keeping track of. You're pretty sure you told someone (a teacher? parent?) you'd volunteer for the spring book fair back in September, when it seemed oh-so-far away. Then there was the email asking you to be on the fundraising committee, and you haven't chaperoned a single field trip this year. You worry about your child's teacher and other classroom parents resenting you. After all, they are the ones picking up the slack when you don't participate. But what are you supposed to do? There are only so many hours in a day!

Meanwhile, what do your *children* think of how little time you invest overall in their school community? Are they comparing you with the other moms who seem to have oodles of time to say an unhurried goodbye, check in with the teacher, make double sure everything is in the kid's backpack, and even remind their child that "tonight is home-made pizza night?" C'mon! While you are almost always flying out the classroom door, they are strolling, even turning back to wave to their child one last time. Clearly your kids notice and, *gulp,* imagine you don't care as much as the other parents. Nothing could be further from the truth. You just don't have time to linger and get to work on time, so how do you set things *right*?

QUIZ: DO YOU PUT IN ENOUGH FACE TIME AT SCHOOL?

1. Your daughter tells you over dinner that she wants you to come to her classroom one morning and read books. So you:

   a. exclaim, "That sounds fun!" and hope she'll forget tomorrow.

   b. pick a couple of days right then that, with some finagling, could work for you and sign up the next day.

   c. tell her that you'd love to as soon as work slows down in a month or two.

2. You agreed months ago to chaperone your son's class field trip to the art museum next week, and now a deadline has popped up unexpectedly, so you:

   a. go on the field trip anyway and turn off all your gadgets so work can't get ahold of you; you'll "overtime it" this weekend.

   b. go, and sneak away to the lobby several times to check your work email, just to make sure no disasters occur.

   c. tell your child and his teacher that you won't be able to make it, and then suffer guilt-induced stomachaches.

3. When an email pops up from the PTA with "Volunteer Request" in the subject field, you:

   a. respond "yes" and will figure out the logistics; you're due for participation.

   b. delete the email without even opening it. If you don't open it, it doesn't exist.

   c. send an email back with a small lie about being out of the country.

Answers: If you answered "b" for number 1, give yourself one point. If you answered "a" for number 2, give yourself one point. If you answered "a" for number 3, give yourself one point. If you received at least two points, you're probably doing a pretty good job of giving what you can to work and school, even if it feels like you're racing around a lot. If you received one or zero points, pay extra attention to the steps in this chapter, because you're likely going to need them until your child leaves for college.

Reality Check

- - - - - - - - - - - - - -

No one (well, no one *sane*) can expect career moms to serve on PTA committees, make homemade brownies for every fundraising bake sale, attend every school concert, and show up to all the holiday class parties (why *are* there so many parties?) each year. Frankly, I don't think anyone *does* expect this. But in between full-throttle parental participation and doing nothing is a huge range of possibilities that we can each take advantage of. After all, most of us want to feel connected to our child's school and feel like a part of the community. It's just that our schedules are so jam-packed with prior obligations that we can't figure out how to participate.

What typically happens, as a result, is that instead of offering to volunteer *sometimes*, we give up altogether and say no to everything. We make it even worse by then feeling guilty each time we say no, and worry about what others will think of our lack of effort. As one mom aptly put it: "When I see an email from my son's teacher, I think, 'Oh, sh*t, here we go again.' I just assume it's going to be yet another thing I won't be able to help with." For this mom, it wasn't that she didn't *want* to help; it was that she "doesn't want to commit and then have to bail due to a last-minute work or family obligation. I feel it's worse to abandon ship than never to volunteer at all."

While this is understandable—none of us want to be labeled "flakey" or "uncaring" in our community—what we really just need is to get smarter about *how* we volunteer. As certified life/business coach Lara Galloway (also known as "The Mom Biz Coach") told me, "We need to focus on choosing to volunteer doing what serves our own interests and those of our children." She suggests signing up two or three times a year for short commitments that we can stick to, adding, "You can have a very powerful impact on your child even if you can only participate for a short while a few times a year. This allows us to drop the 'shoulds' and feel good rather than feeling overwhelmed by taking on too much."

I definitely like this idea of volunteering and feeling good about our efforts, while easing up on the pressure to do more all the time. Wouldn't it be nice to feel that we're doing right by our children and the village that's helping to raise them, without feeling exhausted from overcommitting? That's what this chapter is all about.

Step 1: *Raise your hand before you get called on.*

- -

Remember back in grade school when you avoided eye contact with the teacher if you didn't know the answer to a question? Then you learned that the best defense is a good offense—you raised your hand for a question you *could* answer as quickly as possible so you'd be off the hook for the rest of the discussion. It was insurance. You can apply that exact same principle when it comes to volunteering at the school. Jump in early if you can't necessarily jump often. For example, my friend Betsy, an author and mother of a teen and a preteen, says: "I'd rather go volunteer to read to my daughter's class, which I love, than deal with a request to be an overnight chaperone during the school science camp, so I volunteer for the reading *right away*."

I, personally, have been trying over the past year to add my name to those volunteer sign-up sheets posted outside my child's classroom door as soon as possible, whether it's for being the mystery classroom reader, picking a time for the parent-teacher conference, or choosing an item to bring to the class breakfast (I do not want to get stuck with the heavy items, like watermelon). By committing right away, I boost my chances of scheduling a time that won't conflict with work obligations, so I can likely follow through. The same holds true for email; I'm finally learning to check my calendar immediately after reading about volunteer requests I think I can help out with, and then reply immediately so I don't box myself into a work-conflict corner.

Here's a tip from a mama of three who confessed to me that she has an extremely hard time managing the numerous volunteer requests from *three* teachers at once: "I send my children's teachers a note at the start of the school year, explaining that I don't have much time to volunteer during the year but would like to find a few ways to help the classroom." By doing this, she says—and following through on the teacher's suggestions—she doesn't worry so much about the deluge of email requests throughout the rest of the year and can feel good about her efforts.

Try This:

If you would like to follow suit but worry an open-ended offer to the teacher might backfire (what if the teacher asks me to cut 4,000 triangles out of felt on the day before a client meeting . . . or worse, to fill in as a last-minute driver for an all-day field trip?)—provide specific ways you know you can help. Perhaps you can send in a garbage bag full of craft materials, like magazines, toilet paper rolls, or milk cartons—a good way to get rid of that clutterfest of recyclables sucking up space in your kitchen. Or volunteer to trace hearts from construction paper for Valentine's Day (a relaxing change of pace for your brain, which can be done while watching a favorite TV show).

Step 2: *Be visible when you volunteer.*

- -

When it comes to pitching in at the school, this is the time to think counterintuitively. You're busy at work so it's probably best to volunteer to do something you can do at home, at night, after the kids go to bed, right? Wrong! Forget offering to pick up party supplies that you drop off before school, or tallying weekly class reading logs, or attending a nighttime committee meeting. Your child is not going to appreciate (or even recognize) that you're pitching in, and she's the one you are doing this for, yes?

Instead, suggests Jennifer Berz, a Massachusetts-based child psychologist, think *visibility*. Pick volunteer experiences where your child can see you participating, ones that will also likely lead to a pleasant time together. Sign up to volunteer at the school fair, Halloween party, or trip to the zoo. Offer to read a book or do an art project or explain a holiday ritual for the classroom, where you'll be front and center. You'll get the benefit of contributing to the school *and* spending time with your child *and* meeting his or her classmates.

One mom from my daughter's school told me, "I sign up to volunteer at the school carnival the second the email comes to me asking for parent volunteers. Last year I had a blast. It was easy; I got to know a whole bunch of kids from my classroom, and my son kept running over to the table to say hi. I knew he felt proud that I was there making sure the other kids were having a good time. I don't want to be stuck in parent meetings talking about organizing the fair. I wanted to be playing and having fun, too!"

As an added bonus, the other parents (and a whole bunch of school staff) will likely see you contributing. It's not like they are scribbling notes about which parents do what on any given day, but it's still nice to feel that your efforts are being seen and acknowledged. It feels good, right? More important, you'll likely have fun being part of the crowd and possibly meeting new parents or getting to know parents and administrators better, and your children will surely be happy to see you stepping up for their school. It's a win-win approach.

Step 3: *Avoid the morning rush.*

- -

Consider how many hours you have wasted in any given week trying to find missing school library books (I found one under the living room couch just this week). Or trying to find your car keys or cell phone. How many times would you estimate you've demanded that your child "go find your sneakers . . . NOW!" while looking desperately for your own shoes? How often has your family witnessed you running around the living room muttering, "Who has seen my laptop? It was right here!"

One of the hardest parts of weekdays is just getting out the door when there is clearly a vortex sucking up all the necessary items for the day. If you could get out the door faster, you would have more time to spend in your child's classroom, say hello to teachers and other moms, and check out what's happening in the school hallways. Or, if your kids are older—and don't need classroom drop-off—you could actually fit in a conversation with them over breakfast. Imagine. If only we could be more organized!

If you're like me, perhaps you've fantasized on occasion about having hanging wire baskets and labeled trays around the house to keep everything in its place, but it just seems so time consuming and unrealistic. Never fear! We can employ a *hint* of Martha's organization to bring down daily stress levels in the house without going so far as color-coordinating our child's umbrella with her backpack, or labeling everything with artsy stenciling. Says Sarah Buckwalter, certified professional organizer and owner of Organizing Boston, "Being organized isn't about having a picture-perfect home; it's about planning and having a routine. Especially with kids, organization is the key to a less stressful day. Taking just a few extra minutes at the end of each day can save you time and stress as you rush out the door each morning."

Yes, but what do we *do* in those minutes, you wonder.

My favorite suggestion from Buckwalter: "Put what you can in the car the night before—think sports equipment, items to return, special projects. This will help avoid needing to make multiple trips back and forth in the morning because your hands are too full." She also suggests creating a "landing zone" that includes baskets for keys, hooks for bags, and bins for homework and artwork.

If making lunches in the morning is what's slowing you down, take this advice from Laura, a forty-two-year-old mom of two: "I handle the morning rush the night before. I have to have everything organized before I go to bed to ensure a smooth morning. Lunches are made (up to the point where I can just add an ice pack and cold items in the morning)."

One techie mom, age twenty-nine, told me she saves time by keeping her gadgets all in one place: "I finally set up a charging station where all my electronics get charged at once in the same spot. Between my iPod, laptop, and cell phone alone, I could easily spend hours hunting the house for them every morning before school. Sometimes I feel too lazy to bring one of my gadgets downstairs to the station, but I do it anyway, and then am relieved. It's been life-changing."

Wendy, a forty-three-year-old nurse with two girls under age ten, says that one of the keys to getting her kids out the door is making sure there are clean underwear and matched socks in the girls' drawers, adding, "I couldn't care less about their outer layers of style." She also insists that "the girls need to be responsible for packing their homework the night before."

Try This:

Getting our kids more involved in the process of organizing is essential, says Buckwalter. Her advice? "Incorporate tasks into their daily routine. It can be as simple as adding a step to an existing process—such as putting their finished homework back in their bags or choosing and putting out their breakfast when they have an evening snack. It's never too early to teach kids how to organize."

Step 4: *Show off your skill in the classroom.*

Another option for contributing to your child's class in a way that fits your schedule is to showcase one of your particular skills. What kind of demonstration can you do that would be fun for kids that perhaps ties in to your work? My husband, a 3D artist for video games, felt bad that he never volunteered at the school (yep, dads often feel the heat too). So he asked our daughter's first grade teacher if she would like him to come to class and show the kids an animation program on his laptop. The teacher was delighted; the students loved watching my husband making kooky monsters on screen; our daughter was proud as can be; and my husband served his duty in an enjoyable way, even offering to do it again. We recently saw this teacher, who told my husband that the kids still talk about the demonstration, and that she'd love him to do it again.

If you're thinking, *Yeah, yeah, but my job is not as cool for kids as video-game animation,* that may be true. But that doesn't mean you can't whip up a child-friendly presentation around your skill set. If you work in a doctor's office, show some of the latest equipment kids might like to try out (my daughter and her friends are fascinated by stethoscopes), or tell a story about how a new medicine was recently invented to heal children. If you are in accounting, bring in Monopoly money and give the kids a creative math lesson on what happens when you overspend. You get the idea; just because your job isn't notably creative doesn't mean you can't be creative in showcasing it. Just make sure your explanations are age-appropriate. Discussing tax loopholes or the particulars of DNA encoding to six-year-olds—while wildly fascinating to your colleagues—can be a snoozefest to young kids. Test your presentation on your kid ahead of time (or borrow someone else's child!).

Once you have a specific idea for your presentation, email your child's teacher, volunteering your services, and ask whether she thinks it's a good fit for the students. What's great is that you can plan it around *your* work hours. If your presentation is a hit in the classroom (you'll know when you hear your audience yelling "COOL!"), offer it again next year. If it's met with mixed reception, tweak it for next year. If snoring or booing is involved, well . . . you'll find another way to help the classroom in the future.

Try This:

If you have a high-pressure job where you just can't leave the office on weekdays, think about contributing with cash. (Hey, when aren't there donation requests in this economy, right?) One entrepreneur and mom from Austin, Texas, said: "I know I can't be there to lead crafts for the holiday parties or chaperone the kids to the museum 99 percent of the time, so I am the first to open my checkbook when the request comes for money to buy classroom supplies. That's one way I know I can help out, and the teachers can bank on me—literally. Those classroom books and supplies don't pay for themselves!"

Step 5: *Get smart about teacher meetings.*

- -

It's not just about contributing and volunteering in your child's classroom. Sometimes it's about trying to find time to connect with the teacher to discuss an issue that your son or daughter is facing. There are moments during the year (maybe a slew of moments) when you'll want—even need—to talk to the teacher, whether it's about a bullying incident, missing homework, or any other concern involving your child's classroom experience. If you try to approach the teacher in the morning, you have to fight for the teacher's attention because every parent, it seems, has something important to discuss at that very moment. It's the same dynamic at the end of the day, and now you're starting to worry you're never going to get a chance to bring up your concern unless you take off work or kidnap the teacher (don't).

Ask your child's teacher whether it's okay to use email for communication, if you don't already. If she says yes, email with your concern, and be *as specific* as you can to avoid multiple rounds of emails before coming to a solution or understanding. For example, I've found that it's much more helpful to say, "My daughter seems to be having a lot of trouble focusing this month. When she's telling me a story, she stops mid-story and then forgets what she was saying. Is this something you are seeing too in class?" than to say, "My daughter seems spacey this week. Do you think so?"

I've also found it helpful to ask the teacher whether she has any feedback, and what *I* can do to be helpful as well. I don't want to be labeled a hyper-demanding parent who expects teachers to find the solution. I want to help my child. There have also been times when I needed to talk to the teacher in person because she needed more concrete examples or I didn't understand her feedback. But at least we had a starting point when we met, which made the meeting more efficient for both of us.

> ### *Try This:*
>
> *When emailing your child's teacher, use this sample email letter from Lynne Kenney, author of* The Family Coach Method, *as a model:*
>
> > "Dear Mrs. Bales: I notice that Jessica is doing her school work but forgetting to turn it in. This has resulted in a series of failing grades on her homework assignments. May we meet to discuss how I can help my daughter turn her homework in and succeed in your classroom? I am available before or after school M W F, if that suits you. I appreciate your time and look forward to talking with you. Sincerely, Jenny."
>
> *If the problem has something to do with the teacher's style or method, be careful. Advises Kenney: "Write a succinct email, and try not to be angry or defensive because teachers have feelings just like you. Use phrases like, 'I observe that' or 'Do you have ideas about . . . ?' Then ask if you can meet to discuss the concerns before or after school. Face to face, make a plan with the teacher and follow-up in brief intervals so that you all uncover success. Keep communication short, succinct and focused on solutions."*

Step 6: *Barter your way out of it.*

There may be times and situations in which you need to meet regularly with your child's teacher, making the work-parent juggle even more stressful. Take Laurie, a fifty-year-old New Hampshire business owner and mom to an eleven-year-old boy, who told me: "My son was diagnosed with ADHD and needs support from his school, and the school has resisted providing adequate support. This tug-of-war has resulted in endless time spent in meetings at the school. At the exact same time, my business needed my attention in a big way during the worst economic downturn in my lifetime. I honestly don't have enough time in a day to do it all, and both have suffered."

There are going to be times when you can let the school or office know you're up against a crazy deadline or family crisis and could use a little slack. As long as this is on occasion and not an everyday occurrence, most of us probably find we're usually given some leeway. But there are some times when our life just goes off the rails, and we need a whole lot of slack. For instance, your son has the flu and you need to stay home with him, but you took off several days in a row last week when your daughter had the same sickness. Your partner can't help because he/she is on deadline at work too. Now what?

At these times, we have to get resourceful, which is not easy to do when we're running on empty emotionally. This is where we can think *barter*, the exchanging of services and goods. As Bob Myer, editor of *Barter News*, put it in an article titled "Economics Outside the Box": "Bartering is a matter of creatively using what one has to get what one desires" and a way "for the real entrepreneur (individual, business and nation) to look beyond the limits of cash."[1]

Moms barter all the time without thinking twice. My friend Linda, a professor and mom of two boys, told me she "convinced a friend to take my boys for a sleepover so I could celebrate my husband's birthday, and I promised in exchange to take her dog for a weekend." Karin, a massage therapist, swaps masseuses for family haircuts from a friend who is a hairstylist. Another mom who works from home told me she walks her neighbor's dogs in the morning in exchange for babysitting in the evening. Why not use bartering to help us out when we're in a parent-work jam?

If you're a decent painter, offer to paint one room or a mural in your neighbor's house next season if she can take over your carpool slot for this month. Offer your colleagues a homemade meal once a week for a month if they'll take over some work portion for this deadline so you can focus on your child's health. Good at tax codes? Offer to do taxes for a dad this winter if he brings your daughter to soccer practice for the rest of the season. Hey, it beats pleading for more time off or babysitting help, which is unappealing to everyone concerned—and especially you.

> **Try This:**
>
> *My business brain advises that you write down the terms of the barter agreement so that everyone is on the same page. The last thing you need after a hassle-filled time are friends or colleagues insisting you promised to make meals for two months when you are sure you said one. If you offer to do someone's taxes, get it in writing that you need all the person's forms, receipts, etc., two months before deadline, so you don't end up pulling out your hair the day of the deadline because you still don't have what you need. The idea is to ease your stress—not amplify and prolong it.*

Step 7: *Stick to the game plan.*

- -

You have every intention of pulling through when you say you'll help at school or in the community. But each time you come up with a concrete plan to contribute, a code-red alert seems to pop up at work. Now you have to tell everyone you can't help as planned, and you've got an annoyed child, parents, teacher, or coach you've inconvenienced, and a migraine on the way. *Argh*.

Ask Hanna, a Washington, D.C.–based journalist and editor of a popular women's blog, who has three children, ages nine, seven, and one. Hanna says she wishes she had more time to invest at her children's schools and has experienced tough moments of over committing. In particular, she struggles with the "one-hour gap between my son's schoolday and the soccer program. Usually the other moms of the soccer team volunteer to fill that gap and watch the kids. Twice I've volunteered and had to back out because of other commitments. I definitely felt like the jerk those days and hated feeling that way."

Most of us have been there. Realizing how much other parents pick up the slack during "one-hour gaps between activities" or carpooling or leading a school activity, we happily say, "Okay, my turn!" We put it in our calendar, and we're set to go. Invariably, less than 24 hours before our big helping moment, a work crisis arises and we have to humbly ask another parent to cover for us. In addition to feeling the stress of the work crisis, we've got severe guilt to contend with. Boo!

Given that we can't control office fires, what can we do? The answer: everything in our power to try to prevent them and create backup options. We do this at work all the time, right? We try to foresee what could go wrong and figure out how to prevent that from happening. The same applies to volunteering our time at school; we need to come up with the steps to boost our chances that we can follow through. A few moms told me, for example, that they check ahead of time if a colleague can cover for them for those hours when they're scheduled to be at school *should* something come up at the last minute at work. Great idea!

Try This:

Professional certified executive coach Lori Link says in one of her newsletters, The Link Letter, on follow-through that once we define our goals, we have to really think through the game plan: "What steps will be needed to accomplish the goals? Who will do which steps and when? What is the desired timeline? If a strategy does not address the hows, it is almost certainly doomed to failure."[2]

Moms told me that as soon as they agree to volunteer at school, they mark the time as "busy" on their work calendar, so everyone knows. You can also remind everyone at work before the event that you'll be out and they should let you know in the next day or two if they anticipate needing anything from you. Cover all your bases; at the very least, you'll know you did everything possible if you have to skip out of a school obligation.

Step 8: *Douse with appreciation.*

When we're feeling conspicuously MIA at our child's school, there's something else we can do (and should do anyway): Send a thank-you note to his teacher, coach, or mentor expressing our gratitude for the guidance, attention, and support he gives our child. Some may call this "sucking up," but as long as the sentiment is *genuine*, I call it "proper thanks few teachers receive." How many times do you think a teacher gets a letter of gratitude in any given year from a parent? It's not often, according to my friend Jill, a teacher in Colorado: "I very rarely get notes from parents—it's usually from ex-students. Whenever I do get any notes of appreciation, I read them over to remind myself of why I do my job and why I love it still!"

What should you say? Advises Dr. Robyn Silverman, child and teen development specialist: "When writing a thank you letter to the teacher, don't fall back on overused phrases and colloquialisms.

It's important to customize the letter so that it can only be for that one person—that teacher—impossible to interchange with another. What is it about that teacher that you appreciate?"[3]

Says Caroline Berz, mom of two who taught for ten years and leads teaching workshops: "Sending emails to a teacher is a great way to show support and enthusiasm for what your kid is learning in a particular class. Articulate a specific appreciation for a lesson taught, a reading assigned, or a discussion pursued in the class. This means two things that good teachers are interested in: the kid is talking about what he/she is learning at home and that the parents care about what their kids are learning. It's not just about a grade, it's about the journey of discovery, questioning and learning."

One working mom of three emailed me with the right idea: "Last year, I was creating a start-up and the only time I wasn't working was when I was eating breakfast and dinner with my family or putting the kids to bed. Every other second of my time was accounted for, and I was losing my mind. I also felt bad at how little I was able to do for my child's school, especially when I had always tried to do my fair share in the past. It just wasn't possible. So I wrote my children's teachers an email explaining why I wasn't volunteering this year, apologizing, and saying how much I appreciated that during this rocky time they had a strong teacher to guide them. I think my honesty went a long way. They both emailed me back and told me they so appreciated my email and not to worry about it. I felt so much better after that exchange, and now that my business is sailing more smoothly, I am volunteering to the extent that I can and happy to do it!"

Hey, while you're in appreciation mode, thank the moms of classmates who deserve recognition for all the time they spend making sure the class runs well. I'm talking about those classroom parents (working or not) who update us about the class trip to the aquarium, lead a fundraising event for earthquake victims, purchase a gift for the teachers at the end of the year, etc. Instead of rolling your eyes at these do-gooders, thank them. It feels good! Hey, you don't have to do this stuff *because* they do it. Consider even going one step further and inviting classroom parents over for wine and cheese one night (don't wait for a holiday), or organizing an evening out to get to know one another better. Unless you've got plans to move out of state, you're going to know these parents for a long time, so a little effort now will go a long way. These parents will be looking out for your child, and it's in your best interest to get to know them.

Proceed with Caution If . . .

your child's teacher scolds you for not doing enough volunteer work (while a few moms told me this happens, it seems to be pretty rare). Do not blow up at her or list the plethora of responsibilities you have this week. She, too, is overextended and exhausted. Take a deep breath, exhale, and tell her you would love to volunteer at one of the next after-school activities for the kids. Ask for a few specific dates, check your calendar so you know you can commit, and choose one. You and the teacher have the same goal, which is to make sure the class (including your child) has a positive experience this year, so make sure you do your part.

On the Flip Side . . .

maybe some days you're trying too hard to prove that you can be super-involved, and you end up wearing yourself ragged. It's good to commit to activities throughout the year that you can take part in, but it's definitely a mistake to cram in as many as you can scribble into your calendar so your children feel loved. We need time to replenish *ourselves* in order to be present for others. Says Shann Vander Leek, founder of True Balance Life Coaching, "Allow yourself an hour to go for a walk, get a pedicure, or take a nap. Not only is it okay, it's actually necessary in order to be able to fully function in the other areas of your life." So choose a few wisely selected activities, ideally with your child, and enjoy them.[4]

SHOUT-OUT TO . . .

the thirty-four-year-old doctor and mom from California who emailed me with this: "I found out this year that it's better for me to bite the bullet and take off the whole day instead of volunteering for an hour here and there over the school year. Yes, it was hard taking the day off to chaperone my daughter's class on the trip to the science museum, and I was a little panicky about losing one of the kids. I must have counted the heads of the kids in my group 400 times. But on the other hand, I wasn't thinking about work like I tend to do during PTA meetings or classroom breakfasts, where I know I have to race back to the office after the meeting. Knowing I wasn't going back to the office meant I could quit worrying about it and fully engage. I've got to say . . . it was a good day! Now I stand behind the motto 'go big' when volunteering."

Chapter Wrap

- - - - - - - - - - - - - -

Step 1: *Raise your hand before you get called on.*

It's far less stressful volunteering early in the year than going undercover to avoid requests.

Step 2: *Be visible when you volunteer.*

When you do volunteer, make sure that your child can actually see your efforts.

Step 3: *Avoid the morning rush.*

You'll stop mocking efforts to organize when you notice the reduction in morning screaming.

Step 4: *Show off your skill in the classroom.*

If you can't make your work schedule mesh with the school calendar, offer to share your talents with the class.

Step 5: *Get smart about teacher meetings.*

Save time by emailing your child's teacher instead of fighting the morning drop-off crowds.

Step 6: *Barter your way out of it.*

Instead of pleading for favors, swap goods or services with a parent or coworker when life gets out of control.

Step 7: *Stick to the game plan.*

Plan for ways to clear out your calendar on the day that you're scheduled to volunteer.

Step 8: *Douse with appreciation.*

Expressing thanks doesn't take the place of volunteering on occasion, but it does show you care.

Chapter 6

FRIENDSHIP HIATUS

Confession: "I put so much time into family and work that I end up neglecting my friends!"

Remember back in the old days when a random call to a friend typically resulted in a lengthy discussion over which celebrity was hotter (Clooney or Pitt), which foreign country we'd most like to move to for a year, or how long it was acceptable to go without shaving our legs? Or we'd stay on the line for hours working through maddening office politics ("Can you believe my boss is making me go in every weekend this month?"), decoding the mysterious actions of a significant other ("What does it mean that he made an off-the-cuff remark about our future child?"), or recovering from foot-in-mouth syndrome ("How was I supposed to know that he wore a toupee when I made the Rogaine joke?"). From the ultra-mundane to the emotionally heavy-duty, we hung up the phone with our pals feeling lucky to have someone in our lives who just *gets* us.

It's no wonder most of us would love nothing better than to catch up with our friends in a café where no one could interrupt us, except possibly the barista delivering drinks. The problem is, when is a get-together supposed to happen with everyone's calendar so chock-full of appointments and meetings? These days, it seems there is only time to crawl into a hot bath at the end of the day and maybe skim a few pages of a book before passing out. Each time we think, *Oh, I need to call Emily, it's been too long!* we are just sitting down for a meeting or starting a bedtime story with our child. So we text, "Let's talk soon, Em . . ." and hope she can read between the lines ("I promise I am thinking about you far more than I am contacting you!"). More weeks pass, and we're left thinking, "*Eesh,* how can we even *begin* to catch up at this point?"

We think we will never be the type of working mom who drops off our friends' radar because we're too busy. In the past, we took pride in nurturing our friendships, reaching out to pals when we needed support, being there for them in return, and staying in touch frequently enough that we knew exactly what they were up to in any given week. So how did we get to this place, one where we're no longer even sure how old their kids are or what our friends are up to? How do we navigate back to our girlfriends? More important, *can* we?

QUIZ: ARE YOUR FRIENDSHIPS IN DANGER?

1. **When your best friend emails you, it takes you about how long to respond to her?**
   a. About one week (and by that I mean one month).
   b. Oh shoot, I never emailed her back!
   c. Sometimes right away but definitely by the next day.

2. **Whenever you and your girlfriends plan a get-together, the following happens:**
   a. You have a blast. Given that it happens only a few times a year, you make the most of it.
   b. You are so glad that you meet up regularly with them because they truly keep you sane.
   c. Ummm, a get-together?

3. **You are most likely to call your friend when:**
   a. you're crying from all the stress or in desperate need of advice. One of these days you'll call just to say hello.
   b. you have at least twenty minutes to catch up, typically after your child is asleep.
   c. Never. You're an email friend and Facebook poster only these days. If you're not working or parenting, you're sleeping.

Answers: If you answered "c" for number 1, give yourself one point. If you answered "b" for number 2, give yourself one point. If you answered "b" for number 3, give yourself one point. If you received at least two points, you're on the right track for keeping your friendships alive and well. If you received 1 or zero points, pay extra attention to the steps in this chapter because it's time for a friendship-boosting program.

Reality Check

- - - - - - - - - - - - -

Most of us would agree that to be truly content with our lives, we need our girlfriends. They help us regain perspective when it's hard to see straight because we're so tired or worried, wave their proverbial pom-poms when our confidence dips, remind us of what we're doing right when we're desperate to hear it, and even make us laugh so hard we snort (which only makes us laugh harder). Marriage therapist Cyndi Sarnoff-Ross sums it up like this in her article "The Importance of Friends": "Friends give *texture* to our lives that differs from that of our mate, colleagues, or children."[1]

No matter how wonderful our immediate family is, it's our girlfriends that frequently provide us with much-needed support. If you pay attention, you can *feel* it. Clinical psychologist Aurelia Palubeckas, EdD, says: "There's something about real human contact that stimulates our hormones—not just spiritually, psychologically, and emotionally but *physically*. We need human contact—and the kind you get with your kids and husband doesn't always feed that. You need someone paying extra attention to you, giving you a hug, saying 'I'm so glad to see you!' In fact, if you are really present, you'll feel a pleasant physical surge that happens with a friend." By the way, this is vital not just for us, adds Palubeckas, but for our kids: "When our kids grow up, they are not going to feel good because we spent our every second with them, but because they were with a mother who felt good."

Given how much energy we expend caring for others, we need friends who help care for us, while, of course, we do the same for them. I consider my husband a fantastic source of support, but it's often a woman's perspective I crave when problems pop up that leave me unsure. I am reminded at this moment of sitting with my friend Betsy at a coffee shop when I got the call from the school nurse saying that my daughter had head lice (yes, if you read Chapter 2, you know this happened again right before I was scheduled to do an online live chat with *The Washington Post!*), and I needed to come get her. Waves of panic rolled in because I knew we were up against endless sheet and blanket washing, obsessive combing, vacuuming, and uncontrollable weeping—and I wanted to stay in that café with Betsy for all eternity. But my friend kept me grounded by reminding me that this wasn't catastrophic, just *irritating*, and that this ordeal had a definitive ending. Five minutes later, breathing easier, I gave her one final hug and was able to face what needed to be done. My friend Jenny knew the perfect metal comb to use for maximum nit removal, and showered me with warmth and sympathy when I got grossed-out. Other girlfriends made silly comments about how cool buzz cuts could be on girls, and how overrated hair is. My husband was a true partner when it came to getting rid of the biblical pests; but my girlfriends (who, yes, also had the benefit of distance from the situation) got me through with my humor intact.

It's understandable that we sometimes stop tending to our friendships when our lives get so overloaded that we don't have much to give. What energy we do have, we tend to save for family or work. But we need to remember that it's not all or nothing with friendships. We may not have the endless hours to devote to them that we used to, but we can continue nurturing our relationships and enjoying how much they replenish our reserves, not deplete them. This chapter is loaded with strategies on how to do just that.

Step 1: *Give yourself a friendly nudge.*

My friend Pam, thirty-eight, an assistant professor of forest ecology, is looking forward to resuming friendships once (oops, I'm supposed to say "if," due to any potential jinxes) she gets tenure—a process that to me seems longer and more arduous than becoming an astrophysicist. Right now there is a tremendous amount of pressure on Pam to get tenure, and almost all her energy admittedly goes into this and parenting her two girls (ages five and three). Unfortunately, she says, that means that her life feels out of balance *a lot* of the time. She especially misses spending time with her girlfriends. "It feels like my whole life is work and the kids right now," she says. "I really miss taking walks with friends like you," she tells me, "to discuss how life is going. I always feel better after we do this. I have this dream that if I get tenure, I'll take a whole weekend to go away with my girlfriends to reconnect."

Pam isn't the only working mom I spoke to who's experiencing the "lapsed friendship" phenomenon. Kids and work simply take priority. Here's some of what I heard: "I'm going to get back in touch with my friend once this damn project is finally over." "If I can just get through this school year in one piece, I'm going to call my girlfriends again." "I miss my friends but since having the second baby, it seems impossible to find any extra time to hang out with them." "As soon as this kid is done with breastfeeding, I'm going to get moving with my social life."

If we wait for a calm to descend before getting back in touch with our friends, we may never make contact again. As we know all too well, if family is running smoothly for the moment, that's when we typically find out that our company may be going through layoffs. If our job is running smoothly, it is likely that our kid will come home with some weird illness like "Fifth's Disease." If work and parenting are both on track, our significant other will probably have to leave for a week to take care of an ailing parent. There's always something. That's why we can't wait for "the right time" to reach out to friends, and more important, the wrong time is when we most *need* them. According to women's health expert Dana Crowley Jack, EdD, of Western Washington University, "Our physical and mental health *depend* on having close relationships with people we can turn to, especially in times of crisis or stress," she says.[2] I also like what Anne Bogel, who examines family dynamics, etiquette, and literature on her blog *Modern Mrs. Darcy,* had to say: "One of the bright spots of my own tough times has been watching my friends rally to help me through. There is a joy in knowing you're not facing your hurt alone, and that there are people in your life who will stand by you in times of trouble."

We need and deserve those bright spots, and sometimes must remind ourselves that spending twenty or so minutes talking with a friend is the exactly right use of our time. So instead of holing up when life gets stressful and prolonging contact with a close friend, we need to reach out. We also need to make time to return the favor when our pals need our soothing words. I don't think any of us will ever look back at our lives thinking, "If only I had made less time for friends and more time for work."

Step 2: *Make the call—literally.*

Now that it's time to pick up the phone, you may be excited about the reconnection—or you may feel sincere regret for letting the relationship with your close friend lapse. You may even have concerns that her feelings have been hurt due to the unintentional neglect, or feel guilty for letting a friend down in her own time of need. Life happens, and none of us are perfect, right? Says author Peter McWilliams, author of several books on healing depression, "Mistakes, obviously, show us what needs improving. Without mistakes, how would we know what we had to work on?"[3] It's a mistake not to make more time for a friend—not an act of malice—and one we can certainly learn from. Reaching out in a kind, humble, and compassionate way to let a friend know she's important to you, and that you're sincere about wanting to reconnect, is the perfect step in rekindling a friendship that hit the skids when your own life went full-throttle.

So where do you start? There's been so much distance between you two. Okay, here's what you're NOT going to do. You're not going to send her an email! As Scott H. Young, author of *How to Change a Habit*, points out in his blog *Get More from Life:* "A phone has immediate feedback, adds tone of voice, and can't be skimmed."[4] Also, rather than yell "Hi!" or "Hey, it's me. Whatcha up to?" when she answers your unexpected call, particularly if there's been some water under the bridge, have a sense of what you want to say. I've found it's always better to cut to the chase and be accountable right away rather than dance around it. Perhaps when she answers, say hello, and consider something like, "I realize that I have been completely MIA for the last several months and I am so sorry. I got caught up in a storm of work and parenting, and I let a lot of things slide. I miss you and would love to get our friendship back on track." Most likely, if this is a close friend, she's going to understand and cut you some slack; certainly, she's going to appreciate your taking ownership of letting the friendship slide and apologizing for it.

She may want to know *how* things will be different moving forward (especially if she has experienced this before with you or in another friendship), and she has every right to. Frankly, it is a good idea for both of you to sketch out mutual and realistic expectations. As clinical psychologist Dr. Mary Grogan says on mindfood.com, "Often, setting high expectations comes at a high cost, the painful thud as you fall back to reality."[5] You don't want your friend thinking you're back to once-a-week dinners if once-a-month tea is what you had in mind. How often can she expect to hear from you? When is her best bet for actually getting ahold of you? You don't have to pin down every potential scenario or concoct a full-on game plan (friendships should be pleasurable and low-stress, not something you have to plot out), but having some idea of what works for one another will help you both as you get your friendship back off the ground.

Okay, hopefully at this point, you and your friend are pleased and relieved to have the relationship back on track. But what if she is reticent, even a little miffed at you for dropping out of her orbit, especially if she'd been trying to get in touch with you for weeks? Be open and prepared to listen to her without getting defensive. Remember, your friendship is based on shared affection and kinship, being compassionate and understanding, even in the face of difficult truths.

Try This:

"If your friend sounds distant or angered," advises psychologist Palubeckas, "say, 'I really regret that I dropped off the planet. I missed our contact so much. I didn't know how much that being a mom and working would consume me. I can't believe it's been a year since I talked to you. I'd like to meet with you and see if we can pick up where we left off,' and you can say, 'I agree, I was the one who didn't reach out but I'm wanting to give it another try.' If they still say no and won't budge, then you probably have to say good bye."

Step 3: *Nail down a date and time.*

- -

I'm going to assume here that the phone exchange went well, because most likely that will be the case. Wait! Before you hang up, suggest to your friend that you pick your next outing right then and mark it in red on your calendar. Do not hang up with an agreement that you'll connect sometime next week to come up with a plan. Without a specified date on the calendar, it's unlikely to happen. Every day, life and obligations seem to make sure of that. If time spent with this friend always leaves you feeling lighter on your feet and puts a pep in your step, consider scheduling a regular time each month to meet up so you can avoid having to figure out new logistics every time you'd like to get together. It gives you something to look forward to, and you're more likely to accommodate social time together if it's already built into your calendar, despite your busy work and family life. But a note of caution: If you only *talk* about doing it, it stays just that: talk.

Take my aforementioned friend Betsy and me. We had this grand idea that we should meet regularly for coffee every week and do our writing together, given that she's an author too—but it never transpired. We suggested it every time we connected via phone, text, or email, but months passed without us seeing each other. Finally, one of us called with a specific date, we met up, chatted for a bit, and then got to work. The experience ended up being so productive and nourishing, we decided to meet once a week in a coffee shop located halfway between us (a twenty-minute drive for each of us). Blocking off the same time each week in our calendars eliminated scheduling conflicts and ensured that, short of an important obligation or emergency, we'd get together. We go to the same café each time—*easy*.

Now that you have a date—or possibly a slew of them—*go*. Make it happen. Do not call it off or otherwise renege because you're stressed-out, unmotivated, overworked (it will still be there tomorrow!), or are feeling the urge to zone out in front of the television, if given the chance. Treat your friend date as seriously as you would your monthly staff meeting or your child's doctor's appointment— attendance mandatory. Afterward, take stock of how rejuvenating it felt to be with a supportive friend, whether you initially felt tired, stressed, or not. Be mindful of how it improved your overall well-being, and remember this the next time you're toying with the idea of bagging out. Once you get into the rhythm, you'll never look back.

Try This:

If you're looking for ways to break the coffee-shop rut and add adventure to your social life, suggest that you and your friend take turns coming up with new things to do during your meet-ups. Rent a canoe, find a nearby hike on a trail you've never tried, volunteer at a soup kitchen, enroll in a guitar lesson, or visit a tarot-card reader. In addition to the joy of spending time with your friend, you'll experience the rush of trying new things.

Step 4: *Remember that it's a two-way street.*

- -

If you haven't hung out with your friend for a while, it may be tempting during a high-stress time to unload all the angst, frustrations, and work/life issues churning in your brain. After all, here's a warm, compassionate person who knows you and cares about you, and it's been so long since anyone has asked how you're *really* doing. Even though we know better, it's easy to fire away with all the injustices, big and small, occurring in our life—the mean-spirited comment our boss made about parents in front of a client, the frustration of feeling like your child's chauffeur on weekends, the hassle of coming up with new dinner options each night only to be told, "Gross, I'm not eating that!" Before we know it, it's time to leave and we haven't even asked our friend a thing about her *own* life. Oops.

Yes, your friend most likely does want to hear details of your life, but try to refrain from spilling it all—even if your friend is looking at you with sympathy all over her sweet face. I like how leadership expert Dan Rockwell (a.k.a. "Leadership Freak") puts it in his article "10 Power Tips for Leaders Who Talk Too Much" (substitute "Friends" for "Leaders" and it's just as true): "Avoid fire hoses when people want sips. Short simple questions call for short simple answers."[6]

Be honest about the fact that life is chaotic at the moment, and do share *highlights*. Just don't get so lost in the minutiae that an hour later she hasn't gotten a word in edgewise. (If you're rolling your eyes and thinking, *Lady, I know how to be a friend, thank you,* I believe you, I swear. But from my own personal experience, I can say it's easy even for the socially savvy to become self-absorbed when we haven't had sweet contact with a friend for a while.)

Ellen, a New Jersey mom of three, admitted that she didn't realize she'd hogged the whole conversation until she was on the way home from hanging out with the first friend she'd seen in months: "I swear, I had one beer—that's it—but you'd think I'd had five from the way I was blathering. Honestly, I hadn't been asked in so long how I was doing that I just started yammering and couldn't stop myself. My friend was a good sport about it, luckily, and I called the next day to apologize and tell her we were going out again next week, and I was just going to listen and not utter a word!"

"It can be especially hard to hold back for single moms hungry for adult conversation," Beth, divorced mom to an eight-year-old shared. "I am divorced, and the thing I really miss is having a partner who I can share things with at the end of the day, whether it's a snarky comment a coworker made or a funny thing that happened during the day. My kids are little, and they certainly aren't asking about the particulars of my day. Last week, I actually spilled my guts to a telemarketer when he asked, 'How are you, ma'am?' I don't think he'll be calling me back anytime soon!"

> **Try This:**
>
> *How do you avoid monopolizing the conversation unintentionally? If you realize it's been ten minutes and you're the only one catching up, turn the conversation around quickly and ask your friend about her life. Also, make a mental note that this is a clear indication that you really need more face-to-face time with your friends.*

Step 5: *Schedule "Friends' Night Out."*

Maybe for you, it's a whole circle of pals who have fallen by the wayside. You miss all your women friends but can't figure out how to squeeze in time to see more than one or two of them a month. Yes, you realize what a decadent "problem" it is to have *too many* friends to try to fit into your schedule. It's just that they are all genuinely valuable to you, and the last thing you want is to appear to play favorites and potentially hurt anyone's feelings by only making plans with one or two of them.

Easy fix: Arrange a monthly get-together that allows you to see everyone at once. Pick a spot central to everyone, or take turns hosting at your homes. Catch up over takeout dinner when the kids are asleep, or keep it to desserts with the host providing one. Keeping it simple allows you to avoid the pressure of having to spend hours cooking, cleaning, and preparing food. Even if you enjoy throwing parties every once in a while, and even secretly fantasize about doing it professionally sometimes, this is a time to focus on connection, not orchestrating a major event. What you don't need is a group of already overstressed moms feeling like they have to keep raising the bar when it's their turn to host. The whole meet-up plan will disintegrate quickly because working moms need fun—not more work. I like Los Angeles event planner Alan Dunn's suggestion: "Don't pressure yourself! It won't be perfect, and no one will mind. When we have people over, everybody knows they're just there to have a good time."[7] Consider a fluid night where you simply crack open a bottle of wine and hang out together. Food? Ask everyone to bring a simple hors d'oeuvre.

How to get things started? Send an email to your friends telling them you miss them and toss out your idea. Ask who's in—letting them know there's *no pressure*—and suggest a few meeting times. Let "majority rules" when it comes to picking a date, since it's not always easy to find a night or day that fits everyone's schedule, even if that's the goal. If your plan involves more than a few people, advises "Chris," founder of the website succeedsocially.com, it can take a surprising amount of time just to get in touch with everyone. For the first one, he suggests, "You may have to talk to them all in person individually." Then you can work out the details during the ensuing flurry of emails. Chris also states that once "everyone's agreed to your plan, and you are working out the details with each other, it's not totally yours anymore. Don't get too hung up on it going one particular way." The good news about everyone weighing in is that it means your busy mom friends are just as eager for a break as you are.

> **Try This:**
>
> When it comes to friends' night out, there's no limit to the possibilities. Consider organizing a book club or movie night or craft night. If you're all bummed about never getting to the gym, throw a dance party and laugh over your lame, outdated moves (sorry, I may be thinking of my own) while breaking a sweat. Play your kid's Wii Tennis game now that he's asleep. Take your daughter's hula hoops for a spin.

Step 6: Set realistic expectations with child-free friends.

I'm aware of how fortunate I am to have a friend like Lindsey, thirty-three, who doesn't have kids yet and is completely flexible and compassionate about making plans with her friends who have babies. As she put it, "I'm really sympathetic to friends who are new moms and am happy to spend time with their little ones. Or, if my friends need space to figure out those first few months, that's fine too." My child-free friend Jacquie has been a super-supportive friend not only to me but also to my daughter Risa, and they share their own unique relationship, which thrills me to no end. In fact, at least once a year, Jacquie and her husband, Gabe, invite Risa for a sleepover, which is my daughter's dream come true and allows my husband and me to enjoy a night out and even a quiet morning together. *Sigh*. So . . . I'm the last person to say that child-free friends can't be supportive.

That said, there often is a big difference between child-free friends and "been there, done that" mom friends. Our mom friends have been in the trenches and know what it's like to walk around half brain-dead from sleep deprivation, trying to figure out how to extricate themselves from a staff meeting to pump the breast milk that's threatening to pump itself, or how to chauffeur the kids to dance and baseball practice when their boss has just given them a last-minute task that *must* be done by the end of the day. These moms, for the most part, understand all too well that your life is not your own in many ways, and that you're sometimes hanging on by a thread.

It's not surprising that *some* child-free women don't comprehend why you can't figure out how to go out for dinner once a week or ditch the family to go hiking on a Saturday afternoon. It's only a few hours, after all. What's the big deal? While their lack of understanding may be frustrating, it most likely comes from not having been in your shoes as opposed to them being selfish. Hey, before having kids, it was impossible to imagine the exhaustion, mental and physical, that we would be swamped by once we finally got the kids to sleep after a full day of being mentally present at work.

"Oh man," Jen, mom of two, told me, "I remember feeling like my mom friends were wusses—and that I'd never be like that when I had kids. I really thought I would put those kids down, dress in my coolest jeans, and meet my friends out on the town. Ha! I am lucky if I have enough energy to *call* my good friends, much less go out for cocktails!"

Point is, you may have to explain to your friends that you want to see them and would love to set up a plan, and that you hope they'll understand you have less time than you used to. Do not give them a list of all the reasons why you're so busy, because as Meagan Francis puts it in her blog *The Happiest Mom,* "There's little in life more boring than listening to a full-on play-by-play of the scheduled minutiae of another person's life—heck, mine is boring enough that I can barely pay attention to my own calendar."[8] Also be careful of sounding condescending ("Oh, you can't *possibly* know what it's like . . ."); instead, focus on the fact that your limited time is no reflection on how you feel about her, and you intend to spend as much time with her as possible. Also, there are courtesies we can extend to our friends without kids, like making sure we talk about things other than our children, getting a babysitter on occasion so we can spend time alone with them, and never forcing our girlfriends to "talk" on the phone with our infant unless they absolutely insist.

If your friend, for whatever reason, remains irked that you don't make enough time for her, the friendship may not be sustainable in this particular stage of your life. It doesn't mean she's a bad person or dud friend, just that she's likely to feel let down constantly, which is no good for either of you. You don't want to be considered a crappy friend when you prioritize family; she doesn't want to feel perpetually dissed by you. So on the off chance that the friendship fizzles out, you might tell her, "I can see you're frustrated that I can't put more time into hanging out, and I'm doing all that I can. I'm worried that we just can't meet one another's expectations." Who knows? Maybe your lives will verge together again in years to come.

Step 7: *Start from scratch if necessary.*

- -

If at this point you are thinking, *Wait, do I even* have *friends anymore?* you're not alone. Between friends relocating and starting families, switching careers, and being at different life stages, there are a slew of reasons women who were once rich in friends find that their compadre list has dwindled if not vanished altogether. But it's never too late. Says clinical psychologist Irene S. Levine, PhD, author of *Best Friends Forever* and founder of *The Friendship Blog,*

"When you realize that you don't have enough friends, or enough friends of the right kind, it can feel daunting. It's common to feel like everyone else is paired up and it's too late to make friends. This simply isn't the case." The most important thing to do, she advises, is "Once you realize that you have a friendship deficit, you need to carve out time to find friends. You need to give people a chance: Two friends may not click right away and it takes time for people to feel comfortable enough to share intimacies with each another. You need to find ways to interact with people whether it's at work, in your neighborhood, or as part of a group."

First, remind yourself why you're doing this. Says Ann Pietrangelo, a regular contributor on health issues for the site care2.com, "We all need to feel part of something meaningful, and we owe it to ourselves to make an effort to connect and reconnect with our fellow human beings. Our health and well-being depend on it."[9] Now it's time to get looking. The first and easiest place to look is at your child's school, whether it's the classroom, after-school program, or volunteer experiences. (When it comes to making friends with school parents, bonus points if your kids are friends.) "Mama Bee," founder of the *Mama Bee* blog, which looks at women, work, and the politics of motherhood, says her child "has always made good choices for us—frequently his good friends have parents we like too. Since our kids know how to play with each other from their daily routine, we can relax and have a glass of wine without having to entertain [them]."[10]

Maybe you'll meet new friends at the sidelines or bleachers of the athletic field where your child practically lives these days. Instead of texting clients and colleagues or doing work or research on your conveniently portable iPad (nothing like taking the office with you!), engage with another mom—or two. Strike up a simple conversation and see where it takes you. Or find friends at the pre-school playground or local park if your kids are young. Many a friendship has been born beside the sandbox and slide. If you *do* find a new friend, be sure to get her email right away. I'm not the first mom who's met a potential new friend at the playground only to lose out because we assumed we'd see each other again within a few days. Big mistake. Months passed before we ran into each other again.

Scout for friends at work (see next chapter for specific strategies on how to go about this). Jamie, mom to a one-year-old, works in a large corporate office and told me she looks for family pictures when she walks into a coworker's office: "It's not like I would only be friends with another working mom," she said, "but I can guarantee you that the woman and I will be able to swap stories about family and job, and might even end up covering for one another down the road." What's trickier about an office mate, of course, is that friend-ships (like office romances) that go sour can turn awkward. Ease your way into the friendship, starting with lunch together or stroll-ing to a coffee shop, before making plans to get together outside of the workplace.

Other potential haunts: your gym (sign up for a workshop, or show up early for a class and strike up a conversation with some-one else who's waiting), religious community, book club, or a low-key adult class, like wine-tasting or sushi-making. If you do connect with a friend, you have the added benefit of regular built-in social time. You may find you don't even need to extend the social-izing beyond these contexts. It's a safe testing ground for a budding friendship and guarantees that you at least engage socially. Don't discount word of mouth, either: If you're new to a community, post a Facebook status or tweet, asking friends if they know anyone who lives in your new town and can introduce you. Even if you don't totally connect with that *particular* person, you may meet a friend through *her* group of friends.

Last, keep in mind what life coach Rachel Wilkerson has to say about giving it a few tries with a new friend: "While sometimes it takes a little time to decide if you really click with a new friend, unlike in dating, you aren't keeping yourself from meeting more friends if you 'settle' for someone. So if it's a no-chemistry thing, hang in there and say yes if she invites you to group events."[11]

Try This:

Many working moms should win gold medals for their extraordinary technique in web-surfing. Use your mad skills to find websites that allow you to create local friendship get-togethers (meetup.com, for example, helps people connect who live nearby and share similar interests, from cyclers and skateboarders to reggae-lovers and pug-owners). I also heard recently of a site called grubwithus.com, where you can browse dozens of upcoming gatherings at local restaurants and book seats at a table of strangers who also want to meet new friends. At worst, you'll have a delicious meal; at best you'll leave with contact info for a few new pals.

Step 8: *Keep the friendship ball rolling.*

No matter how thrilled you are to reconnect with a friend, you're going to go through batches of time when you can't tend to the friendship as much as you'd like. It just takes one new deadline at work, or realizing your child needs extra attention, to fill out your Google calendar, and suddenly you realize you haven't even talked with your significant other in days. Friendships, new or old, have to take a backseat sometimes, and unfortunately, that's just how it goes. You keep thinking to yourself, *I'll send my friend an email tomorrow,* but then some other task pops up or you get the call from the school nurse saying your son has a stomach bug, and once again you fall off the edge of the friendship universe. It's not all or nothing. Okay, you may not have an hour of get-together time to spare, but you can take *a few minutes* to send an email to your friend telling her that you can't wait to see her again once you come up for air. That can turn even the most aggravated friend compassionate immediately.

Take two minutes first thing in the morning and let your friends know you haven't forgotten about them, that you've been sucked under by work, and that you shall resurface. This is especially important when dealing with a new friend who is likely to feel blown off if she doesn't hear from you for weeks. New friendships need nurturing, so dash off a quick email saying, "Just want to let you know that I'm swamped at work but really looking forward to getting through so we can go out for coffee again."

Thanks to having more technology than ever at our fingertips, we can also reach out to all our pals at once easily and quickly during chaotic times. Thanks to Facebook and Twitter (and any other new social media that arise by the time this book comes out), we can let our friends know that our radio silence is due to an overwhelming project—even attaching an Instagram picture that illustrates how crazy life is at the moment (perhaps looking bleary-eyed while double-fisting cappuccinos). Laurie, a forty-five-year-old New York writer and mom to a nine-year-old, says: "I know that some people hate Facebook, but for a mother it is a godsend. I am in frequent virtual communication with most of the women I care about."

> **Try This:**
>
> To make sure you sustain the friendship in busy times, psychologist Aurelia Palubeckas suggests that you tell your friend to check in with you if she doesn't hear from you in a stated amount of time. If you know you're going to be swamped for the next ten days until you meet your deadline or get back from business travel, say, "Hey, you might not hear from me for a couple weeks because I'm crazy busy with work, but please give me a call if you don't hear from me by mid-month, because I want to make sure we stay in touch!"

Proceed with Caution If . . .

you find your group of friends stops getting real with one another, which can happen when moms feel insecure about how they're handling the work-family balance. Attempt to start an authentic conversation, admitting some of your own insecurities. That's what Tami, a thirty-four-year-old director of marketing and mom to three young boys under the ages of seven, did during a girls' weekend trip she arranged. She told her friends that when a woman asked how she manages so much, her response was, "Yeah, but . . ." as in "Yeah, but I have a babysitter helping." Another friend chimed in that her own "Yeah, but . . ." was "Yeah, I do all this, but my in-laws help out," and another friend responded with her own "Yeah, but . . . ." According to Tami, it opened up a terrific discussion about why we feel defensive about our accomplishments. The exchange deepened their bonds and helped build more trust. Can you find your own opportunity to start a similar discussion with your working-mom friends?

On the Flip Side . . .

it may get to a point where *you're* the one constantly being rebuffed by a working-mom friend backing out of social plans. If you keep putting out invites to a friend who says yes and then cancels, talk to her. Don't accuse or attack her; you'll just amp up her stress level and make it harder to get the friendship back on track. Instead, suggests Jan Yager, PhD, author of *365 Daily Affirmations for Friendship*, "Cut her some slack if she's going through a tough time. Especially be kind to your longstanding friends, because you can't ever replace those memories or years with newer friends."[12] Tell your pal that you understand her schedule is really busy (as is your own) and that you really miss her. Ask her what would work for her, and let her know that even an hour get-together would be a treat. If she consistently bails, it may be time to rechannel your energy into another friend (or find new ones) who will make your relationship more of a priority.

SHOUT-OUT TO . . .

Megan, a forty-three-year-old government consultant and mom to a seven-year-old son, says, "The best way to stay close and spend time with my friends is to include our families and then be very flexible with our kids during that group time. We pretty much ignore our children, letting them run totally wild, not monitoring what they eat, and sticking them in front of a movie right around the time they should be going to bed so the grown-ups can drink more wine and visit without interruption." Megan adds, "I'm stunned by how few people actually have company over, and I think it's because it just feels like so much work. It doesn't have to be. If you're close to people, they'll forgive anything to have a little time off and good company, including takeout on paper plates and spaghetti dinners with sauce from a jar."

Chapter Wrap

- - - - - - - - - - - - - -

Step 1: *Give yourself a friendly nudge.*

No procrastinating—as soon as you feel the urge to reconnect with friends, make it happen.

Step 2: *Make the call—literally.*

When you get your friend on the phone, own up right away to the fact that you've been MIA and that you plan to prevent this.

Step 3: *Nail down a date and time.*

Make sure you end that first phone call with a planned get-together written on both of your calendars.

Step 4: *Remember that it's a two-way street.*

Even if you're starved for friendship sympathy, make sure you don't accidentally monopolize the conversation.

Step 5: *Schedule "Friends' Night Out."*

If you have a bunch of girlfriends you've fallen out of touch with, organize a monthly hang-out session.

Step 6: *Set realistic expectations with child-free friends.*

Try not to get irritated with friends who genuinely don't understand why you can't make more time for them.

Step 7: *Start from scratch if necessary.*

If you're on a search for working-mom friends, start with the easy places.

Step 8: *Keep the friendship ball rolling.*

Let your pal know when you're planning to disappear due to work or family overload instead of telling her after the fact.

Chapter 7

ODD WOMAN OUT AT WORK

Confession: "I'm afraid that if I don't make time to socialize with my colleagues at work, I'll be the odd woman out."

At 4:55 PM on a Friday, a coworker invites you to join him and a crew of fellow employees for "happy hour" at a local bar. There is definitely appeal in kicking back with coworkers at the end of a long day, but you're also ready to go home and spend time with your family, who is waiting for you. When you say you can't make it again, he responds by rolling his eyes. Great. Well, come on, what does he expect? Does he think that in the ten minutes before the day ends you can magically find someone to pick up your children, get them home, and arrange dinner for everyone? Or maybe your employer is planning a four-day office retreat at a ski lodge this year and everyone is expected to attend. Uh, how exactly are you going to explain to your significant other that you'll be off skiing and drinking hot cocoa or brandy by the fire for several days so . . . best of luck holding down the fort! And if you're a single mom, how are you supposed to get that kind of major coverage—even if you wanted to? Does no one in your office have kids to attend to? I mean, seriously, you can't be the only one with parenting responsibilities, can you?

Whether or not you are the only one among your colleagues who's a parent, you feel sad about being the office buzz kill that never takes part in out-of-office socializing. Of course, if your coworkers stop asking you to join them, that might be even worse. Plus, here's the thing: Even if you could logistically go away on a multiday staff retreat, grab drinks with colleagues once a week, and attend networking events throughout the month, perhaps you wouldn't choose to spend that much time hanging with your office mates. Sure, on occasion it would be fun, but, like all working moms, your kids need you, and we all want to be there for them—we chose to have them. Heck, for many of us working moms, we're with our coworkers all day long, five days a week. If, by some miracle, we have any spare hours in a week, we'd probably prefer to spend them talking with close friends, going on an actual date, or getting to bed early for once. But still, there's that looming feeling that if we're not more social at work, we're going to become the odd woman out and it might hurt us professionally.

QUIZ: ARE YOU THE BAILER AT WORK?

1. **When you hear your colleagues gathering in the lunch or break room, you:**

   a. join them. It breaks up the day and lifts your spirits to hang out with them.

   b. don your iPod headphones so you can ignore them and get back to work.

   c. pretend you're on the phone with a client so they won't invite you.

2. **The idea of planning the next staff social event makes you:**

   a. break out in hives. You don't need yet another task that takes you away from your family.

   b. kind of excited. It would be a relief to have your colleagues see you making an effort for once.

   c. feel anxious because you have no idea what your colleagues consider fun.

3. **The last time you volunteered to help a colleague with his work was:**

   a. before you had kids. You don't want to foster the expectation that others can come to you when they need help.

   b. within the last couple of months. You do it with the understanding that it's not okay to ask others to cover you when you aren't offering help.

   c. never. You can barely get your own work done, much less help out someone else at the office.

Answers: If you answered "a" for number 1, give yourself one point. If you answered "b" for number 2, give yourself one point. If you answered "b" for number 3, give yourself one point. If you received at least two points, you're on the right track for putting in social face time at work. If you received one or zero points, pay extra attention to the steps in this chapter because you're at risk for becoming the office outsider, which can have personal and professional repercussions.

Reality Check

- - - - - - - - - - - - -

In 2009, Mom Central Consulting, a firm specializing in marketing to mothers, surveyed 1,300 moms with an in-depth questionnaire about their online and offline behaviors. The focus of the survey was working moms' attitudes toward networking, community, and sense of self. More than 80 percent of the women said they do not get enough support from coworkers. Respondents also said they feel pressure to maximize office productivity in order to make day-care or after school pick-up, and they therefore typically avoid post-work socializing.[1]

Unfortunately for these moms, research shows that spending casual time with coworkers and colleagues is as essential to our success on the job as getting our work done. In April 2010, Gallup consultants interviewed millions of workers in hundreds of companies around the world and found that lack of an emotional bond among coworkers can lead to lower productivity, anxiety, and depression; additionally, having no "social reward" can lead to a lack of interest in one's work.[2] Why? According to Kerry Patterson, coauthor of the *New York Times* bestseller *Influencer,* "Much of what takes place in companies is done through the informal social network," she says. "For instance, people solve important problems over lunch—and if you work out at a health club alone, you find yourself out of the loop."[3]

According to Beth Braccio Hering, a regular contributor to Careerbuilder.com and other outlets, some of the best bonding and information-sharing goes on outside of the office. She advises, "While nobody should be expected to attend every after-hours social event, making an effort to join in office socialization builds your likability and can increase your sense of belonging."[4] When you're having one of those days where the ink from the toner spills onto your hands, your computer freezes, and you accidentally hang up on a client twice, you're going to want that friend at work who lets you hide in her office and cheers you up with jokes or pep talks. But you can't expect this gift unless you're kindling the relationship—which calls for going outside of your work space and showing your face.

This is not to add more pressure to your life. You don't have to attend every networking opportunity, chug beers every week with the crew, and befriend everyone on your floor, but you do have to make yourself available sometimes. It's time to shed your "no thanks" default policy and open your office door (even if it's a pro-verbial door). The good news is, there are plenty of ways to bond with coworkers without falling far behind on your task list or giv-ing up family dinners. You just have to get a little creative in your planning and schedule social events around your calendar.

Step 1: *When possible, make decisions on the spot.*

- -

Melanie, an entrepreneur mom of two boys that I spoke with, con-fessed, "I was invited to the back-to-school picnic and the company outing on the same evening, and I couldn't figure out who to say no to. My husband couldn't make it that night to the picnic either, so it would mean my kids would be there with a neighbor . . . that just felt sad. Or, I could tell my boss I couldn't make the company out-ing, which would piss her off, since it's only twice a year. So I said yes to both events and figured I'd work it out later. I didn't think about how I was going to work this out. I just didn't want to deal with it. Ultimately, I went to the school picnic, and my boss was even more irritated with me because I told her I'd be at the outing. Next time, I'll give an answer right away and stick to it so I don't have to keep thinking about it!"

No matter how much assertiveness training women have had over the years—and no matter how many strides we've made—we still need to get better at saying no and letting the chips fall where they may. Dr. Cathy Greenberg, executive coach and coauthor of the national bestseller *What Happy Working Mothers Know: How New Findings in Positive Psychology Can Lead to a Healthy and Happy Work/Life Balance,* says that learning to say no is one of the best things we can do to preserve our sanity. It's not just meek women or shy women who have a hard time with this; it's super-competent, strong businesswomen. Says Greenberg: "You need to decide where you want to spend your energy because your energy is not an unlimited resource. If you don't say no to certain things, you're not going to be successful at anything. You'll end up saying 'yes' too much and using up your energy and not having enough for yourself and your kids."

As a result, we waste too many hours changing our minds and worrying about potential repercussions, and then changing our minds again. This flip-flopping can be excruciating, right? So even though it feels awkward, just say no when you need to—and without procrastinating. Yep, you're going to be left out of some things and you'll likely upset someone along the way. That's one of the unfortunate prices of having a family and career. Instead of going back and forth on which events to skip, try to figure out early in the game whether it feels worse to skip the work event or family gathering this time (look at each event as case by case), accept it as a done deal, and let the people affected know in advance so they can plan ahead. It stinks letting them down, but at least everyone is clear from the get-go and you don't have to waste any more time going round and round, which is bad for all.

Step 2: *Connect with another office mom.*

It's always a treat to chat with my coworker Debby at The Hadassah-Brandeis Institute, where I edit *614,* an online magazine. In addition to providing me with work suggestions on potential authors for specific topics, we sometimes swap stories about what our children are up to. I get glimpses of the future when she tells me about teaching her teen daughter to drive *(Oy!),* picking a dress together for the prom, and visiting her son at college. When I tell her about what my seven-year-old is up to, she has the wisdom to offer advice on how to handle the occasional nightmare or teach my daughter how to ride a bicycle (which is less stressful than having your child learn to drive, but still panic-producing when she begins veering into a tree because she's trying to tell me she's thirsty). No matter whose kid we're talking about, we usually enjoy a good laugh before getting back to work.

We covered friendships and why maintaining them is so important in the last chapter. That said, it's essential to point out that working-mom friendships in the office have their own unique perks, whether you socialize outside of work or not. This is not to say that all working mothers are kind and helpful to one another, but you certainly have good odds that this other mom not only is going to understand the unique predicaments that come from juggling work and career, but will also implicitly understand how you can help each other ease the stress. These women can be emotional lifesavers; they understand how it feels when you have to leave early to pick up your sick child from school or daycare, or come in late because you had to take your kids to the dentist in the morning.

This is not to say you have to be best friends with these women—or even that you'll enjoy their company outside of the office. But it's worth investing in some kind of relationship if only to have a coworker who doesn't shoot you death looks when you bolt out of the office during crunch time because you have a child-related emergency or obligation. She may also be the only one who doesn't cringe or laugh at you when you show up in a sweater with baby vomit or mismatched shoes. So if you've been overlooking the new mom who works three office doors down from you because she looks kind of stuffy or seems shy, introduce yourself.

Another reason it's worth the effort is that those with friends who emotionally support them at the office live longer—for real. *Health Psychology* reported on a study in Israel that found employees who on average were forty-one years old (one third of them women), had worked for twenty years for 8.8 hours a day, and who didn't have emotional support at the office faced a 2.4 times greater risk of dying within those twenty years.[5] Coauthor of the study, Dr. Sharon Toker of the department of organizational behavior at Tel Aviv University in Israel, said in a *USA Today* article, "We spend most of our waking hours at work, and we don't have much time to meet our friends during the weekdays. Work should be a place where people can get necessary emotional support."[6]

So how do you go about setting up this emotional support? Nicola Taggart, certified executive coach and founder of Nicola Taggart & Company, a corporate consulting agency, suggests: "Have the courage and make the effort to invite at least one other working mom to lunch. Just be honest about your desire to connect with others who are in the same dual-role. More formally, consider starting a Working Moms group in your office. Although some may be reluctant to draw attention to this role, it can actually be very liberating to embrace the challenging position you are in and create a circle of other women who understand. Plan a once-a-month lunch gathering, bring in a speaker for a lunch-and-learn topic that would be helpful to working moms, or create a way to communicate virtually about working mom—related issues." Greenberg, author of *What Happy Working Mothers Know,* suggests posting a note on your internal internet system at work and/or on the bulletin board in the lunch room saying you're hosting a brown bag lunch for moms, and women who want to participate should bring their lunch and a positive story about being a working mom so everyone can learn from one another and feel good at the end of the session.

Step 3: *Spell out the b-o-u-n-d-a-r-i-e-s.*

Cynthia, a thirty-two-year-old banker from New York and mother of six-month-old twins, remembers all too well the twelve-hour days she experienced when she returned to work. "After my maternity leave, I had to repeatedly set my foot down with my boss and colleagues that I had to be home by 7:00 PM to relieve my nanny. It was much harder than I had anticipated! I hated being the first person to leave for the day, and I hated to have to tell people in a meeting or on the phone that I had to leave early for the day. Eventually my coworkers all got up to speed and understood that I now have two little people in my life who need me more than my work. As long as I still deliver good-quality work, communicate timelines well, and am reachable, the respect I worked so hard for is still there."

When we're exhausted and/or stressed-out, it feels impossible to put our foot down (what we want is to put our feet up). That said, it's essential to your well-being to make boundaries clear to those you work with. If you have to leave at 4:55 PM sharp every day to make the daycare pickup on time, don't sneak out hoping that no one will notice. They will notice. Instead, sit down with your supervisor or staff and let them know you will need to leave at a specific time each day and explain how you intend to deal with it (i.e., "Any work that hasn't been completed I'll do tonight from home after I put my child to bed," or "I will be in early during workdays to make up for any work that might not have been completed before I left"). If you are the boss, let your staff know your schedule, how they can be in touch with you if a work emergency pops up, and what you classify as an emergency (i.e., not "We looked everywhere and we can't find the copier toner" but "Our client just called and is pissed off").

Setting boundaries is all the more challenging at a time when coworkers can reach us at all hours of the day via cell phone, Black-Berry, email, and instant messaging. If you don't establish parameters for communication and someone wants to get ahold of you, he is going to try. This means we have to be even more vigilant about verbalizing our expectations. If a colleague announces, "I'll call you tonight to figure out the next steps," as you're packing up for the day, stop and explain what time frame is acceptable (i.e., "Sure, if you call me between eight and nine, I'll be free . . ." or "I'm sorry, we'll have to connect in the morning. I'm not available"). Or if a team member says she will email her report to you to look at tonight, don't just say "fine"; let her know what she can expect from you (i.e., "Sounds good. If it's after 10:00 PM, I will look at it first thing in the morning and get it back to you before 10:00 AM").

Sandi Stewart Epstein, a Washington, D.C.–based work/life coach, suggests remembering that you and your employer are "both on the same team trying to accomplish the day-to-day tasks at your work," and "If you're willing to work late during occasional crunch times, chances are your employer will be more receptive to letting you leave early for an occasional school play."[7]

So keep your boundaries in place, with a willingness to be flexible when you are able—considering these exceptions. If you find that exceptions quickly become the rule, sit with your employer or staff and see whether you can come up with a more reasonable solution.

Step 4: *Build goodwill whenever possible.*

- -

There are plenty of workers out there who are tired of picking up the slack for working moms (I know because I've read many anonymous comments over the years on the Internet). And, to be fair, they have a point: Why should they have to stay until 9:00 PM to get a job done because we have to leave at five? Why should they have to come in on a Saturday because we can't find coverage for our child's February break? I'd be resentful too if I had to do someone's work because she had to get her child to the pediatrician and couldn't make the deadline. These experiences, unfortunately, can foster an "us versus them" mentality, and many working moms feel that separation on a regular basis.

Kathryn, thirty-seven, a researcher from British Columbia and mom of a thirteen- and a three-year-old, admits, "I work full-time, Monday to Friday, in a small office with coworkers who don't have kids, and I sometimes feel like I'm taking too much time with sick kids, orthodontist appointments, school functions, etc."

It's tough when you don't have much choice about handling family obligations, particularly if you're a single mom or are with a significant other who can hardly ever take time off from work for appointments and non-emergencies. And to make matters worse, there's always that underlying concern that your colleagues will resent you.

Amy, thirty-three, is a corporate communications specialist and mom to a four- and a two-year-old. She says the hardest part of juggling work and family is "keeping up appearances—people expect working moms to slack or let life creep in—and we do! So we have to work doubly hard to act like we don't!"

In theory, we all know it's an awful idea to expect coworkers to pick up our slack when we can't finish a task because of a family priority. But when we have to take a few days off of work because our child has a broken arm and we need help finishing a report, we have no choice. Nor do we when we have to dash off to the school concert but still need to ship out a FedEx package to a client and the proofs aren't back from the production department yet. We look over and see a coworker sitting there laughing and texting with a friend, and think, *What's the harm in asking? She's clearly got time.*

Sure, it's not a big deal asking a coworker to lend a helping hand here and there (as in once or twice a year). It's another thing to ask for her help on a consistent basis because of an overabundance of family obligations and setbacks. After a while, that effusive "Thank you, you're the best!" as you rush out the door is going to lose its charm and you'll end up with a resentful colleague—or two or more. Is there any way to call on coworkers to help without fostering resentment?

Yes.

One thing you can do is pick up the slack for coworkers voluntarily when you can. As Barbara Pachter, an internationally renowned business etiquette and communications speaker and president of Pachter & Associates, says, "Working moms need to establish rapport with their coworkers, being friendly and interested in their lives. And when coworkers pick up the slack for a working mom, she needs to make it up to them." On a day when you finish a project a little early or your phone call gets cancelled or a meeting rescheduled, ask a coworker who has covered (or could cover) for you if she needs some help with anything. Think of this as your rainy-day fund, in which you're investing time in them with hopes they will return the favor when you really need it. You're going to be in a much better position to ask your coworker to lead a staff meeting you were supposed to direct if she remembers that you handled a client's needs when she called in sick one day. An added bonus is that it just feels good to do something nice for a coworker you appreciate.

Try This:

On a day when you do get caught up or even ahead of schedule, give the gift of help to a stressed-out coworker. Say, "Hey, I have an extra thirty minutes today, and I know you're working hard on the [fill in blank] project. Do you need some help?" If you can't take on someone else's work because your brain is basically fried from catching up on your own, offer to get your coworkers coffee and treats. Also, when they help you in the lurch, go beyond a simple thank-you. If the task they did for you took more than ten minutes, bring them appreciation gifts (cookies, bubble bath, a gift card to Starbucks).

Step 5: *Save adorable stories for grandparents.*

- -

In the *New York Times* magazine column "That Should Be a Word," author Lizzie Skurnick coined the term "brattle" in 2011, a verb meaning to "discuss one's children, often at length." She even used it in a full sentence: "Anne hid in the basement to avoid the cocktail brattle."[8]

One of the reasons working moms are sometimes avoided at work is that, sadly, nobody appreciates our office brattling. Who doesn't want to hear about our child eating solids for the first time, scoring a touchdown, or doing her first split in gymnastics class? Who wouldn't want to watch that split on our flip camera (it'll only take a sec and it's so cool!)? But the bummer reality is that Fred in accounting—who is single and child-free couldn't care less. The single gal you are networking with does not want to hear about the Diaper Disaster of 2011 or how your son shoved peanuts up his nose that wouldn't come out. Wait, I take that back, almost everyone wants to hear that story—especially if it involved going to the ER at midnight. That aside, any story involving the question "Do you want to hear the cutest thing my daughter said?" should probably be saved for best friends, grandmas, and your husband.

As Betsy Shaw, writer of *Babe's Blog* on Babycenter.com, eloquently put it: "I know what it's like to get cornered by someone who wants to talk about her kids, whether it's an office or cocktail party setting, and as soon as you hear the words, 'You won't believe what my pre-schooler said this morning,' your brain just kind of yawns."[9]

Along these same lines, if and when you bring your child into the office to pick up important papers or get some work during a school vacation day, be courteous of your coworkers. It may be tempting to parade your child around so everyone can get a good look at your little one, but it's probably best to keep it very brief. Sure, some might ooh and ahhh over your child and invite your child to check out the cool toys they stash in their desk drawer, but others—including those without kids, those trying to cram in work, and those who desperately need a break from kids—may not appreciate your toddler grabbing paper clips from their desk or older kids bombarding them with questions. Try not to see this as a reflection on you or your child; it's just about being at different life stages or having work priorities.

Advises Beth Braccio Hering: "If the child is old enough, prep her ahead of time by reminding her to use an indoor voice and explaining that she cannot be running around because people are trying to work. For a child of any age, come prepared by bringing a snack and quiet, age-appropriate toys (crayons and paper, a favorite stuffed animal, etc.) to keep the child occupied while you tend to your work. Use your best judgment as to how long to hang out with coworkers. Some will be delighted to interact with your child, while others may be busy or not particularly fond of being around kids. A polite introduction suffices in the latter case."

Try This:

Hering also suggests trying out the "Pied Piper Effect": Simply make your way to your desk or office. Those who are interested in a lengthy interaction will follow you there, leaving the rest of the workplace free for other activities to carry on with minimal distraction. If you can choose your time to come in, consider first thing in the morning or right after lunch. This allows colleagues to socialize with you and your offspring before settling into work rather than be interrupted."

Step 6: *Plan the next company outing or event.*

- -

You dread the staff email reminders about the company softball game, company picnic, or other "optional" company events that take place after hours. Every time you reply back that you can't make it, you imagine the others rolling their eyes and sharing a knowing "I told you so" look, or worse, writing you off as part of the team, so that you feel like an outsider during those rare moments you linger with them in the break room or catch a few in the elevator. "I'm a good person and I'm doing my best trying to juggle work and family!" you want to scream-type in your reply email. Even though you are, it's not going to win over any coworkers. It's time for you to plan the next event, and on your own terms.

Why not find one night in the next month that you actually can go out and then organize the staff event? We're not talking rocket science here, ladies. We're talking about picking a date and sending out a group email suggesting everyone go miniature golfing, go bowling, or take part in improv night or a walk-a-thon . . . whatever. If you're thinking, *No, no, no, I can't take on one more thing,* I get it. But let's look at this for a second: The email is going to take all of five minutes to whip up, plus about ten minutes beforehand coming up with the location and suggestions for best day and time.

One word of warning: Beware of outings with alcohol. If it's been awhile since you've been on a social excursion, remember that drinking with your staff is in no way the same as having one too many with a close friend. Says Bill Lampton, author of *The Complete Communicator: Change Your Communication, Change Your Life!* "Sometimes we assume that two more drinks will help us talk more easily. That's a mistake. Two more drinks will encourage you to talk more—period. The impaired speaking and unsteady walk that follow those extra cocktails could brand you: 'lush,' 'a drunk,' 'undisciplined,' or something similar."[10] So perhaps skip the moonlight booze-cruise, and initiate something a little tamer, like the suggestions mentioned.

That's it! Everyone will be pleased (if also startled) to see that you're actually planning an event rather than trying to figure out a creative new way to get out of it again. You no longer have to dread the next invitation because you actually planned one and even showed up! Hey, you very well may enjoy your night out with your colleagues—and find out that Andrea in accounting is a whole lot more fun playing paintball with than when she's chastising you for overspending on your work trip.

Once the event is over, you've just bought yourself a good few months before you have to attend the next event (unless, of course, you had such a blast that you're game for the next one too). You have proven you don't think you're too good for the others; instead, you've shown you're interested in being part of the team. Also, take plenty of pictures at the event so you can post them the next week—a reminder of the good times everyone had because of your planning.

Try This:

If getting all your coworkers to agree on a destination proves too challenging, plan an event inside the office. One mom emailed me to say that she created an in-office contest during the holidays so she didn't have to do anything off-site. She created a "Holiday Desk Design" challenge for her employees, where staffers had to make their desk as festive as possible (using whatever supplies from home they wanted), and the winner got an extra day of vacation. "I don't know if my staff was excited about doing something creative or desperate for an extra day of vacation, but they totally got into the spirit of this contest and there was a lot of silliness! I took photos of the top picks and posted them around the office to help remind everyone of how much fun we had together. I'll definitely do it again next year."

Step 7: *Ease up on the self-created pressure.*

Kiki, thirty-four, from Oregon, is a marketing and sales director for a small company and mom to a fifteen-month-old. She struggles with self-induced guilt, even stress, worrying about how hiccups between work and family might foster resentment from her supervisor. She had this to say: "We had just come back from a four-day weekend to visit my parents. It was Sunday night when we got back home, and my daughter came down with a fever almost as soon as we walked in the door to the house. It spiked in the middle of the night. My husband was scheduled to leave for a work trip that next morning so there was no way I would make it into the office. I had to struggle with the feeling that people at the office would think I just wanted another day to be on vacation, when in fact I had my sweet toddler drooling and sneezing all over me as I logged into my computer at work and did my best to prove that I could still connect in and work. I had no choice, something I'm sure a lot of moms face all the time. I had to improvise and thanked the powers that be (for the millionth time) for inventing the BlackBerry, which allows me to answer emails, IMs, phone calls, etc., all while my poor little one snoozes on my shoulder."

Yep, we've all been there—more than once. It's tough enough to deal with the family crisis du jour without worrying about how resentful a coworker may be because they think we're playing hooky. Instead of obsessing, take action. Talk to your boss or colleagues—or email them—explaining your situation. For example, "I'm home taking care of my child today and I'm upset that I've left you more responsibilities. What can I do when I get back?" If you put it out there on the table, only someone with a heart of stone is going to beat up on you rather than reassure you that it's okay (of course, most of us have had at least one boss with a heart of stone, but nothing you can do about that).

Even more important, go extra-easy on yourself when you're in the midst of an unexpected crisis. It's not like you've ditched work to go to Vegas for a weekend bender; you are being a good mom who is taking care of her child to the best of her ability. What you need is understanding, even compassion—not extra panic about what everyone at work is going to think. As my stepfather, a wise therapist, always says, "You do you, let them do them." They'll figure out what to do at work to keep things on track. You worry about getting yourself and your child through the day with sanity intact.

Step 8: Connect with your people online.

- -

If socializing at work just doesn't seem to be an option (it's impossible to break into the clique, or you just can't swing the time required), or you work freelance—and many of us do—there is another option for socializing with working moms. Go online. Award-winning journalist Linda Lowen, who writes the "Women's Issues" column on About.com, says, "Online moms can spend quality time with old friends and make new ones. And with support and guidance available 24/7, even if the baby's sick and it's too cold to go out, community and companionship are just a keystroke away."[11]

Personally, I use an online documentary filmmaker forum called D-word (there's your shout-out, d-word.com!), and I'm instantly connected with fellow documentary filmmakers around the country. We ask each other questions ("What do you think of my new film website?" "Does my trailer seem compelling enough?" "What kind of light should I use for this scene?"). One of my favorite sections is "Doc Maker as Homemaker," where parents swap tips on how to balance filmmaking with family life and gather tremendous support and encouragement from one another. For me, this site isn't a substitute for sitting face-to-face with other filmmakers and musing about our projects, but it is a wonderful complement to it and gives me a way to connect professionally at any hour.

If you haven't used these online sites yet, go forth and conquer. Just a few finger clicks away is a world of advice on technology; what to do when your boss is being, uh, difficult; what to do when you are the boss and your staffers are slacking; ways to "chill out" during the holidays; how to hire; how to fire. More than anything else, you will find a whole sea of listening ears that make you feel less isolated. You may not be able to carpool with these gals or roll your eyes at the same client, but the connection you experience will more than make up for it.

Try This:

Here are some of the working-mom forums I discovered that cover a whole range of topics, from daycare concerns and finding time to pump to asking for a raise and success tips for working from home. One suggestion from Greenberg (What Happy Working Mothers Know): As you start using online forums, make sure that you're feeling energized from taking part in the discussion after you log off and not drained because others are venting.

Real Working Mom: http://realworkingmom.proboards.com/index.cgi
The Bump: http://community.thebump.com/cs/ks/forums/4236752/Show Forum.aspx
WAHM (Work at Home Moms): http://www.wahm.com/
Moms Network: http://www.momsnetwork.com/
Freelancemom: http://www.freelancemom.com/

Proceed with Caution If . . .

you overhear a coworker talking about how you don't take part in any activities outside of work. Instead of getting defensive, take a deep breath and think about this: These coworkers want you to take part in their extracurricular activities. Hey, isn't that a thousand times better than them not noticing you're not at the event? Or worse, they could have experienced relief that you didn't show up. Bathe in the joy of being wanted, and then show up at one of the events to show them what they've been missing all this time.

On the Flip Side . . .

maybe you simply can't attend after-work activities because you're a single mom who can't always find a babysitter when you'd like. Or maybe there's something serious going on at home that needs your undivided attention. If this is the case, make a point of lunching with your coworkers. You may be tempted to scarf down your sandwich in front of the computer so you can complete all of your tasks by the end of the day, but that lunch is where everyone exchanges stories, jokes, mini-exasperations, and the intimate stories that make relationships stronger. Work lunches are also rich in opportunities to learn something about the boss or staff members, any challenges or issues that other departments are dealing with, and all manner of things that make an office tick. An added bonus: Socializing with these people means they will be more likely to help you when you need a refresher on how to use the new phones or restart your crashed computer—or even help you out in a pinch. So head to the cafeteria/kitchen, and if you can't do the full hour, hang out for a half hour at least.

SHOUT-OUT TO . . .

Lorie Marsh, a forty-four-year-old film producer from Minnesota with a three-year-old daughter, who says it has been helpful to be really clear with herself and her coworkers about her priorities. "Everyone I work with knows that my first priority is parenting my child," she states, "and that if push comes to shove and both work and my kid need me, my kid is going to come first—end of story." As a result, Lorie says, "I experience no guilt about saying I won't be working on the days my child needs me. That's just how it is."

Chapter Wrap

- - - - - - - - - - - - - -

Step 1: *When possible, make decisions on the spot.*

People are much more likely to forgive you for not showing up if you tell them in advance.

Step 2: *Connect with another office mom.*

You don't have to be BFFs, but this woman could end up being your lifeline.

Step 3: *Spell out the b-o-u-n-d-a-r-i-e-s.*

Let coworkers know exactly what they can expect (and not expect) from you.

Step 4: *Build goodwill whenever possible.*

It's worth investing in helping coworkers during your downtime so you don't end up the office mooch.

Step 5: *Save adorable stories for grandparents.*

Your kids really are remarkable, but seek out confirmation from relatives rather than coworkers.

Step 6: *Plan the next company outing or event.*

Take twenty minutes to set up the next event and show that you consider yourself part of the team.

Step 7: *Ease up on the self-created pressure.*

Most coworkers will be kinder than you think when you have a family crisis— so long as you don't leave them in the lurch.

Step 8: *Connect with your people online.*

If you can't find supportive colleagues at work, track them down on the Internet.

Chapter 8

HEADING TOWARD BURNOUT

Confession: "I spend so much time trying to meet everyone else's needs. I worry I'm not taking good care of myself."

When I asked working moms to describe the *best* part of maintaining both a career and a family, many of them talked about "maintaining their own identity," having "a sense of purpose," and/or "feeling engaged." While "being stimulated" is also a fabulous payoff for straddling these two realms, unfortunately the very idea of relaxation is but a misty memory for many working moms. "When exactly are we supposed to kick back?" women balked. "Wait, what is this word 'relaxation' you speak of?" one commented. "It sounds vaguely familiar." Sure, there are a few hours when the children are in bed for the night that is "our" time . . . but many of us need to get back to work, get some sleep so we can at least start the next day feeling rested, or try to get somewhat organized for the upcoming week. "Relaxing" is one of those unrealistic goals, like "finding a way to get rid of the cellulite on our thighs" or "remaining calm as our mother-in-law judges our parenting style while we're standing *right there*." It's recognized as a legitimate concern by working moms, but not nearly as essential as figuring out how to get our child to the dentist without missing an important conference call.

When you get right down to it, the act of relaxation is pretty much the great oxymoron of a working mom's life. Not only is it a challenge to find "me time," but we also have to deal with the guilt of not creating enough of it because every women's magazine seems to be shouting at us to replenish! Are you recharging?! Why the heck *aren't* you doing "downward dog" in yoga class on Saturdays or cleansing your pores in the sauna or curling up on the sofa to knit yourself a sweater on a winter afternoon? According to all the messaging we get, if you were a healthy, whole person, you'd be all over this art of relaxation. You'd find a way to go with your girlfriends to Kripalu or Canyon Ranch and have your feet massaged in lavender oil. But here's what the experts don't address: When exactly are we supposed to indulge in "filling up our tank"? There's always—at every second—something we could and probably should be doing. Yes, "me time" sounds just lovely—and perhaps we can jump right on that when our last child is off to college.

QUIZ: ARE YOU IN NEED OF SERIOUS DOWNTIME?

1. **While tucking in your child at bedtime, you are most likely to:**
   a. give one last kiss goodnight, and then look forward to quiet time for Mama.
   b. read the same paragraph of your child's book two, maybe three, times because you keep zoning out.
   c. fall asleep next to him/her and wake up hours later confused.

2. **The last time you accomplished at least thirty minutes (consecutively) of exercise was:**
   a. folding and putting away the clean laundry last month (hey, it isn't easy pairing all those socks together).
   b. that time last week when you had to staple several reports together at work.
   c. this week, when you donned exercise clothes and got your heart rate going.

3. **The idea of hiring a babysitter so you can go out at night makes you:**
   a. weep with sorrow. How can you leave your little one with a virtual stranger?
   b. weep with joy. Oh, to put on a little lip gloss and hang out with real live adults who aren't coworkers!
   c. weep with exhaustion. You wouldn't even know where to start when it comes to finding an adequate babysitter.

Answers: If you answered "a" for number 1, give yourself one point. If you answered "c" for number two, give yourself one point. If you answered "b" for number 3, give yourself a point. If your sum total is two or more, then you probably know a little something about staying replenished. If your total is less, pay careful attention to this chapter so you can veer off the road to burnout before it's too late.

Reality Check

How much downtime you need is dependent on your personal energy level, which we all know can change from one day to the next (or even between morning and afternoon). How do you recognize when you need, not just desire, "quiet time"? Remember: You have a honed skill for reading energy levels. You can probably tell within mere seconds of looking at your child's face whether a nap is needed, and how many minutes you have left on the clock before a total meltdown occurs. You can also tell by the changes in your child's tone and demeanor—maybe he gets cranky, or the whining kicks up a notch, or perhaps he even starts yelling over some seeming injustice, like not getting his sippy cup refilled *right this instant!* Now, look in the mirror: Does this ever sound like *you?*

Says Dr. Kathleen Hall, CEO and founder of The Stress Institute, when it comes to losing our balance in the work-parent juggle, "You can't [avoid it]! It happens to the best of us. But you can develop practices that will warn you when you are out of balance and help you return to balance easily and effortlessly." It's all a matter of tuning in to what nourishes you, Hall says, whether it's a call to a friend or spouse, a short meditation, a nap, or something else. You have to find out "what feeds you."

First, we need to tune in to these signs and deal with them as soon as possible. If all signs point to you needing to recharge, do what you would for your tired child and assign yourself quiet time—even if it's only fifteen minutes. "But I can't," you say, "because I need to put away the laundry, finish my speech, shop for dinner, call Mom, [fill in the blank]." Well, as you tell your child (as she insists, "I have to finish this LEGO tower," or he demands, "I need ten more minutes to finish my picture!"), it can wait. Time *out*. What do you do in these spare minutes when there's not enough time for the full-on nap you're craving? That's what this chapter is for, to remind or teach you what you can do, while providing easy ways to bring down your stress level so you don't top out to begin with. And guess what? I'm not even going to *mention* exercise. You know it's good for you; the last thing you need is yet another source of pressure pushing you to get that body moving.

Step 1: *Tune in to your body, especially when pain is involved.*

- -

Tiffany, a twenty-five-year-old human resources manager, says while she's blessed with an enjoyable job that boosts her confidence, she learned this past year what can happen when you don't listen to your body's signals. As she tells it: "Less than a year ago, my back gave out. I had two herniated disks in my lower spine, and I couldn't walk. I think it was stress related, and because I pushed myself through the pain, I ended up tearing those disks and making it worse." Tiffany says her health bottomed out at the Christmas party she organized for her company. In spite of the pain she was feeling, she forced herself to go. Because her husband was playing the role of Santa, she "felt she had to attend." Of course, her back got even worse, and it took about three months to be able to stand up with her back straight and pick up her daughter again.

What is your body telling *you* right now? Sometimes it's hard to know, especially when you're running around trying to get to the bank before it closes, or making sure the overnight package gets into the mail, or returning a half-dozen phone calls before picking up your child at school. In order to listen to our body, we need to recognize it as a priority for our well-being and take a few moments to get a proper read.

Life coach Julie Zeff of Vivid Living, who specializes in working with busy moms, suggests doing a "body check": Find a quiet space, close your eyes, breathe, and notice what sensations are present in your body. Simply breathing and noticing these sensations—letting them be and move through you—can help them to dissipate. Common sensations include tightness and pressure around the chest or around the heart, constriction at the back of the neck, and breathing shallowly. As you notice these sensations, she says, just keep breathing and see if they dissipate fairly quickly. If not, it's a sign we're overstressing our bodies.

And what if we simply ignore these aches and pains? The more symptoms will become intense. Don't make your muscles and joints scream to get noticed (like when your child starts with "Ma?" and, if ignored, escalates quickly to "MOMMMM!!"). Anne Louise Oaklander, MD, PhD, an associate professor of neurology at Harvard Medical School, warns, "Pain in the body is a red alert. You must always listen to it."[1] Go to your doctor for a checkup at once when you notice your body is feeling "off" or you're in pain. If your doctor can't seem to help, says Oaklander, get a referral expert, and "no matter what," she advises, "if you have chronic pain, don't ignore it—and never accept it." Of course, we should also do whatever possible to address our aches so they don't turn into chronic pain. I've definitely found it helpful to stretch my back and neck after sitting too long at the computer; take breaks, like a short walk around the neighborhood; keep a bottle of water at my desk so I remember to drink plenty; and soak in a long bath with Epsom salts if I feel sore or tight. Your body will thank you for paying attention to it, and reward you by not stepping up the pain.

Of course, it's not just physical symptoms that can alert us to our stress. I can usually tell my energy reserves are dipping below normal when I get overly annoyed by tiny problems (say, when my husband signs us up to bring fruit salad for the classroom breakfast instead of something super-easy and convenient, like cream cheese and bagels), and feel less tolerant of my daughter's stories, which are sweet when I'm in a good frame of mind but seem to trail on eternally when I'm stressed. I'm sure you have your own telltale mental signs that you're in need of recharging. Says Zeff: "When you do, ask yourself if there is any urgent or true danger that needs to be responded to immediately. Is there clear evidence of something gone awry? If so, then trust your instincts and act immediately! If not, then most likely the worries are just stories you are creating in your mind. Let them go."

Step 2: *Create serenity the moment you open your eyes.*

Instead of flying out of bed when your alarm goes off (or your child bangs on your door or dive-bombs you in your bed), take this tip from Jessie Lazar, yoga instructor and mom of two girls: "At the start of each day, sit on the edge of your bed, feet flat on the floor so you feel grounded. Now, close your eyes, and take three deep breaths, inhaling and exhaling from your nose. Repeat the word 'calm' on the exhale." Everyone in your family can wait a few extra moments for you to do this—especially when they see how it makes Mommy less *crazy*. If there is any pounding on the door while this is going on, open said door and announce to the little person that you will be out in just a minute while giving your best "back AWAY from the door" look.

End your day mindfully, too. It's tempting to fall into bed after doing the last dish or emailing the last work message. Or we zone out during an hour of bad television and then pass out on the couch. Then before we know what hits us—*buzz!*—the alarm is going off again and it's Groundhog Day! Give yourself fifteen minutes before going bed to unwind. You can do the same exercise above, or try this one from Joan Borysenko, PhD, director of Harvard's Mind-Body Clinical Programs: "Let out a big sigh, drop your chest, and exhale through gently pursed lips. Then imagine your lower belly, or center, as a deep, powerful place. Feel your breath coming and going as your mind stays focused there. Inhale, feeling your entire belly, sides and lower back expand. Exhale, sighing again as you drop your chest, and feel your belly, back and sides contract. Repeat ten times, relaxing more fully each time."[2]

Try This:

Sometimes, it's hard to find those spare minutes of alone time to unwind. Consider bringing your child into the experience. Not only do you get to unwind, but you also get to spend quality time with your child and help him or her learn to replenish as well. For example, my seven-year-old daughter, Risa, whipped up a game we call "Salon." The two of us created a menu of spa choices (back massage, foot massage, hair brushing, etc.) on my computer, and I let her choose the name of the spa, the font, and any other choices that would get her excited. Then we printed out our menu, and headed to the living room with a basket of nice-smelling lotions. We lit candles, put on classical music, and pretended that one person was the client and the other was the salon owner and masseuse. This is my daughter's favorite part of "the game," taking on various roles she can act out (her masseuse tends to have a British accent). I always like to be the client. Often, to keep her attention, I add in random elements of silliness: I might pretend to be a rude front-desk person or a bad masseuse that keeps tickling her feet, just so she stays engaged longer. In the meantime, we both get to hang out, enjoy each other's company, laugh, and forget about whatever else happened during the day.

Step 3: *Block out twenty minutes a day as mental recovery time.*

For many of us, days and weeks fly by. You glance at your watch, note you have another sixty minutes to go before you have to run out of the office, and the next thing you know it's time to grab your coat. How did that happen? Where did an entire hour go? As you review your day, you realize you accomplished about one quarter of what you set out to do, and that means even more work tomorrow. Now you're frazzled *and* you have to make the difficult transition from career girl to supermom, but it's hard to switch gears. How are you supposed to build in time to decompress, especially when it's essential to your well-being?

Well, one thing is for sure, no fairy godmother is going to do it for you, so you might as well do it yourself. In your Outlook or Google calendar, block off fifteen to twenty minutes each day as "busy" so no one can schedule a meeting or phone call with you. During that time, shut your literal or proverbial office door and have a high-level meeting with yourself. The objective? Mental recovery time. Lest you feel blocking this time out is self-indulgent, think again. According to business coach Tanveer Naseer, "By not giving ourselves time—to rest, relax, or simply enjoy the fruits of our labor—we're actually doing more harm than good because we're not giving ourselves the chance to catch our breath so that we might take on new opportunities with a fresh outlook."[3]

So what can we do in this pocket of minutes to help get ourselves grounded and relaxed? Here are some ideas, told to me directly by working moms: Call a friend who makes you laugh, read a pal's blog, go for a walk while listening to music, play a few rounds of word games on the computer, engage in a little meditation using a cell phone app, stand up and do yoga stretches, or sit on a bench facing the sun. Here are a few more of my own: Close your eyes and take deep calming breaths, sip a cup of herbal tea (okay, that's a lie, I drink dark-roasted coffee but felt compelled to say tea, which sounds healthier), look at a picture of an island getaway on your computer screen and envision yourself lounging by that swaying palm tree, or place a lavender eye pillow on your face and inhale the calming scent. Whatever you do, working moms agree that we need to tune out all the to-dos racing through our mind and really experience each decadent minute for all it's worth. You are guaranteed to feel more grounded, and the extra bonus is, this replenishing time will actually *improve* your productivity. A study conducted by *Cognition* journal in 2011 pointed out that short breaks allow people to maintain their focus on a task without the loss of quality that normally occurs over time.[4] So consider your meetings with yourself an opportunity for highly productive, mental recovery.

Step 4: *Peer into the future to decide what's worth stressing over.*

- -

Joy, thirty-seven, is a project manager in Washington and mom to two kids, ages six and ten. "Today, I had three priority projects at work, displacing my full-and-overdue to-do list," she wrote me. "Then a high-stress home appointment forced a change in schedule so I came home to help prepare. Now EVERYONE is a stress case, and I am absorbing everyone's angst. I'm also avoiding the two hours of writing/thinking I still *'owe'* my job for today."

Stressful? Yes. Enough to make a tired working mom weep? Check! This is the perfect opportunity to say, "There is no way I can manage three high-stakes projects today—especially given the situation at home. It's just not going to happen. Given that, what's the best choice I can make today? Okay, now . . . will this choice ultimately matter in a year? In five years?" Likely the answer is no. It may make life extra-stressful for the rest of the week (maybe even a few more weeks after that, while you play catch-up), but in the scope of years—*meh*, not such a big deal. So follow the advice of Catherine Pulsifer, author of several motivational books, including *Wings of Wisdom* and *Wings for Goals*: "When you find yourself stressed, ask yourself one question: Will this matter in five years from now? If yes, then do something about the situation. If no, then let it go."[5]

Test out the "future impact" barometer for yourself. Think about a difficult choice you have to make this week and ask yourself, "Whatever I do, is this going to matter in a year? In five years?" It may be irritating, but it probably isn't worth letting it consume all your energy. Make the conscious choice to keep the problem small ("I know it *feels* like a big deal that I am going to have to miss tonight's family dinner to speak to a client who lives in a country with another time zone," or "It feels stressful that I can't put another late night in to finesse this project, but the project will get done, and truthfully, I won't remember it in a year." Pay attention to how it feels as your anxiety starts shrinking.

Step 5: *Stay in the present, squeeze a stone.*

- -

For Barbara, a thirty-nine-year-old journalist in Massachusetts and mom to children ages two and six, the problem is that she sometimes literally needs to be in two places at the same time. She recalls, "I got a plum writing assignment from the *Boston Globe Magazine* when my second child was six weeks old. Since I was breastfeeding, I couldn't be away from him for more than a couple hours. So I took him to Vermont with me on a research trip, left him with friends for the day, and ran back and forth doing interviews and pumping my breasts."

Like Barbara, I know that one of the most wearing things about juggling parenting and career is trying to be in (at least) two places at the same time. We're making playdough farm animals with our child when thoughts about a work deadline start vying for our attention. Or we're in the midst of delivering a PowerPoint presentation at work when we are hit with an inspired idea for our child's birthday party (*Rollerskating theme . . . yes!*). My friends and I have debated whether parking our child in front of *Sesame Street* while we sit beside her working on our laptops counts as quality time, and who hasn't concocted shopping lists or babysitter options while nodding our head during a staff meeting to make it seem like we're focused on the matter at hand? Most of us have pretended we were fascinated by our child's painting process as we pondered what to write on our annual evaluation. Over and over throughout the day, we try to be engaged in two places at once, and then suffer from the mental exhaustion that comes from leading a double life. This is nothing new for working moms—this multitasking mayhem (as covered in Chapter 2)—but the truth is, we're not doing ourselves any favors here. Says business consultant Patrick O'Neil, author of *Visionmaker: Making the Journey from Possibility to Outcome*, "We are like time travelers . . . We are operating in multiple time zones with one important exception, the present moment."[6]

All this racing around is a major problem; in addition to sometimes making us scatterbrained and cranky, it's terrible for our health. According to Lama Surya Das, national bestselling author of *Awakening the Buddha Within* and *Buddha Standard Time*, "The thinner we spread ourselves the more disconnected we become. That leaves us vulnerable to high blood pressure, heart attacks, stroke, insomnia, digestive ailments, and depression."[7] The only way to truly avoid this is to be mindful, and while I've heard many explanations for what this means over the last year, I like how pediatrician and Zen teacher Jan Chozen Bays defines it in *The Mindfulness Revolution*: "Mindfulness means deliberately paying attention and being fully aware of what is happening both inside yourself—in your body, heart, and mind—and outside in your environment."[8]

That doesn't mean you need to meditate every day (although kudos to you if you do). Says Sarah Napthali in her book *Buddhism for Mothers of Schoolchildren*, "Even those who do not feel ready to commit to regular meditation can still insist on making time to pause and consciously relax for a few moments every day."[9] We can also make the conscious choice to pay attention, as Bays suggests. For example, if you're with your children, you're tuned in to the stories they're telling you and how it feels to be listening to them. If, instead, you're doing yoga or lying still on your bed, that's what you are doing—and nothing else. Only the very space you're in exists, and you're aware of how it feels.

When you catch your thoughts drifting into that other world, stop the action as quickly as you can and gently bring yourself back to the present by noticing what's happening right in front of your eyes. Ways to get back into the present moment, says Marcia Reynolds, PsyD, author of *Wander Woman: How High-Achieving Women Find Contentment and Direction,* include: "Get a daily dose of going outside, smelling the air, appreciating the trees and feeling the ground beneath your feet. When I reconnect with nature, I reconnect with my soul." Don't tell yourself you screwed up or you're never going to get this if you find your mind journeying back to the past ("Why did I have to point out my own mistake to my client?") or the future ("What if he doesn't trust me to get it right the next time?"). Just take a grounding breath, and begin again. You might have to do this dozens and dozens of times while you're trying to change the habit, and that's fine. According to O'Neil, it really does get easier, and one thing we can do to help ourselves practice staying in the present is to "find a little stone that you can keep in the palm of your hand. When you find yourself drifting give it a squeeze. It will help you transition back to the now."[10]

Step 6: *Shut down your gallery of gadgets.*

You've got your cell on your desk, a couple of browsers open at once so you can toggle between work and personal email, and maybe you're on IM and you have your Facebook page open. There are buzzes, dings, chirps, and other alerts reminding you to "LOOK OVER HERE!" and "DEAL WITH ME!" Not only is all this techno-intrusion distracting you from getting your work done, but it's also pulling you in different directions for much of the day. Why not turn it off? It's a case of FOMO: the "fear of missing out," whether it's good or bad news.

"What if the school nurse has to get ahold of me? I'm the primary contact," one mom asked. A corporate mom of three stated, "I can't just 'tune out.' What if my kids need to get ahold of me after school? It's bad enough I can't be there. I'm not going to cut off all connections." Another mom confessed, "I think it would be too quiet if I didn't have all my gadgets on and buzzing."

That's exactly the problem, says *Wired* magazine writer Steve Silberman in his essay "Digital Mindfulness" in *The Mindfulness Revolution*: "Restorative intervals of silence and solitude have become an

endangered species of experience."[11] Yes, we are all used to the pinging, dinging, and bleeping going on all day long, but is that a good
thing? Regarding the nurse or emergency contact getting ahold of
us, how many outlets does someone really need to track you down?
Wouldn't one phone line cut it? Here's the thing: If there is an emergency involving your child, you *will* be found. Most of the ringing interruptions have nothing to do with emergencies, unless you count your
son's after-school babysitter texting to say, "I can't find the remote
control for Nintendo," as one. See what life feels like when you unplug
for at least an hour. We forget that we have the power to turn gadgets *off*. In fact, according to a national survey conducted by the Pew
Research Center's Internet & American Life Project, only 29 percent
of cell phone users turn off their phone to get a break from using it![12]

The one exception to unplugging? Music. According to medical
experts, listening to music can calm the nervous system significantly. According to health researcher Jenny Stamos Kovacs in her
article "Blissing Out: 10 Relaxation Techniques to Reduce Stress on
the Spot" on WebMd.com, thirty minutes of classical music may pro-
duce calming effects equivalent to taking 10 milligrams of Valium.[13]
Of *Valium!* So if you're allowed the luxury of playing music in your
office, tune in to Beethoven or Brahms and enjoy the high.

Of course, find the music genre that most calms you. One freelance mom confessed, "I listen to oldies love songs while I'm working—with my headset on, of course, because I would be mocked
to death if anyone knew. We're talking the kind of music you hear
when you're in the dentist's chair. I'm only twenty-nine years old.
But I find it soothing. When I'm getting overwhelmed with how
much is left to do on my task list or I can't think of the right words
for my report because my brain is fried, I just close my eyes and let
the cheesy lyrics wash over me for a minute or two and feel better."

Step 7: *Don't let others peer-pressure you into their ideal of "relaxing."*

- -

One of my working-mom friends complained to me that her mother-in-law is always asking her, "When do you relax?!" with an accusatory tone. I can relate. I've had the experience where someone asks me what I do for work, and when I tell her about my various projects (which are all ones that I enjoy, mind you), she says, "I don't know how you do that *and* parent! You must have no time to yourself at all!" First of all, I have plenty of time to myself, given the nature of the projects. Second of all, her statement is usually said with no compassion. Instead, it feels judgmental. Suddenly I feel like I have to explain the different ways I relax, as if trying to pass a well-being exam. Marcia Reynolds gave me good advice: "When someone says 'How do you do it?' or 'You look exhausted!' say, 'I am so lucky to have a life where I'm doing what I love, that sometimes I forget to rest.'"

Also, how much R&R we need built into our weeks, as mentioned, is different for each of us. Says Zeff, "Your body knows and will tell you if you listen. Just think of a time when you knew you had just the amount of R&R time you needed to unwind, relax, breathe, nurture yourself, or play. What sensations do you notice in your body when you remember this time? Maybe you could breathe easier, felt a fullness in your belly or chest, noticed your shoulders feeling open or relaxed down, or noticed a smile on your face. When you feel these same or similar sensations, you'll know that you have gotten the R&R you need—or that will serve you best."

Then again, some women are just built differently, and often, the quality of their work offsets the potential burnout that might come from less fulfilling work. Instead, they just feel . . . busy. I was emailed by a forty-two-year-old art director from California with a six- and a four-year-old, who told me: "My close friend is always telling me that I work too hard and that I should slow down or I'll burn out. I know she says this because she cares about me and wants me to be healthy. But here's the thing: I am just kind of built with lots of energy and I'm always on the move. Yoga and massages bore me, even the idea of them. My way of relaxing is by sitting at work with other adults and exchanging art concepts. This is when I feel *calmest* and most joyous. For whatever reason, she can't understand this—or maybe she thinks I'm deluding myself."

If you, too, fit this category, well . . . good for you. You certainly don't have to justify to anyone else that you're doing okay and are wired differently. Just know that the people close to you are most likely not trying to attack you; they just want to make sure you're okay. Let them know calmly, "Thank you for caring so much about me. I'm pretty good at paying attention to my body." Then switch conversation topics. If they won't ease up ("But your schedule is too much . . ." "I'm so worried you're going to crash . . .")—and you know full well that your schedule works for you—explain gently, "Again, thank you for caring about me. What I'd like you to understand is that we are built differently and our bodies have different needs. I respect that you know your limits, and I hope you will respect that I know mine." End of story.

Step 8: *Delegate at home and delete the need for perfection.*

- -

One of the big balance busters for working moms is household tasks, which women still do in large majority. If you're a single mom, all the tasks fall on you. But even if you're married, most of them pretty much fall on you anyway. According to 2010 Bureau of Labor statistics, women with full-time jobs and kids under age six do close to two hours of housework a day, while men do one.[14] Hey, no fair! And according to Anna Kudak, coauthor of *What Happy Couples Do*, men don't see the work.[15] It's somewhat invisible to them because women are so used to doing it on their own.

Pam, a forty-four-year-old journalist from Illinois with a three-year-old daughter, admits that "it's very easy for me to be the one who makes sure everyone else has what they need to get their work done, but—despite having a wonderful partner—I am really the only one who will make sure I have the childcare support and other supports I need to get my work done. It often means spending time arranging playdates for my daughter at friends' homes or throwing money at the problem, which creates its own difficulties, but sometimes that's the only solution."

Another working-mom friend told me she does the laundry because her husband throws the clean clothes in drawers without folding them. She does the shopping because her husband won't follow her list and "his idea of a healthy dinner is peanut butter and banana sandwiches," and she is the designated dishwasher because . . . well, you can guess and you get the idea. My friend is not so different from a lot of women who buy in to the theory that if you want something done right, you do it yourself.

This is swell if the goal is to have things look exactly the way you want them to. But if the goal is to clear your daily to-do list so you can breathe, and maybe, possibly, even sneak in a yoga class or time on the couch to read your book, something has to give. That something is your expectations. Who *cares* if your clothes aren't folded perfectly? Or if you eat peanut butter and banana sandwiches once in a while? Or there are more Cheetos in the house than *you'd* ever buy? If you're hitched, thank your hubby so he'll keep doing his part, rather than scold him for handling the tasks poorly.

If you're single, make a list of what you can delegate. Order your groceries from a company like Pea Pod, one of America's leading Internet grocers, where you can send your grocery list and they deliver it to your door for a fee ranging from $6.95 to $9.95, depending on your grand total. Is there enough money in the bank account to hire a housekeeper, even if it's once or twice a month? Can you send out your laundry to a service that will wash, dry, and fold it (you just pick it up)? My friend sent out his dirty laundry to a laundromat service in college, and I thought he must have been a trust funder. I later found out it was pretty cheap—cheap enough to make me wonder why I hadn't thought of that. Make a list of the errands/tasks you hate the most and see which ones you can get rid of tomorrow, in a week, or in a few months.

> **Try This:**
>
> When you delegate at work, suggests Caitlin Friedman and Kimberly Yorio in their book The Girls' Guide to Being a Boss, you have to understand that it "doesn't just mean telling your team what to do. You have to make sure they understand the project and how best to achieve the goal."[6]
>
> Applying that advice, here's my suggestion for deciding when it's time for your child to start doing his own laundry. Don't just say, "Figure it out." Let him watch you do the entire process, start to finish, one time, and even suggest he take notes if he might have trouble remembering the proper washing machine and dryer settings to use. If you take the time to make sure he truly understands the process that first time, he won't come to you with questions every time he does the laundry.

Step 9: *Keep quiet time alive.*

- -

It's not always possible to get away from the house for a restorative weekend away. In fact, it's rarely possible. As one mom emailed me, "Sure, I'd love to do a weekend away, but it's not going to happen. I am not going to spend all this time at work away from my kids and then leave for a weekend to 'restore' myself." Another told me, "Sure, I can get away with girlfriends once a year, but that's hardly enough to sustain me for the *rest* of the months in the year."

It's one thing to build in twenty minutes here and there at work to help ground yourself, but that's not enough to keep you consistently sane in the membrane. For that, we need *daily* quiet time, even on weekends. I build in an hour of quiet time for my seven-year-old daughter on Saturday and Sunday (obviously, you can pick the amount of time that works for your family if you go this route). It used to be the time when my daughter napped, which of course she outgrew before she was two and therefore hated. In fact, the director at her daycare at the time jokingly voted Risa "Least Likely to Nap." So we transformed nap time into "You need to do something by yourself time," which I will continue to do until she moves into her own home someday. Right now she's seven, and she might play with her dolls, color, use her sticker books . . . it's up to her. As long as there are no sharp objects or matches involved, we're cool. While she'd much rather be playing with her friends or the cats or anything with a beating heart, I think it's good for her to know how to entertain herself. And I *know* it's good for me. I don't use this time to vacuum, pay bills, or do anything useful. Quite often, I grab a catnap—sans the cats.

When nap time phases out, many moms have shared that they pine for that blessed gift of literal quiet time during the day when they get to take a load off and enjoy some peace. If it sounds appealing to you, why not reinstate it? You may get some resistance at first, but it will soon become a habit. The trick is to explain it to your child simply: "We're going to take an hour of quiet time now and during that time, you can [fill in blank] . . ." Make sure he understands that it's a way for everyone to replenish, not a time-out or punishment, because some kids will automatically wonder what they've done wrong to deserve this. But keep your explanation simple and to the point. My daughter, for example, would ask, "Why do we *have* to do this?" and I had to tell myself over and over that this was a stall tactic and not a legitimate question. There's no reasoning with resistance. Simply state that it's a house rule, for everyone's benefit, and you'll look forward to reconnecting in an hour. Remind yourself that having quiet time is going to make for a more relaxed mama, and that's good for everyone. I like what Anna, a thirty-seven-year-old business technology vice president and mom of two kids under five, advises: "Put on your own oxygen mask first. That has helped me a lot to be a better and more enjoyable mom when I am with the kids."

I've even heard there are kids who create their own quiet time, who love to go spend time by themselves with only their imagination for company. I haven't seen this rare trait myself, but several moms tell me it's true, so I believe it. For you moms, I have no advice except to be grateful . . . and enjoy.

Proceed with Caution If . . .

the reason you can't relax is that you're sleep-deprived and grouchy. You're not alone. According to the latest poll from the National Sleep Foundation, 20 percent of Americans sleep less than six hours a night, and only 28 percent of people report getting eight hours or more of shut-eye a night, in spite of the fact that most adults need seven to nine hours.[17] Make getting to bed early a top priority and have a lights-out policy that will let you get the full amount of sleep you need.

On the Flip Side . . .

maybe you feel you don't need more time for R&R and detect no warning signs telling you differently . . . but plenty of loved ones in your life are advising you to reconsider. When you tell them you're looking out for yourself, they look skeptical and worried—collectively. Before you dismiss them altogether, ask some questions. Maybe they are seeing warning signs you're not, and if the concern is coming from a reliable and trustworthy source, pay attention. Ask, "What do you see that I'm not seeing?" or "I feel like my schedule is working for me, but maybe you could explain what worries you so I could check in with myself?" After you get an answer ("You look physically exhausted . . ." "You seem very distracted when we're talking . . ."), stay open to that possibility. Agree to sit with the idea and see if there is any truth behind it. Sometimes, we are so locked into our habits and routines that we aren't able to see or feel issues that our close friends can detect.

SHOUT-OUT TO . . .

Nina, a Washington, D.C.–based filmmaker and mom of three twentysomethings. "One of the things I realized about going out with friends," says Nina, "is that if and when you do go out to be with your women's group on the weekend, don't waste your time feeling guilty about it if your child gets upset. Yes, that's time that you won't be with your child, but you don't need to apologize for it or overexplain why it's important to keep up your friendships. Your child doesn't care why; he or she just may not want you to leave. So accept that, understand that you'll spend time with your child before and after your outing, and then go enjoy the experience. I would say to my kids, 'I'm going to my women's group and I'll be back at noon.' Then I'd go have a good time—and look forward to spending time with my children afterward."

Chapter Wrap

- - - - - - - - - - - - -

Step 1: *Tune in to your body, especially when pain is involved.*

Pay attention early to any body aches and pains resulting from stress so the symptoms won't get worse.

Step 2: *Create serenity the moment you open your eyes.*

Start each morning with deep breaths and an intention to move into the day feeling grounded.

Step 3: *Block out twenty minutes a day as mental recovery time.*

Block off time in your calendar each day to relax so you can feel your best while boosting your productivity.

Step 4: *Peer into the future to decide what's worth stressing over.*

Minimize problems by asking if they are something you'll even remember in a year or so.

Step 5: *Stay in the present, squeeze a stone.*

Make a conscious decision to tune in to what you're experiencing only at the present moment.

Step 6: *Shut down your gallery of gadgets.*

Unplug from all your technology for a span of time each day to create serenity around you.

Step 7: *Don't let others peer-pressure you into their ideal of "relaxing."*

Check in with your body and mind to determine whether your energy level is too low or just fine.

Step 8: *Delegate at home and delete the need for perfection.*

When you're feeling overwhelmed with obligations, figure out which tasks you can hand off to someone else.

Step 9: *Keep quiet time alive.*

When nap time phases out, continue to build in regular time for your child to do something alone and low-key so you can both replenish.

Chapter 9

BLURRED BOUNDARIES AT HOME

Confession: "If I created clearer boundaries while working from home, my family and career would fare better."

There is a pervasive myth that work-from-home moms have some hidden advantage that allows them to address their family's needs on a par with any nonworking mom while also managing a home-based business or freelance career. In this fantasy, these double-duty moms somehow get their work done in time to pick up their kids when the school bell rings and juggle client phone calls while whipping up delicious dinners. They spend mornings at the gym before settling into their well-appointed home office, taking a few minutes here and there throughout their half-day's work time to empty the dishwasher, load the dryer, pay bills, consult with the plumber who comes to fix the broken garbage disposal, and clean up the cat vomit. Again. They are also calm and relaxed, not to mention efficient. And they are totally present to everyone's needs, including their own.

It's not called a myth for nothing.

If you're a mother who works from home, you're probably laughing right now—or crying—because you know just how ridiculous this fantasy is. Sure, there are good days—even productive ones—but for the most part, you probably feel like it's a big mad juggle, and balls drop regularly. You're always scrambling to get things done, and your focus is forever pulled in competing directions. While filling out your child's permission slip during a work call, you get distracted and forget why you're calling. Or you can't focus on finishing your child's Halloween costume because you are worried about getting client materials shipped off before FedEx closes. And you're often stuck having to address immediate issues (like a clogged sink or finding a vet who will examine the hamster) at the expense of work time. If you were at an office, these non-emergencies would be non-issues. But at home, there's no obvious divide between family and work, yet the expectation exists that we can keep them separate but equal. Problem is, just by way of working out of your house, your home life has, well, home-court advantage. It's not surprising if you sometimes crave the security of office walls.

Then there's the fact that no one in your family seems to appreciate that you're actually *working* and earning *money* when you say you are. Hey, you're not wearing office attire, and, well . . . you're HOME. How could you possibly be *working?* As you try to crank out two last work emails, your kids barge through your office door (if you have a door) yelling about whose turn it is to pick a television show, asking you to mediate the latest aggravation, or begging for a playdate. You tell your kid(s) to please shut the door NOW because you need to get these dang emails out. *Now what the heck were you emailing about?* Or perhaps you hear the baby crying because she just woke up but you just need to type . . . this . . . last . . . sentence. *Hold on, Mommy is coming, sweetheart!*

We work-from-home moms want to be there for our kids—and we want them to feel like we're available. But if it's always *family time,* how are we supposed to get work done (because, yes, we really are working!). Not to mention it's hard to foster a feeling of family time when we've got the business phone ringing constantly, demanding our attention. Who can focus? What we all need—for our own sanity, as well as for those around us—are clearly stated boundaries. Having had the last seven years to figure this out, I finally know what does and doesn't work.

QUIZ: DOES YOUR FAMILY RESPECT YOUR HOME/WORK BOUNDARIES?

1. There is a good chance that when a contract comes through your fax machine:

   a. your child will grab it and transform it into a hat.

   b. you will pick it up, wander around the house, and leave it somewhere random.

   c. it gets signed and faxed back as quickly as possible.

2. During your work time, your child wants to show you a magic trick she just made up involving napkins. You:

   a. say you are happy to watch it in twenty minutes, when you are finished with work.

   b. tell her, "Go for it!" Hey, you want to encourage your daughter's creativity!

   c. not only watch her trick right then, you also show her several good ones that you learned as a kid.

3. In the midst of family dinner, a client calls. You know it's not an emergency so you:

   a. grab the phone and run into another room so your family can eat in peace.

   b. bring the phone over to the dinner table while you're talking; hey, they don't call it multitasking for nothing.

   c. let it ring through to voicemail; you'll call back after dinner.

Answers: If you answered "c" for number 1, give yourself one point. If you answered "a" for number two, give yourself one point. If you answered "c" for number 3, give yourself one point. If your sum total is two or more, you demonstrate some strong abilities to set limits when it comes to working at home, and this chapter will help you even further. If your total is less, check out the steps below so you can stop freaking out at your child, client, or supervisor on a regular basis.

Reality Check
- - - - - - - - - - - - - - -

According to the U.S. Department of Labor Women's Bureau, about 600,000 mothers of children under six reported some job-related home-based work.[1] Of this multitude, I'd like to know how many of these women have successfully set up true boundaries between work and family time—and then stick to those boundaries. Because I'll be the first to tell you: It ain't easy.

Recently, Dr. Jeanne Moore and Tracey Crosbie of the University of Teesside contacted over one hundred "homeworkers," mostly in the north of England and Wales, for the Economic and Social Research Council to find out how they felt about working from home. One thing they discovered—which is no surprise to those of us with an office in our house—is that working from home is a double-edged sword, particularly the *flexibility* it brings. Most of those who were interviewed for the study thought of flexibility as a *benefit*, but "also admitted it resulted in their working in the evenings and weekends, and that one of the big challenges facing professional homeworkers is "a tendency to overwork."[2]

Sure, we do not have to rush to an office by 9:00 AM in a power suit and heels, but nor do we experience the elation of saying sayonara to office workers to mark the end of a workday.

So it's up to each of us to carve out a reasonable schedule for ourselves and make sure we articulate the game plan to the family. We also need to set up visible boundaries. Jane Applegate, nationally known small-business author and advice columnist, claims: "You really need some sort of boundary so that on one side you can say, 'This is my business,' and on the other, 'This is my life.'"[3] But nobody teaches us how to go about doing this, so it's no wonder we flail around and make ourselves sick with stress. The good news is that we moms have plenty of experience when it comes to setting limits. We've established no cookies in the bedroom (unless we're the ones eating them), no tossing Frisbees in the house, and no permanent magic markers on the couch. Now it's time to set ground rules around Mommy's work time and play time.

Step 1: *Get a room!*

In 1929, author Virginia Woolf declared: "A woman must have money and a room of her own if she is to write fiction."[4] I'm declaring that in order to make money while working from home, a mom must also have a room of her own—and that room must have a door that closes all the way shut. It doesn't have to be an actual office if that's not in the financial cards, but it needs to be a space with a barrier to entry. If you're new to this and thinking, *Yeah, but my child will stay upstairs while I work, which we talked about,* I respond, "HA!" The very need to be left alone inherently means you have no chance of being left alone; it doesn't matter who agreed to what. If you're visible and working, you will be found and interrupted.

But I have a nicer view in the living room, you may be thinking, or *I feel more inspired creatively in the kitchen.* That's fine as long as you're working in this public space while everyone else is out of the house. One mom shared via email, "I prefer working in the kitchen because I've got the coffeepot going and it just feels like my space. But I know I can only work there while my kids are at school. As soon as they're home, my sweet little office turns, *poof!* back into kitchen, and I go back to my closet-size office. So I just have to be hyper-efficient and organized with my time so I can maximize using this space."

Another working-mom friend told me she works in the dining room because she needs to spread out all her work stuff. When I asked her what happens when her kids get home, she told me they know that she is not to be disturbed for the next hour. "Wow," I replied, "and that actually *works*?" She smiled sheepishly and said, "Well no, it's more of a theoretical idea."

And so I say again . . . find a room with a door! An added financial incentive: A portion of your total household expenses is deductible as a business expense if you have an office in the home.

If you're the type who sits down to start working and feels instantly compelled to put away the dishes, fold the laundry, or even scrub tiles in the bathroom with a toothbrush, your designated room may be *out* of the house. Rather than cursing yourself for not being able to focus, get your laptop or whatever you need to get your work done and get *out*. If you decide on a space like the public library, bring a drink and snack so you have no excuse to come home early (oldest trick in the book). If you like more "atmosphere" when you're working, your nearest coffeehouse will serve you fine.

Step 2: *Explain to your family what you're doing behind closed doors.*

It can be hard for young ones—and adult relatives and friends, it seems—to understand what it means that you *work* from home. All they know is that you hole up in a small space with coffee and get all crazy when they come in uninvited. What do they *think* you're doing? Mostly, they think you're ignoring them. "What do you *do* in there?" my daughter still asks me. I swear she thinks I'm playing Angry Birds or updating my Facebook status half the time.

Because they don't understand you're working, children see no problem with interrupting you and peppering you with questions like "Can I have a snack," or "Can I have a playdate this weekend?" or "Have you seen the glue?" or "Do you wanna play Candyland?" Mouth agape, you exclaim, "Do you not see that I'm *working?!*" No, they really don't. You have to explain.

I realized this when I told my daughter for the umpteenth time, "I'm working here," and she responded, "What are you really doing?" It finally dawned on me that she had no idea that I'm an editor for an online magazine. She would see me typing away on my computer with no understanding that I was creating a publication, especially since there was no physical magazine to show her or let her hold in her hands. So I had her pull up a chair next to me, showed her the online magazine, and took the time to explain exactly what I do. It was helpful for her to understand what my work entails, why I do it, and, oh yeah, that I get *paid* for it—which allows me to buy her clothes, books, and cups of hot chocolate. It doesn't stop her from bursting into my office to ask whether I want to see a funny scene on Nickelodeon's iCarly, but when I say I can't because I'm finishing work on my magazine, it *means* something now.

Once children reach age five or so, you can sit them down and ask, "Would you like to know what I work on when I'm in my office?" They'll probably say yes (if they say no, don't take it personally; try again at a later date). Explain your job in a few clear sentences, and then expand your answers as they ask you questions. In addition to explaining that you get paid to do your work, let your child know that you *enjoy* work. It's a valuable message to impart: that working can be personally fulfilling and satisfy our desire to contribute to the world.

"I used to tell my daughter that I work to pay for things like her ballet lessons and groceries and helping to pay for the house," says Jenna, mother of a twelve-year-old. "I think I didn't want her to realize that I do the work, in large part because it's something that's *mine*; I thought she'd be jealous of the work. But then I realized that it's a good thing for her to know that I seek out work that is interesting, because it adds to my life. I want her to know that I choose to do this work and that it doesn't take anything away from how much I love spending time with her."

Step 3: *Make yourself accessible by designating family time.*

Sometimes, it's hard to remember that when your children (or husband or partner) interrupt you, it's often because they simply want your attention. They're not actually trying to drive you mad. It could be that your child needs help reaching the milk in the refrigerator, or that he just wants to spend time with you. The reality is, says Alexis Rodrigo, author of *The Savvy Freelancer's Website Secrets*, "Your young child will be more demanding and clingy if you're always busy and distracted." Furthermore, "if your child's basic need for attention is met, the more likely he'll be happy to play by himself."[5] So, set aside a span of time when you will be fully accessible to your kids. It's family time, and nothing competes for your attention.

During this stretch of time, resist any and all work temptations: Unplug the phones, the fax; heck, yank out the cords for your computer, if need be. Shut off any alluring gadgets that may try to seduce you with flashing, pulsing, pinging, or vibrating. During this time, do not check your iPhone while scratching your child's back, think through a work issue while your son recounts a story, or surf the net for new funding opportunities in between helping your children with their math homework. You are Mom, present and accounted for.

Deborah, a thirty-two-year-old marketing manager from Iowa and mom to a one-year-old, can speak to the temptation to sneak in work. Her advice? "Turn off your cell phone and shut down your computer. This is now a time I look forward to every day. I'll often work some more after my son goes to bed, but for that window of time before then, my husband and my son know they have my undivided attention."

When you share this new schedule with your child, establish the parameters—as much for you as for them. You can say something like "It's important to me that we get to spend time together every day, just me and you. Plus, sometimes I know you need my help with homework or other things. So from 5:30 PM to 7:45 PM every day, it's just time for family. Obviously if there's an emergency at *any* time, you should get me, but I'm purposefully setting aside this time for us." Now little Emily knows that she doesn't need to run through your office in an all-out ribbon parade to grab Mama's attention, nor does Jason need to launch a space rocket through your office window while you're trying to finish your progress report. Everyone wins, as long as you stay consistent.

Take it from Lynn, a forty-eight-year-old college professor in California and mother of seven-year-old twins: "My schedule is very flexible, including several weeks of part-time work or no work in the summer. While this seems like it would be a dream come true, it sometimes fills my children with confusion. I'm home, and then I'm gone again. I can do the morning routine, and then sometimes—like during the school year—I can't."

Once you develop a system that works for you and your family, it's best to stick with it.

Step 4: *Call for backup when you need it.*

- -

If your child is home by midafternoon, or too young to go to school at all, you may be thinking, *The only way I can get any work done is if my child takes a lonnng nap.* You wouldn't be the first mom to wonder, *Is it horrible if I let the TV babysit my child for an hour or two if it's something wholesome, like* Sesame Street *or* the Electric Company? (I don't know how I would have met some of my deadlines years ago if the Teletubbies weren't on the boob tube!)

The problem is, these are temporary solutions. Eventually, your child is going to get glassy-eyed from too much TV or refuse to go down for a nap on the day you have a deadline (your scent of desperation keeps him awake). Do you find that you consistently struggle to meet deadlines because you simply don't have enough free time? If so, seek help when you see crunch time coming, or consider having a sitter or nanny come in on a regular basis. Says Leslie Truex, author of *The Work-at-Home Success Bible,* "Many moms choose working at home to be with the kids, but it's not possible to earn any significant, regular income during nap times. So I'm a big advocate of finding someone else to occupy the kids." Other reasons to track down a sitter: You are turning away work because you don't have enough time, you're not getting enough time with your family, or you're falling asleep on your keyboard.

Debora, a thirty-five-year-old event planner from Massachusetts and mom to twin five-year-olds, says, "One thing that I constantly struggle with is when I am trying to read and respond to emails and my children are trying to talk to me and get my attention. You just have to be honest with yourself about the number of hours you have in the day. If you can afford it, hire a sitter to come into your home when you are trying to work from home."

It may feel weird hiring a caregiver when you're right there at home. As one mom put it, "You feel you're supposed to be able to manage everything without outsourcing parenting." But if that's how you're going to get work done and have focused time with your child, then so be it. It may not be what you pictured when you imagined working from home, but it's better than freaking out on your child who doesn't want to nap or watch reruns of *Arthur* and *Dora the Explorer* . . . again.

If you have limited financial resources, consider hiring a "mother's helper" (no, not Valium)—a young person to come into your home for a few hours while you're there. Basically, this person is not old enough to babysit alone but can come play with your child for a couple of hours while you're in the house. This will run you somewhere between $5 and $10 an hour, depending on the helper's age. Your child will likely adore having an older kid to play with, and you're going to get time to complete your tasks. Cull your neighborhood or condo complex for a likely suspect. Not only will you know this person (and her parents, even if just in a cursory way), but you also avoid the big time-suck of having to drive her to and from your house.

Another option, which is becoming increasingly popular as more moms work from home, is to swap childcare with fellow moms. If your kids are school age, you'll have a wealth of connections from your child's class alone. Several moms shared how they swap regular weekly "playdates" after school, with a 5:00 PM pickup time, thereby giving each other an actual eight-hour day! The added bonus? Your child gets more bonding time with her buddy in a safe, nurturing, and informal environment.

"I share childcare with two other moms who work at home. All our boys are friends, so it's a natural," says Erin, a forty-four-year-old freelance magazine writer and mom of two boys under twelve. "And since we have designated days, we can schedule client calls or work-related errands and meetings outside the home. As a freelance jour-nalist, this is a huge help when I need to schedule interviews in the field. Neither my sources nor my children would appreciate them being dragged along."

If swapping childcare isn't an option, consider enrolling your child in some type of daycare or after-school activity. Jennifer, a thirty-two-year-old graphic designer from Georgia and mom to three children under five, says, "When I left my full-time job to freelance, I thought I could do it all. What I didn't realize is that my kids need stability. Too often, the flexible schedule worked for me but caused unnecessary stress for them. After a year of juggling different babysitters, family members, and dragging my kids to meetings, I put them in preschool and worked my schedule around them. Everyone was happier. The mornings were mine to work, afternoons were about them, and then I pulled the night shift once they were in bed. It's tough, and I'm tired, but it works."

Step 5: *Don't try to fake it with contacts.*

It may be hard to imagine telling your new boss or client, "I can't talk to you at 4:00 PM because I will probably be making sock pup-pets with my daughter," or "I'd love to set up goals with you, but five o'clock won't work because that's when I chauffeur my son to band rehearsal." It doesn't exactly sound *professional*. However, you don't have to spell out the details. Simply tell your boss or cli-ent that you have a scheduling conflict. It's really that easy.

But what if you deal with clients or businesses in different time zones? Scheduling calls or Skype conferences gets even trickier. For example, when I was working on my first documentary, my producer, Kerry, worked on the West Coast, while I was on the East Coast. We became friends quickly, but it definitely felt strange at first that we couldn't talk during her afternoon hours (my dinnertime on the East Coast, followed by my daughter's bath and bedtime rituals). During her early evenings, I was sound asleep. So, *uh,* when were we going to talk? At first, I picked up her phone calls during dinner, shooting my husband an "I'm so sorry!" look and signaling with my hand I'd be off in five minutes—which, of course, I never was (who completes a business call in five minutes?). Eventually he called me out, saying these phone meetings were disrupting family time—and he was right. So Kerry and I agreed that for any action items with deadlines, we'd use email. If we needed to talk out how to execute said action items, we'd chat while she was sitting in traffic on the way to work. If we needed more phone time, we'd trade off who got called during an inconvenient time (I'd have to stay up past my bedtime; she'd have to wake up early). It wasn't a perfect system, but we made it work.

Granted, I was lucky to be working with someone flexible. It may be that you have a rigid client who refuses to meet you halfway, or one who has about as much flexibility as you. *Can* you make it work? What is the cost of making it work to you and to your family? Or maybe you have a boss who requires you to call in to staff meetings at the exact time you're trying to get your youngest dressed for late-start kindergarten? The anticipation of these meetings alone makes you break out in hives. The first step is to figure out whether there is leeway with your client or boss. Present one or two alternatives: Can you communicate mainly through email, particularly if you know agenda items that relate to you beforehand (e.g., status of a project)? Can you attend every other meeting in person? Can you schedule a late-afternoon catch-up call rather than a morning one? Or, simply be straightforward about your scheduling conflict. Perhaps the staff meeting time can be moved up or back an hour. You don't know until you ask, and it will always go better if you provide a few options rather than announcing you will be incommunicado.

Step 6: *Get real about taking calls when you're with your children.*

- -

There will be times when you are hanging out with your kids and the phone will ring. It's an important contact and you know she is calling to give you a vital piece of information that should only take a few minutes. Do you pick it up? What if this key person hears your child screaming at you, "Mommy, I need to go poo-poo!" or something equally cringe-worthy? Bad scene. But surely you can sneak in a super-quick phone exchange, if you stay on point?

Maybe . . . it depends on your child's age. Tammy Harrison, mother of four and independent creative representative for hbwm .com (Home Based Working Moms), advises, "Realize the attention span of your children. Little ones are good for about *three minutes*, so be aware that you need to have a short, direct, and efficient conversation."[6]

Taking the call while immersed in mommy-and-me time also depends on the nature of your relationship with the caller. Colleen, a thirty-year-old freelance writer and mom to a nine-month-old boy, says, "The hardest part for me is scheduling phone interviews for stories—especially if Henry is supposed to be napping at the time but isn't. If the interview is with someone like a high-powered doctor, I now make sure my husband is home, so I can focus on the call. Or sometimes I reschedule the interview."

If you have a fairly casual relationship with the caller, let her know you are on parent duty and have one or two minutes before chaos will likely hit. Can you get all the information in that short amount of time, or should you call back? That way, if your child yells, "I swallowed a nickel!" this person will have been warned. My rule of thumb: If during this phone call you would be humiliated to have the caller hear your child blurting out something about boogers or farting, let voicemail pick up. It's easier to return the call later than it is to recover from the stress and mortification.

When the exchange goes well—your children are relatively quiet while you get the necessary info—reward them with praise. Say something like "I so appreciate you waiting to talk to me so I could hear the person on the phone. Thank you." Also, shower your children with appreciation when they let you get your work done without interruption, especially when you're just starting to work with the boundaries you've set up. You might even say, "Because you gave me the time and space to get my work done, I finished it early. What should we all do together?" Now your kids know that giving you space to work equates to more time with them.

Step 7: *Know when to call in experts.*

- -

As any wise person will tell you, sometimes you have to know when to surrender. Your time working at home is valuable. If something is eating into that time that's not essential, it has to go. If you're not techno-handy, don't spend more than an hour trying to fix your printer. If you're design-challenged, don't devote endless weeks to designing a blog that will end up looking crappy. Know your weaknesses and throw money at them. As expert Gerry Hartigan, entrepreneur and author of nine business books, says: "Unfortunately, about 80 percent of all new businesses fail in the first five years of operation. One of the main reasons that this happens is because business owners are not aware of their strengths and weaknesses."[7]

Once you know what your weaknesses are, call in a pro. Author Alexis Rodrigo puts it this way: "Sometimes it just makes better business sense to hire somebody to do some of your tasks. If there's a work task that needs to be done and you don't have the skill, why insist on doing it?" She suggests outsourcing anything essential to your business that isn't your core competency. "Even though it means paying extra, it will be worth it in the long run in terms of time saved and higher-quality work."[8]

This concept tends to be hard to give in to, especially if we're on a tight budget. We say, "Oh, it's too expensive to bring my computer in for a repair. I'll just tinker with it for a few days and see if I can get it to cooperate." But we *should* invest in things that make our businesses and lives run more smoothly. I like how Mikelann Valterra, founder of the Women's Earning Institute, states it: "[Self-employed women] must actively tell people how much they are 'worth' on a daily basis." She goes on to say, "They must believe in their gut that they are worth making good money."[9] The same is true for *spending* money to make your business go well. Need a confidence boost? Tory Johnson and Robyn Freedman Spizman, authors of *Will Work from Home,* suggest keeping handy a list of your past work successes and accomplishments, which will "remind you of your own worth as a worker and add to your confidence" when you need it.[10] Believing in the value of your time and investing wisely in yourself are the only way to get your business off the ground.

> **Try This:**
>
> *If forking over cash is not a possibility (i.e., the wallet is bare), barter with working friends and community members. If you're a strong writer, offer to create press releases for a friend who can fix your computer when it crashes. Babysit for a friend on a Saturday night in exchange for having her design your business cards. Ask a pal to proofread your important business letters in exchange for double-checking her Excel spreadsheets. Post on craigslist.com or ask parents at the schoolyard who is particularly skilled at the area you need help with. Does your child's school send a weekly email with classified listings? It's a perfect place.*

Step 8: *Create your own pep squad.*

Even as you become increasingly successful at setting boundaries while working from home, you may still have mixed feelings about it. You might feel bad about closing your door during your designated work hours, knowing your child is counting the minutes until you reappear. Perhaps you're feeling anxious about telling your favorite client that you can't talk during family time, worrying he will lose tolerance and ditch you.

No one knows the hardships about blurred boundaries and faulty assumptions better than other moms in the same working-mom boat. Kate Lister and Tom Harnish, authors of *Undress for Success*, state that the "stigma home-based employees and business owners face is that folks think they have it easy," adding that coworkers, neighbors, and even families picture them "sitting around eating bon-bons while they giggle at reruns of *The Office*."[11] Too true! Plus, these people expect you can help them with last-minute needs the second they call, figuring you can just make up the work any old time. *When?* Other moms who work from home know all about these aggravations and can be supremely helpful in boosting your spirits.

If you know two or three other women who work from home, you have a potential support group right there. Consider asking them if they'd like to be a part of it. Tell them you can decide together how you can be most helpful—and that it can be through email if you don't want phone calls disrupting your work. Emotionally, maybe you can act as a support system when one of you is trying to figure out a boundary or explain to the new teacher that you aren't home watching soap operas or that you are going to scream if your child saunters into your office one more time to let you know it's not raining and she wants to go to the park *now.* Consider creating a shared Google document that pools together your lists of repair people, reliable services, and babysitter recommendations. Why not consider working together once a week if you tend to feel isolated? Desiree M. Frieson, president and CEO of Mahogany Communications, a marketing firm in Brooklyn, New York, even suggests inviting someone into your home and working in the same space. "Sometimes when it is too quiet, you end up doing other things; having a peer or group of colleagues around you can help you focus," she says.[12]

Step 9: *Play hooky because you can.*

- -

Yes, we moms who work from home do indeed get to wear sweatpants and T-shirts (I opt to ignore experts telling me that I should dress in corporate gear each morning to sit and write at my desk. The best part of working from home is wearing my soft bathrobe until noon). But the flip side, as discussed, is that it's often hard to call a day "a day." There is a lot to be said for *not* having access to

your files once you leave an office. Working moms are always trying to pack in work around home life so we can spend time with
our families, trading hours in the day to address household needs,
figuring we can catch up at night. Sometimes, there's simply too
much work to juggle to begin with, and we're either left impinging
on family time to get it done or filling every spare hour—morning
and night—to address it.

As Lorie, a forty-four-year-old film producer and mother of a three-
year-old, says, "It's hard for me to feel relaxed. My brain is always
full, and I'm stressed about what's not getting done. When she's at
daycare, I think, 'Oh my God, what am I going to do? I don't have
much time!' I feel like every moment I'm not with her, I'm working!"

It's a relentless cycle of obligation and no downtime, which can
make for a cranky, unhappy, uninspired mom and entrepreneur. Consider playing hooky to regroup and decompress. Every two weeks,
escape your house for a few hours and *play*. Because you can. I'm not
talking about running around doing errands, like going to the bank,
grocery store, or dry cleaners. That is not *play*. I'm talking about
treating yourself to lunch and a matinee or meandering through
your favorite boutique. Go for a bike ride around a pond, snowshoe
around the neighborhood with a thermos of hot chocolate. Nothing
beats stress like fresh air, says psychotherapist Christine Webber
and Dr. David Delvin. "Walking in a leafy environment seems to
soothe our minds" and "we tend to feel healthier and more energized
if we can sit or walk somewhere there are plenty of trees."[13] It beats
staring at an empty screen and flashing cursor, right?

A word on shutting down: Understand that there will always
be more work to be done, but it can wait until tomorrow. There's a
cost to burning the midnight oil beyond feeling tired and cranky; it
becomes harder to focus on the next step. Linda Wasmer Andrews,

author of *Stress Control for Peace of Mind*, states, "When you work from home, it's tempting to never really leave the office. There's always one more thing to be done, and it's calling your name from the next room. Ignore it. Learn to close the door and walk away at a reasonable hour!"[14]

> **Try This:**
>
> More tips for unwinding: When the kids go to sleep, leave time to soak in a hot bath, read, or catch up with friends before you turn in. Set an alarm in your office if you need a reminder to shut down. This may be the only alarm you will truly come to look forward to.

Proceed with Caution If . . .

you realize you're not getting enough work done at the end of *most* days. There are always going to be to-do items toward the bottom of your list that don't get done (there are only so many hours in the day). But if you are noticing that the *majority* of your goals aren't getting finished, it's time to make a dramatic change. As discussed earlier in the chapter, you can always grab your work materials and get to a library or coffeehouse. If there's still too much distraction, however, ask a friend if you can "house-sit" with your laptop while she's at work for the day. Hey, you're not going to be tempted to put away her dishes or get a jump-start on folding her laundry, right?

On the Flip Side . . .

you become so good at setting up boundaries between work time and family time that you forget you made the rules and can break them every *once in a while*. For instance, if you're toiling away during your "office hours" but know that your child is suffering from a harsh experience (a rumor was started about her; he got pushed down on the playground), suspend the rules and spend extra time doling out TLC to your child and screw the work hours. That is one of the upsides of working from your home! Your child will understand this is a special occasion and that it doesn't mean all bets are off with work boundaries; plus, it's important for your children to know that their well-being will always come first.

SHOUT-OUT TO . . .

Juliette Fay, bestselling author of Shelter Me *(a* Good Housekeeping– *featured book pick and Target book club pick) and* Deep Down True. *She has four elementary- to high-school-age children and says her schedule is "pretty much dependent on five other schedules." Mostly she writes while the kids are at school, but Juliette also checks herself into a hotel a few times a year for 24 hours. "I bring everything I need to eat so that I don't need to leave and I can just work," she says. "I pick only hotels that have a microwave, a refrigerator, and a window with a pretty view, and I just spend the time writing. During my last hotel stay, I wrote 6,000 words!" When I asked Juliette whether she ever feels guilty for taking this time away from the family, she says, "Well, I try to pick times that will have the least impact on everyone else. But, really, I feel great about it!"*

Chapter Wrap
- - - - - - - - - - - - -

Step 1: *Get a room!*

To truly separate work and family, you need your own space and a closed door.

Step 2: *Explain to your family what you're doing behind closed doors.*

Let your child know what work entails for you.

Step 3: *Make yourself accessible by designating family time.*

Build time into each day when it's all about family so your children can anticipate when you're completely accessible to them.

Step 4: *Call for backup when you need it.*

If you're swamped with work, call in backup to help with childcare.

Step 5: *Don't try to fake it with contacts.*

If your client or boss tries to contact you while you're with the family, be realistic about whether it will be more helpful to try to talk now or reach out later.

Step 6: *Get real about taking calls when you're with your children.*

Young kids can't wait patiently for more than a few minutes when you're on a work call.

Step 7: *Know when to call in experts.*

Honor that your time is valuable by paying for help when time-sucking obstacles show up.

Step 8: *Create your own pep squad.*

Only other work-from-home moms can truly understand your work-from-home challenges, so lean on each other.

Step 9: *Play hooky because you can.*

The biggest perk you can give yourself is time off to refresh and energize yourself.

Chapter 10

FRENEMIES AND FAMILY CRITICS

Confession: "I resent that some people think I'm a 'bad mom' for not staying home with my kids."

In the big picture, you don't really believe that staying at home would make you a better mother. Working is what's best for you and your family, and that's just the way it is. Still, there may be moments when you experience a teeny-tiny nagging doubt. It's usually when someone—a loved one or complete stranger—voices her belief that working moms unfairly rob their children of valuable time and love. *That is BS!* your mind rears. Yet this other pesky voice wonders, *Wait, is that true? Does my child feel robbed?* And now on top of this terrible internal response, you feel like a traitor to working moms everywhere for even allowing the question to surface.

Whether or not you experience moments of doubt, most of us have had to contend with the disappointment, sadness, even anger that comes from being judged about something so personal. Whether it's out of financial necessity, personal fulfillment, or both, we have all decided that working *and* being a mother makes sense for our lives. When someone close to us tries to make us second-guess this decision, we feel not only misunderstood but also slighted. We expect the people who care about us to boost our confidence and support us, to reassure us that taking care of our families financially and fulfilling ourselves emotionally will help our family, not tank it. So why do these people leave us feeling defensive and insulted, and what can we do about it? How do we get them to KNOCK IT OFF once and for all?

QUIZ: ARE YOU GOOD AT DEFLECTING CRITICISM?

1. In the middle of dinner, your mother-in-law leans over and whispers, "You look so tired. Do you think you'll ever consider going part-time?" You respond:
   a. "Yeah, but you look exhausted too and you stay home all the time."
   b. by excusing yourself, walking to the bathroom, and locking yourself in for the rest of the evening.
   c. by telling her that you have no plan to go part-time and then switching to a neutral topic.

2. Over coffee with a friend who is a stay-at-home mom, your pal asks, "Do you ever worry your child doesn't get enough time with you?" You reply:
   a. "Sometimes, but we seem to be working it out."
   b. "Do *you* ever worry your child has too MUCH time with you?"
   c. "Why? Do you think I *should* be worried?"

3. You overhear your mom telling another relative that she thinks you'll regret having a career while your kids are still so young. You:
   a. ignore it; there's no changing that woman's mind.
   b. butt in, yelling, "Are you out of your mind?!"
   c. tell her later that you overheard her and want her to quit talking about you behind your back, starting right now.

Answers: If you answered "c" for number 1, give yourself one point. If you answered "a" for number two, give yourself one point. If you answered "a" for number 3, give yourself one point. If your sum total is two or more, you are probably pretty skilled already at deflecting criticism, and the tips in this chapter will only help you get better. If your total is less than two, pay careful attention so you can stop spending energy agonizing over others' thoughtless comments.

Reality Check

- - - - - - - - - - - - - -

The sad truth is that pretty much *all* moms worry about whether they're doing a good enough job—whether they work or stay home. According to The Working Mother Research Institute's 2011 report "What Mothers Choose: The Working Mother's Report"—for which more than 3,700 moms were asked about their top worries—more than a third of all mothers say they frequently feel guilty about their contribution to the household. And while 51 percent of the working moms "feel guilty about not spending enough time with their kids," 55 percent of stay-at-home moms worry about "not making a financial contribution to the family finances."[1]

Looks like we're just about even-steven on the guilt front; we've all got it in spades.

But we're dealing with working-mom guilt here, so it may please you to know that the *children* of working moms aren't suffering for it. According to a 2010 study in the journal *Psychological Bulletin,* researchers reviewed fifty—*fifty!*—years of research on the impact that being a working mother has on her children. The findings: Kids whose moms went back to work before they were three have no worse academic or behavioral problems than kids with stay-at-home moms.[2]

Some researchers have even argued recently that kids with working moms fare *better* overall: A recent UK study in the *Journal of Epidemiology and Community Health* evaluated 12,000 young children at three different stages: infancy, age three, and age five; the study concluded that not only does a mother's job not *harm* children's social and emotional behavior, but boys and girls with two employed parents exhibited the least emotional and behavior problems.[3] Susan Newman, blogger for *Psychology Today*'s *Singletons* blog, reported on this study in "Go to Work Mom, the Kids Will

Be Fine," commenting: "The results were independent of a mother's education or household income. Working mothers, whether they work because they need to or because they want to, can relax and enjoy both their roles." She adds that what very well may be driving this outcome is that a working mother's income helps reduce the family's financial stress, which, "in turn, creates a happier, calmer atmosphere for growing children."[4]

So we can all just relax a bit here and put some of those lingering doubts to rest. It's time to stop stewing over rude comments and start setting boundaries that protect you from feeling attacked. This chapter will help you establish clear boundaries with misguided family or friends.

Step 1: *Know where you stand . . . and stay there.*
- -

You're going to be far less susceptible to feeling attacked if you are clear with yourself about your own viewpoint. You will feel less compelled to justify yourself by convincing others that working is the best way to go. Mark Tyrrell, therapist and founder of Uncommon Help (www.uncommonhelp.com), advises: "You build and convey genuine confidence when you can relax with other people who have their own perspectives and do not see things your way."[5]

Examine why working is good for you. Ask yourself: What is it about work that makes me feel more fulfilled? What does working bring to my family? What would I like to model for my child by working? If your answers make it clear that working is, overall, best for your family, *own* that. It will serve you well.

Eleanor, a thirty-two-year-old attorney with a four-year-old daughter, says, "The moms at my daughter's school are about ten years older than me, and a lot of them stopped working. One of them said to me recently, about my work schedule, 'I don't know how you do it!' But I don't take it as a slight because we're just at different life stages, and I know that I'm making choices in my life that are a good fit for me. I don't feel I have to explain myself."

On to handling the emotional strikes: If you're dealing with someone whom you *aren't* close to (a third cousin you barely see, the mail carrier, a stranger on the subway), know that you don't have to explain to this person why working moms are not awful people, or convince the insulter that it's good for moms to work. Just say, as calmly as possible, "My choice works for me and my family," and switch to a neutral topic. If the person persists, cut her off, reiterating, "Yes, I heard your belief and understand that is how you feel. I'm doing what I think is right for my family." Done.

If the person keeps trying to engage in battle, *disengage* with a line like "Well, I have to get going now, see you later." Now you're free! Do it for your own mental health. In an article on PositiveSharing .com, Alexander Kjerulf, author of three books, including *Happy Hour Is 9 to 5,* says that getting annoyed just makes the memory stronger. "Anything you experience while having a strong emotion will be etched permanently in your mind." The problem with this? "The memory becomes so strong that it keeps coming back to you and keeps annoying you for years," he says.[6]

So make the choice to stay calm and end the conversation. It's their problem if they consider it dismissive.

Step 2: *Let yourself off the hook.*

- -

Alanna, thirty-nine, is a freelance design assistant and mom of two kids under five. Alanna chose to demote herself from full-time designer after having her second child because "I got tired of getting home in time only to kiss my son goodnight." This was admittedly hard for her, going from making major design decisions to often running errands for a designer. Still, Alanna loves spending two full days a week at home with her kids, but adds that when her two-year-old goes to school, she may go back to full-time. One of her most difficult moments, she admits, was when a friend—a stay-at-home mom—stated over drinks one night: "I just don't know how some women can work until six o'clock at night while their kids are at home. I mean, if both parents are working full-time, why bother even having kids?" Alanna, who has spent more than one or two evenings working until six, says she was shocked to hear someone, especially a *friend*, say that out loud. She decided not to tell her friend how much her comment hurt her feelings, but admits that she still feels slighted by the judgment.

Sadly, some working moms say they experience a regular litany of accusatory questions and cutting remarks from friends and family: "Don't you worry that your kids will feel *unloved?*" "Do you ever think about the fact that you're missing time with your child that you won't ever get back?" "I would never leave my kids at daycare; I don't want some stranger raising them when that's my job," and "I wouldn't even consider going back to work until my kids are out of the house, because it's rougher out there than ever before." *Ouch. Ouch. Ouch.* With friends (and family members) like these, who needs enemies?

Adding insult to injury is our own reaction to the comments. Several moms said they believed they were the type of woman to call out the insult immediately, using diplomacy and reason. But in the moment, they were often so shocked to hear the unsettling comment that they said nothing. Perhaps you've been there? If so, maybe you've changed the topic or excused yourself to the bathroom to weep, or you pretend it didn't happen. It's when we get home, and the reality sinks in that our *friend* said this to us, that we fly into indignant defensive mode ("How dare she!"). We may even internalize it, chastising ourselves as cowards for not calling our accuser out on her insult. Why didn't we say anything *back?* Why didn't we at least speak up for ourselves?!

Cut yourself some slack. It's okay that we didn't handle the situation gracefully (it took me awhile to get to this one, but it's liberating). It is shocking when those we consider our close support system hurt us. You are far from alone if you were too tongue-tied or upset to say anything. In fact, in a 2011 survey conducted by TODAY.com and *SELF* magazine, in which 18,000 women were surveyed (and 4,000 men), 37 percent said they "hid" toxic friends on Facebook when they were upset.[7] Certainly there are more direct ways to deal with a friend who says something cruel, intentionally or otherwise (which we'll cover later in this chapter), but it's common to want to avoid a big confrontation.

Also, allow yourself to feel hurt. Just because we don't fully believe what the person told us doesn't mean that it doesn't sting. However you feel at the moment—disappointed, pissed off, shocked—feel it fully so you can move through it and let go. It doesn't mean you "bought into" the idea that you're not a good enough mom because you work; it just means you feel bad about being judged. I like what life coach and entrepreneur Emilie Wapnick says about giving yourself permission to be hurt: "I don't care how invalid, well-meaning, nonconstructive, incorrect, or misconstrued the criticism is, or whether it's cloaked in positive reinforcement or delivered in the friendliest possible manner; criticism still stings. And being hurt by criticism is nothing to be ashamed of—it's normal."[8]

Step 3: *Keep it simple with "the regulars."*

- -

It's enough to have to deal with the occasional dig by a family member or friend, but then there are the "regulars," folks we have to engage with on a regular basis whom we can't either walk away from or be straight with. I'm talking about your child's pediatrician or teacher or a coworker. You don't feel close enough to have a heart-to-heart with these people, but you find it hard to stomach their accusatory and harsh words about working moms and worry that it's going to keep occurring if you don't put an end to it. And experts will tell you, ignoring the comment often ends up biting us in the butt anyway because it affects the dynamics of our relationship into the future. Will we trust our child's pediatrician on other matters if we harbor resentment or feel he's misjudging us? Can we maintain respect for colleagues who pitch underhanded comments at us now and again, if we don't call them out on it? Says Dr. Jonathan Kandell, psychologist and assistant director at the University of Maryland Counseling Center: "While one conflict may be avoided, future interactions will be tainted by the lack of direct expression of thoughts and feelings."[9] The other person will inevitably notice something wrong but won't know the real reason. So you might as well get the real issue off your chest, right? But what do you say?

When it comes to saying your piece, take a deep breath (or several) to calm yourself. Then tell the person who just lobbed the mean or sarcastic words about working moms: "I need to let you know that your comment is very upsetting to a working mom," or "I don't know if you're aware of it, but your comment is pretty insensitive." If the person gets defensive or flustered, you can tell him, "I'm not telling you that to make you feel bad. I like working with you and just want to clear the air so there aren't bad feelings." If the comment comes from a fellow mom, you might consider saying in a neutral tone, "I appreciate your concern, but I think it's really important for all of us moms to support one another."

It's important to note here that just because you confront someone who angered you, it doesn't mean you're going to convince the other person to change his attitude. The goal isn't to get this person to reconsider his feelings about working moms. Instead, it is to make sure this person doesn't say something offensive about working moms to you again. Even if the confrontation ends badly, with the person telling you that you're too sensitive or take things too seriously, instead of feeling like the victim, feel good about taking control of the situation and standing up for yourself. In this way, it's a successful confrontation, no matter what the outcome.

Step 4: *Get into it with your inner circle of friends.*

Mae, a thirty-six-year-old graphic designer with a toddler, recalls, "I remember my friend coming to visit me at home when my daughter was a few months old and saying, 'She's so cute! I can't believe you're going to go back to work! If she were my daughter, I would want to stay home with her all the time.' I was shocked and hurt. Why would she say something like that? Didn't she know that I had my own worries about this without her bringing it up? The last thing I needed was someone insinuating I was making a bad choice by going back to work!"

Another working mom I met recently told me that a friend of hers actually blamed her son's ADHD on the fact that she was a full-time working mom. *Honestly!* When it comes to a disparaging remark made by a close friend, the issue may run deeper than merely needing to call her out on her comment, especially if it's rude or even nasty. Since these are the people who are supposed to prop us up and comfort us, not make us feel like crappy moms, their insensitive comments can be a dagger to the heart.

Before reacting, consider whether your friend's comment was, in fact, a criticism (maybe Mae's friend was just trying to express how cute Mae's daughter was?) or the motivation for criticizing your parenting. We can deflate our anger if we know her heart is at least in the right place. John C. Maxwell, an internationally recognized leadership expert and consultant to Fortune 500 companies, advises asking yourself the following: "Was it given out of a personal hurt or for my benefit?"[10] If your friend is saying you should be home with your child, could it be because of something that happened in her own childhood? This doesn't make it okay to say mean things, but it will make her comments less painful if you know she's not trying to hurt your feelings. Says Maxwell: "People [who are hurting inside] hurt people; they lash out or criticize to try to make themselves feel better, not to help the other person."[11] Even knowing this can take the sting out of a friend's comment. That said, it's still important to point out to the friend that her comments, motivations aside, make you feel bad.

If your friend persists, there may be a deeper issue. Ask her why she feels this way, especially if all evidence points to the fact that you have a healthy, thriving, grounded family. Is it merely her opinion? Is she resentful? As Maxwell pointed out, maybe it's really more about her than you. We're all products of our own experiences, and they can often have an influence on how we judge the actions of others.

Maybe your friend's mom worked while she was growing up and she missed her. Maybe she was insulted by someone else for *not* working and feels defensive. The only way you'll know is by listening to each other. When she's done sharing, you can say, "I heard everything you said, and I'm clear on how you feel and why. I know that you are concerned for me and what's best for my family. But I'm doing what I believe is right for my family, and I need you to respect that if we are to stay friends." Obviously, pick the words that feel right for you, always remembering to avoid antagonism. If this is someone you care about and want to remain friends with, the goal is to be under-standing, respectful, and forgiving; otherwise resentment stews.

However, if the offensive comments still continue to fly, it may be time to break up. The relationship with this person is a choice, unlike relatives you may be stuck spending time with during holidays and family functions. Advises Charles Figley, a spokesman for the American Psychological Association: "You have to take some degree of responsibility for the situation," which means sometimes you have to end things.[12]

> **Try This:**
>
> When it comes to speaking up, communication experts suggest doing it directly. The next time a friend makes an offensive comment about working mothers in general, or more specifically about you being a working mom, make the choice to say something on the spot. Try, "You know, that's not the first time I've heard you say something like that, and I find it hurtful." If the friend doesn't stop there and apologize, you can add, "I'd really appreciate it if you would stop making comments about my working."
>
> Hopefully after you've said your piece, you will feel some relief and that will be the end of any rude comments.

Step 5: *Put the kibosh on rude family members.*

- -

It's one thing to part ways with a friend who fails to be a nurturing part of your life, but it's another thing entirely to have to deal with family members you will be connected to for *the rest of your life*. Just about every working mom I spoke to could name someone in the family who's made cutting remarks about working moms. Sometimes they are direct ("I really think you should give up that job and spend time with your kids"). Sometimes they are indirect ("I'm just so happy that I'm the one home raising the kids and not some nanny or daycare provider").

"My mom drives me crazy," emailed M, a filmmaker and mother of two boys. "I asked her to help me out one day when I needed childcare so I could work. I had all the meals planned out for my two sons and explained the options to her so there'd be less work for her to do. Her response was, 'Are you *ever* home to feed your children?' It's so hard not to respond to that, especially given that I cook and freeze dinners for my boys so they can always have a homemade meal!"

For Kim, a thirty-seven-year-old executive director of a national nonprofit and mother of two children under eight, the judgment she feels from her mom and sister is less aggressive but still painful. "There's this underlying disapproval I feel, and I think what's worse is that they never ever ask me about my work or even acknowledge what I do."

Practically speaking, it's not really possible to tell family members that you're parting ways if the criticism and icy disregard get extreme, but you can put strict boundaries around conversation topics by acknowledging that you don't see eye to eye, and thus it's not a topic worth discussing. Just be prepared to reiterate the point. As counselor Deborah Hill puts it, boundaries tend to fall apart in many families, so you need to maintain them. "Know what you need and what you accept, and don't get pushed around."[13]

Try This:

Sherrie Bourg Carter, PsyD, has a great idea for how to deal with family members that you can anticipate will make obnoxious comments (like, say, that uncle who seems to start every conversation with you by opening with something like "Do you want to know why the world would be a better place if working women quit their jobs . . ."). She suggests: "Start off conversations with something like, 'I only have a few minutes before I have to [fill in the blank],'" she says. "Once the time is up, politely disengage."

Carter's plan is brilliant because of how simple it is: You've just built in an escape plan. Knowing this will allow you to breathe easier no matter what your uncle has to say about working moms. Who cares? You only have forty-five seconds left!

Step 6: *Foster sisterhood with stay-at-home moms.*

I don't know about you, but I've had it with talk about "The Mommy Wars," pitting working moms against stay-at-home moms. Enough already! I wish the media would stop rehashing this story and find something better to talk about (like why women, for some utterly incomprehensible reason, are still not given equal pay). Given my talks with stay-at-home pals, I know firsthand how much we all have in common. We *all* worry about whether it's taking our child too long to potty train, what to do when our beloved babysitter announces she's moving to a new city (oh, I hate that!), whether our child is eating enough or too much, and how we'll keep it together when our kids are old enough to ask for the keys to the car. The kicker? No matter whether we stay at home or not, we all feel judged about how we parent.

According to The Working Mother Research Institute survey that was mentioned earlier in the chapter, *all* of the more than 3,700 mothers (working or not) who were interviewed said they feel judged: Working mothers feel "most judged" about how clean their house is, not taking care of themselves, and the amount of time they spend with the children, while stay-at-home mothers worry about not contributing financially to the family, how clean their house is, and not using their education.[14] One important question to ask (beyond why the heck do we all care so much about how clean our house is?!) is whether moms, working or not, put each other on the defensive via our differences. Some stay-at-home moms might think we're shortchanging our families by working, or maybe you have strong feelings that women should work, and without even realizing it, look down on women who stay home.

Ask my forty-two-year-old friend Tanya, who took off a year of work to spend time with the baby daughter she adopted. "All of a sudden, people made assumptions that I had nothing to talk about other than diapers. Here I was reading the newspaper and taking hikes and going out of my way to have outside interests and some people just assumed I was boring. It was really hard to handle that."

The issue is much more complex than we might think, and it stems from a culture that has mixed messages about what's valued in women's work. On the one hand, women are told that there's nothing more important than staying home and raising our children, while on the other hand, the job of raising a family and taking care of a household is devalued as an asset by this same society. Working moms, however, are praised for "contributing to the household." Hey, we're *all* contributing to the household. No wonder we're all at odds!

Are you guilty of buying into stereotypes about the world of working moms? Whether you voice them aloud or not, your judgments are probably easy to read. Stay-at-home moms are often made to feel "less than" in their comparisons with working moms—less interesting, less capable of holding up their end of the conversation, less modern. In fact, a few stay-at-home moms told me that working women will ask what they do at parties and events and literally walk away from them when they hear they don't have a paying job. (Talk about snobbish!) Hopefully, these working moms are a minority among us. For those of us regular Janes who respect each other for who we are and not what we do, the issue of "working" or "not working" is still an incendiary issue, and our reactions are often driven by the guilt, assumptions, and insecurity we internalize.

Take Erin, a freelance magazine writer with two kids under twelve. "I was at a company picnic one day, and I was talking to a colleague's wife, who seemed really friendly. We were making small talk, and I asked her one of those typical get-to-know-you questions. 'What kind of work do you do for a living?' I asked, smiling. I just totally made the assumption that she worked. Her expression immediately went flat, and she was suddenly super-curt. She just said, 'I work at *home*,' and then she excused herself. It was the first time I saw the other side of the coin. All this time, I was the one feeling like I had to justify my role as a working mom, and here she was, feeling like she had to do the same as a stay-at-home mom. Kinda sucks that this divide exists between women."

It's easy to feel judged for working by your friends and family members who don't. But it's not quite as easy to see when you are the pot calling the kettle black—and putting *them* on the defensive. If this strikes a chord, make peace with your fellow mom. Initiate a conversation in which you apologize for any assumptions or disrespectful comments you've made. While you're at it, open conversations that help you better understand the perspectives and feelings of your stay-at-home friends and family, and make sure you never offer advice unless solicited.

Says Casey, a thirty-seven-year-old policewoman who has four children under age seven: "I have a best friend who is a stay-at-home mom, and her life seems so Pollyanna to me sometimes. She and her children have picnics in the backyard. She used to be this high-powered career woman. And she hears about my life, in which there are constantly a million things going on, and she'll say, 'Oh God, I am sorry for you that your life is so hectic,' not remembering that I thrive on chaos. We can't imagine each other's lives. But we have a lot of history together and we try not to be judgmental of one another."

If you're thinking, *But I've never voiced my opinions aloud,* don't think you're fooling your pal. I like what Lori Deschene, founder of TinyBuddha.com, says in her article "10 Ways to Deal with Difficult People": "When you think negative thoughts, it comes out in your body language. Someone prone to negativity may feel all too tempted to mirror that. Try coming at them with the positive mindset you wish they had. Expect the best in them. You never know when you might be pleasantly surprised."[15]

You get bonus points for *not* contributing to a conversation in which other working moms are judging stay-at-home moms. You know how it feels to be the one on the defensive, and these types of conversations only fuel the fire between women. Why not say something like "Well, I give stay-at-home moms a lot of credit for [fill in the blank with something genuine]." It's up to all of us to break the cycle and accept that our needs are different.

Proceed with Caution if . . .

your friend or family member apologizes for her disparaging comment—and then shocks you by casting out another one. You may be
tempted to yell, "Well, Miss Perfect, let's look at how you're doing as
a mom . . ." and then prepare to rattle off some war stories concern-
ing your antagonist's kids. Or, perhaps you want to make a dig at
your sister about how boring her stay-at-home life is, or you let your
nonworking friends know about a study showing kids in daycare
fare better in the long run. No, no, no. *You* want to be accepted for
the choices you're making, so it would be hypocritical to attack her.
Instead try, "I know we've made different choices around whether
to work or not, and I want you to know that I think you're doing a
wonderful job raising your child." If you can't do that, take a breath
and say, "I think we should both try to be respectful of each other's
choices," and walk away from the area of attack. Maybe things will
get resolved later when you calm down, but nothing is going to happen during this moment of head-spinning fury.

On the Flip Side . . .

maybe you're so worried about being judged by friends and family that you refuse to open up to them about how damn hard it is
sometimes. It's just giving them ammo, you think, that can later
be used against you. Real friends don't use personal confessions to
torment their gal pals, and you can't have deep genuine friendships
without sharing with one another some of your vulnerabilities. Tell
your close friend or relative—before there is any kind of altercation
or barb—that it's hard for you to admit this, but you sometimes

struggle with the guilt of working while your kids are young. If she's a good friend, she will likely open up to you about her fears around child-raising and then you can prop each other up when necessary. Just knowing that the grass is sometimes greener is a gift you can give one another.

SHOUT-OUT TO . . .

Casey, a thirty-seven-year-old working mom of four, believes in taking action rather than letting bad feelings fester. A couple of years ago, an after-school teacher made a cutting remark to Casey about her being a working mom. She went on to tell Casey flat-out that moms should be home with their kids (an irony, given that the woman was an after-school teacher, dependent on working parents for her job to exist). Casey left feeling angry but didn't respond because she didn't want any resentment to be taken out on her children later. But Casey found herself infuriated every time she went to pick up her child. "Finally, I told her that her comment was extremely hurtful. I also told her that I did not want to go above her to the supervisor, but I would if I heard her make another comment like that to me or any other mom there again. She mumbled an apology and that was the end of that. I felt so much better having gotten it off my chest."

Chapter Wrap

- - - - - - - - - - - - -

Step 1: *Know where you stand . . . and stay there.*

Once you are clear on the benefits of working for your family, you're going to feel less hurt when others call you selfish.

Step 2: *Let yourself off the hook.*

Don't beat up on yourself for not calling out a friend who makes a rude comment about working moms—but do address it later.

Step 3: *Keep it simple with "the regulars."*

It's not your job to convince others that working moms aren't doing a tremendous disservice to their kids.

Step 4: *Get into it with your inner circle of friends.*

See whether you can find a place where you and your accusatory friend agree to disagree.

Step 5: *Put the kibosh on rude family members.*

Just because you can't avoid family members doesn't mean you have to deal with their personal attacks.

Step 6: *Foster sisterhood with stay-at-home moms.*

Sometimes stay-at-home moms are trying to express an emotional struggle, not attacking your choice.

Chapter 11

"SICK DAYS" AND OTHER SETBACKS

Confession: "I stress about falling behind at work when my child needs extra attention."

When our phone rings in the middle of the day, most of us freeze in our tracks and send a silent prayer to the heavens: *Please, please, not the school nurse!* When we see in our caller ID that it's someone else, we breathe a sigh of relief—even if it's the IRS on the line. When it is the school nurse, we pick up the phone knowing full well she is about to say, "You need to come get your child." It takes everything in us not to yell, "Wait! I have so much work to do . . . I can't come!" But we signed on for this parenting gig, and this is part of the deal. So we drop everything and head directly to the school, plagued by anxious thoughts ("What if I miss my deadline?" "Why couldn't she have waited to get sick until I finished my annual report?" or "Why did he have to hurt his elbow today of all days?"). Then we are wracked with guilt because what kind of monster-mother gets upset at her child for getting sick or injured?

It's not sickness that sends our day into a tailspin. It's anytime our routine goes off the rails, because really, most of us can just about manage our lives when everything is "normal." It just takes one situation—winter vacation, a lice outbreak, a week or more of summer with no coverage—to get us spiraling into chaos. You are suddenly on full-time parenting duty while the unfinished work piles up. Your daily structure is shot, and worse, you fear you're taking it out on your child, your babysitter, and the man working behind the deli counter at the supermarket. You've got to get a grip!

This is when the "shoulds" start to pile on: "I should be sweeter to my sick child—it's not his fault that my work isn't getting done"; "I should be at home mothering my child and not sitting here at work"; "I should enjoy this extra time with my child before camp starts and stop thinking about work"; "I should not let my child watch this much TV so that I can at least try to answer some of these work emails"; and on and on.

Unchecked, all these worries can gather into one colossal attack: "I am a horrible mother!" You'd prefer that your child not remember you as the unfeeling crazy lady running around with a thermometer and cell phone. So what to do?

QUIZ: HOW WELL DO YOU HANDLE SHAKE-UPS IN THE ROUTINE?

1. **During breakfast on a weekday, your daughter complains about her throat feeling kind of "weird," so you:**
   a. take her temperature and prepare to stay home if she's got anything close to a fever.
   b. give her a fever-reducing medicine just in case, send her to school, and cross your fingers.
   c. hope she's just complaining for attention, give her a giant hug, and send her to school.

2. **During your family vacation week, a client keeps calling and asking unimportant questions. You don't want to be rude, but this is supposed to be family time, so you:**
   a. explain to your client that you're on a family vacation and suggest she email you her questions, and you will respond at the end of the day.
   b. take all the calls but try to keep them short; you don't want to lose your client!
   c. tell your family to go have fun without you; you'll take the calls and then meet up with your family sometime later in the day.

3. **The phone rings during the afternoon and you have a sneaky suspicion it might be the school nurse, so you:**
   a. don't even look at the caller ID number. If it rings again, you'll pick it up.
   b. run out of your office so you can't hear it anymore; now it doesn't exist.
   c. take a deep breath and answer the phone; you don't want your kid sitting in the nurse's office feeling bad.

Answers: If you answered "a" for number 1, give yourself one point. If you answered "b" for number two, give yourself one point. If you answered "c" for number 3, give yourself one point. If your sum total is two or more, you are probably doing pretty well at going with the flow on unstructured days. If your total is less than two, tune in to this chapter's steps so you can stop driving yourself even more nuts during chaotic days.

Reality Check
- - - - - - - - - - - - -

Being a good mom doesn't require that you feel unperturbed at the idea of dropping your work when your routine shifts abruptly. It may help to know that you are far from alone in experiencing guilt attacks when your child is sick. The stress of dealing with sick days was the number one concern I found in my research with working moms for this book. Just the question of "Do I or don't I take off work?" is pure torment. And yes, just about all of us have sent our children to school or daycare when they were sick, giving them aspirin and praying they made it through at least half the day. In the February/March 2007 issue of *Working Mother* magazine, a study of 689 working moms showed that one third of the moms sent their sick child to school or daycare, most likely because they couldn't take off work.[1] Hey, even teachers deal with the burden. Maggie, a forty-year-old teacher and mom to children ages fourteen and eleven, admitted in an email: "Every time my child is sick, I feel I can't call in to work because I have seventy students who need to be taught. Even teachers send their sick kids to school or daycare so that they can get to work, even if for a few hours to start the day and set up contingency plans."

Your child's illness isn't the only problem that throws a wrench in the works either. Again, there are those unexpected school days off, like "Teacher Appreciation Day" and "National Condiment Day" (okay, the latter might not be a real one), furlough days, parent conference week, "short days" for no plausible reason, countless national holidays and breaks, and summer stretches before camp starts, not to mention all the other planned and unplanned work interruptions. We know we need to switch into flexible mode, but it's not easy. It is only possible by remembering that while these days are stressful, the world doesn't cave in when we let the majority of the daily tasks go undone. Michelle LaRowe, author of *Working Mom's 411,* believes we must remember what matters most. "Ticking items off of your massive to-do list with great efficiency may feel fabulous—but always stay focused on the big picture."[2]

The big picture may be attending to your child and getting one or two necessary obligations checked off. Then we need to congratulate ourselves for getting through the day rather than freaking out about everything we didn't get done. It's up to us to adjust our expectations of "good enough," and this chapter is all about how to do it.

Step 1: *Know when to call a sickie a sickie.*

- -

Just before leaving for school, your child groans and announces, "I feel sick." You get a first stab of anxiety but take a deep breath, trying to remain calm as you ask, "What doesn't feel good?" You listen intently as your child lists the symptoms, trying to grasp whether it's okay to send him to school and hope for the best. You don't want your child to go to school feeling bad, but what if he feels better soon and it was just some fluky thing? That happens, right? Right?!

Yes, sometimes that happens—although it never seems to happen on the days we can't take off easily. The stress of going back and forth wondering *School or no school?* on hectic days is driving you crazy. So first, let's get clear on when it's officially not okay to drop your child off at school or daycare, so you can spare yourself the energy of mental battling. According to Susan H. Terwilliger, a nurse practitioner who works in a school setting, your child should not go to school if he or she has been diagnosed with or is experiencing the following:

* Chicken pox
* Strep throat
* Fever
* Vomiting and/or diarrhea
* Skin infections
* Eye infections
* Parasitic infections such as lice or scabies *(ew!)*

If your child has been targeted by one of these villains, the decision has already been made. You're staying home—probably for the next several days. Just accept it, because who has the energy for denial? Now, let's define a fever once and for all (my husband and I debate this all the time): Most experts agree that any temperature below 100.8 is normal, and your child's temperature should be normal for fourteen hours before sending her to school. So if your kid has a temperature of 100.8 at night—and then has a normal temperature in the morning—it's wise not to send her. Plus, we all know that if you do, your child is coming home that day anyway (and probably the moment you settle into your work). As for colds, it's a judgment call. According to kidsgrowth.com (a website overseen by the members of the Medical Advisory Board), as long as there is no fever or discomfort and your child isn't so uncomfortable that she can't function, it's off to school she goes.[3] You'll also be happy to hear that your child can go to school if she has "Cat Scratch Disease" (no kidding, this is a real illness spread by bacteria from the cat's saliva to a child's open skin). Who knew?

Step 2: *BYOT (Bring Your Own Toys).*

Okay, so let's say you keep your child home and you need to bring him to work with you for a bit. As most of us can attest, it ain't pretty trying to get our wheezing/hacking/sneezing child into the car while trying to stay focused on how not to get sucked into work *(If I avoid Carol's office, I should be okay; As long as I take the back exit door on my way out, I should be able to leave undetected).* With all this going through our brains, it's no surprise that most of us forget to bring a bag of distractions for our child while he's hanging out. Now our kid is going to be feeling unwell and restless, and that does not bode well for being productive and efficient. One way to alleviate the problem: While your child is well, pick out a few activities and games you can bring to your office and leave in your closet or drawer for when you need to bring him to work. Children older than eight will likely have their own books or electronics to keep them busy. For younger children, think about bringing in some crafts, coloring books, a blanket, and a favorite stuffed animal so they can make themselves cozy. Can you leave a sealed bag of crackers or dried fruit in your office for these occasions? The more prepared you are now, the more chaos you can keep from invading your already chaotic universe.

Rebecca, a forty-year-old engineering manager in California and mom to two kids ages nine and eight, learned the necessity of having supplies on hand at the office when her daughter got hurt on the school playground. "My husband was on a business trip and I had a huge presentation to our senior vice president of design, along with six other VPs, on some detailed work I had completed. Forty minutes before the presentation, I received a call that my daughter had fallen off the monkey bars and I had to pick her up.

She was fine but ended up having to come to work with me. I had to take her into our design studio (which is off limits to the public and most other employees) so she could wait for me to finish. Thank goodness the administrative assistant gave her some awesome colored pencils until I was finished!"

Dana, thirty-eight, is the program director for the Personal Genetics Education Project, based at Harvard University's medical lab, and mom of kids ages six and four. She admits, "I've learned that I'm not terribly flexible, especially when one of my kids gets sick and plans go off schedule." Dana recalls one particularly stressful day when she was set to talk to a group of high school students about genetics and her son woke up with a fever. "What could I do?" she says. "I brought him with me, along with a whole bunch of complicated Legos, and prayed for the best." Luckily it went well enough, but Dana said she was stressed throughout the entire talk waiting for disaster to strike. She kept wondering whether she should have canceled: Was it fair to make him go with her when he was sick? Was it fair to cancel an obligation under such short notice?

It's up to you to decide, of course, how essential it is that you be at work while your child isn't feeling well, and how much your child can sustain before losing it. There will be times when it's simply too much for your child to handle (i.e., you do not want to take a kid with a stomach bug into your car, much less your office). It should also be noted that no one at work is going to appreciate you taking your contagious child in to work, deadlines or not. But when your child is healing from an injury or has been on antibiotics for several days, it's fine to bring him in. Just make sure he has some creature comforts.

Step 3: *Take your pom-poms for a spin.*

Michelle, a thirty-six-year-old project manager from Texas and mom to a three-year-old son, recalls: "Once I had to give a big presentation on the phone from 11:30 AM to noon. My nanny was sick so couldn't pick up my son from school at 11:45 AM. I called the school to say I'd be there at noon, left my house at 11:15 AM, and did my big presentation in the car around the block from my son's school. As soon as it was over, I hung up, drove a block, and picked him up. It seems like every mom I work with has a story like this; we switch roles constantly to manage our jobs and families."

Lynn, a forty-eight-year-old community college professor from California and mom to seven-year-old twins, emailed: "When my kids were little, the babysitter arrived one day to say she was quitting and that I needed to make other arrangements right away. I had one day to set up alternate childcare. I had to go to work and teach my class because this was also the first day of the semester. My classroom had been moved, and I had to scramble to notify all the students. While this was happening, I was on the phone making arrangements to bring my children for a visit to the daycare center later that afternoon. There were just two spots left and we got them, but that was quite a harried day of balancing in the moment and shifting based on priorities."

It is amazing what Herculean tasks we can accomplish on days when there's not nearly enough of us to go around. We have a way of getting incredibly resourceful, even as we feel our reserves diminishing. Just because we feel like we are falling apart doesn't mean we are! We keep navigating all the responsibilities, and then collapse at the end of the day and weep or pass out in our bed, hoping for a calmer tomorrow. This is unacceptable, and here's why: We need to congratulate ourselves on getting through a rough situation and take stock of how much we were able to do in such a trying time (even when our house is a mess and dinner was a frozen burrito). Take a minute and walk through what you were able to accomplish, because this becomes a model you can draw upon the next time a wrench is thrown into the works and you are freaking out. You can manage . . . proof is in the pudding.

Step 4: *Drop the bar (way) lower.*

You're home for today, possibly for the week, with your little one. One look at the to-do list for the next couple of days and you're beside yourself. It would be hard enough if there were no interruptions, but given all the hacking, barfing, and yelling going on in the other room, forget it. You're done for. If you think about the running back and forth from your computer to heat up soup, dole out medicine, give back rubs, sneak in some work, call the doctor, and so on . . . well, hello burnout.

Rather than setting yourself up for failure, prioritize the two or three tasks that must get done in the next couple of days and make that your mission. If you can't figure out how to reduce them to three, rank each task, giving an "A" to tasks that truly have to get done or there will be severe consequences, "B" to tasks that would be good to get done if there is enough time, and "C" to tasks that can wait until life is back on track. It's far more efficient to spend time creating this high-priority list of tasks than to try to get through your whole list half-assed. Know that you're not even going to attempt your C-list items (and probably many of the B-listers as well) until you're back at work. One more hint: If any of your items have the word "start" or "explore," they are not an A-list item. This is no time to start anything major. And if you don't finish everything on your A-list, big deal. These are trying circumstances and crossing anything off your list is an accomplishment (including showering), so go easy on yourself.

If one of your high-priority items involves getting something to the boss or a client, you're obviously not going to cross your fingers and hope for the best. This is the time to be proactive and protect your butt by letting this person know what's up as quickly as possible. Suggests documentary filmmaker and writer Sarah Baker in her article "How to Care for a Sick Child and Still Make Deadlines": "Explain that you are doing everything you can to do the job under these circumstances. Chances are, if your boss or client has a kid, they have been in this situation themselves. Hopefully, the shared experience will make them more sympathetic to your position . . . they may offer to extend the deadline."[4] You don't know until you try.

Also, embrace (or at least accept) the fact that life is going to be a hot mess right now. You can't stop it so you might as well get on board. Says Marcie, forty-four, creative principal of a design firm in California and mom to two boys ages nine and five, "My two little boys are on vacation this week—'ski week,' if you can believe that. My husband and I didn't realize they were out of school until just the week before—another one to add to our scheduling mishaps. So now we're tag-team parenting, working from home and staying late hours at the office to make up for it. Ill timed? Yes. My design firm is currently churning out a big client's annual report, a website for a university, and countless other huge projects (with a ton of executive pressure) that all have important deadlines this week. Is there a coping strategy when parenting sneaks up on you? I don't think so. Life is messy. All we can do is work hard to make the best of it . . . we just can't beat ourselves up mentally in the process."

Step 5: *Expect the unexpected.*

- -

If your children are in daycare, school, or within fifty feet of other children, they are going to get sick this year—and more than a few times. It doesn't matter if we give them special preventive herbal treatments, make sure they get all their vitamins, or dress them head to toe in aluminum foil. They're going down. Vincent Iannelli, MD, a pediatrician from Texas, says, "It is normal for young children to have six to eight upper respiratory tract infections and two or three gastrointestinal infections each year."[5] Six to eight— and that's just one kid! What if you have multiple kids? Says Leslie, a thirty-two-year-old community relations manager from New Hampshire and mom to two-year-old twins and an eight-month-old, emailed: "The worst is when they get sick—and honestly, with three kids under age three, when isn't someone sick?"

How are we supposed to take that much time off work to care for them and keep our jobs? Many working moms don't even get a sick day when they themselves are sick. According to Momsrising .org, "Nearly half (40 percent) of private-sector workers are denied a single paid sick day."[6] And with our kids potentially ill that often, we're sure to catch their illnesses and ailments. Momsrising.com also reports that globally, 145 countries offer sick pay.[7]

Jennifer, thirty-six, a loan processor in Ohio and mom to a nine- and a seven-year-old, says, "Anytime the school calls and tells me my kids are sick, I'm stressed. My boss is always angry and disappointed when I leave—shocking, since she was a single mother of three . . . one would think she would understand. I actually think she feels like she had to 'suck it up' and so I should too."

So assuming many working moms are going to have to haul their exhausted butts in to work, what can we do to prepare? First, handle your high-priority tasks early in the day for insurance. Yes, most of us prefer to ease into work—sipping our coffee, saying hello to coworkers, and reading over emails before diving in. But it's a wiser idea to get right to work on the tasks that must get done today or else. Once those are out of the way, we can say a more leisurely hello to our favorite coworkers or take a quick look at Facebook postings with the knowledge that nothing too terrible is going to happen at work if, heaven forbid, we get that unfortunate call from the nurse's office.

Next, establish one or two emergency contacts if possible. Ideally, you have a family member close by, although these days that seems to be less and less the case. Zelma, a thirty-four-year-old stock portfolio manager in New Hampshire and mom to two kids under three, recalls: "The worst moments are preparing for a meeting and having my kids get a fever (therefore not allowed at daycare), and my husband at a meeting also. I have no family around and all my friends are at work or have small kids, so I can't drop a sick kid with them." Yep, that sums it up for most of us.

So think now, while it's calm. Is there anyone else you can ask to be your backup in extreme circumstances (i.e., your presentation is starting in five minutes and the nurse just called)? If you have a significant other who's also busy that day, can you split the day in half for parental duties? If you're single or your partner can basically never stay at home, is there a friend at work who could volunteer to watch your child for one hour while you get through the huge event? Is there a neighbor without kids who can pick up your child and, as payback, you do something very nice for that person? Or a friend who's a stay-at-home mom (in exchange for watching her children one night the next week)? Line up one or two people before disaster strikes and outline for them what the emergency role looks like (i.e., picking your child up if you are out of the country or leading a major presentation in less than thirty minutes).

If you expect the unexpected, you'll face it prepared.

Try This:

When your child spikes a fever at 3:00 AM, can you bank on having a stockpile of grape-flavored chewable fever reducers in the medicine cabinet, or do you desperately shuffle through bottles of Midol and outdated antibiotics, hoping you'll find something, anything, a child under twelve can ingest? This is not the time to come up short! Be prepared. Stock up your bathroom now with pharmacy needs so you don't have to run out in the eye of the sick-storm—assuming you even could. Have on hand children's pain- and fever-reducing medicine, allergy medicine, thermometer, and Pedialite. May as well stock up on exta tissues and (for kids old enough to suck on them) cough drops. I also recommend purchasing—when you do not need it—a metal-wire comb for lice (get the one with the comb teeth that are corkscrew—trust me). Keep ginger ale, popsicles, soup, and crackers in the house for recovering post-flu bellies.

Step 6: *Delegate all that you can.*

- -

As we mentioned in Chapter 8, delegating tasks is a godsend, and you're hopefully already on board with this idea. However, maybe when you hear the word "delegate," the first thing you still think is *I can't, I have no time to delegate!* By the time you explain to someone else what needs to be done and how to do it in the way you like, you could have just done it already. It's like hiring an intern at work: You want an intern to take some of the tasks off your plate, but the idea of hiring the right person and then training her is more than you can bear. So you keep slogging away, trying to make a dent in the endless to-do list and muttering "If only I had an intern!"

It's time to change your attitude and get help, because let's face it, when the kids are home with us and work is due, everything else slides (or drops off the face of the earth). So suck it up and share the workload. What can you dole out? If you have a partner, can he (or /she) bring home dinners (everyone will survive having takeout for a week). What tasks can your child take on (if your kids are feeling well enough and are old enough to fold laundry and clean dishes, they should get going). What can you off load at work? Hand over as many tasks as you can to someone on staff you trust, vowing to get his back next time. Go into your savings account if possible and hire someone to clean your house—even if it's just the one time.

This week, things may not get done as well as you would do them. Ask for help and deal with it. Then be totally thankful you got help, even if your favorite sweater didn't make it through the laundry or the clean dishes got put away in the wrong places. Sabrina O'Mallone, president of Working Mom Enterprises, advises in her book *Moms on the Job:* "Don't shoot yourself in the foot by expecting everyone to do things to some impossibly high standard. Accept the help you can get, and be grateful for it. Once you learn to relax a little bit, you'll be glad you did."[8]

Jaime, thirty-two, a high school teacher from Illinois and mom to a one-year-old, recalls, "My daughter was very sick in early January. It was the week before finals and my students are freshmen who are taking finals for the first time. I had parents calling me asking if I could give their student some extra help, and my department chair was sending out several emails about how we need to stay connected to our students during finals time—a stressful week. But my daughter was really sick, with a 104-degree fever, not eating, just sleeping all the time. It was the first time she was very ill. So my husband (a teacher as well) and I alternated days off to take care of her. Also, I got a colleague to take my freshman classes so they wouldn't feel as stressed."

Did it go perfectly for Jaime? Probably not. Did she and her family make it through the day from hell? Yep, they sure did. D-e-l-e-g-a-t-e.

Step 7: *Take the vacation for real.*

- -

I remember taking a family vacation in Florida one year and agreeing to look over some work emails for the film I was making. How long could it take—a few minutes, maybe? I'd wait until after my child was asleep and just get it done, no big deal. Except it was. I had all sorts of technical issues trying to open the attachments, my stress levels were on the rise, and I was up much later than I wanted to be on what was supposed to be a fun family trip. What the hell was I thinking? Why hadn't I expected technology to go awry, since it always does at key moments? Next time, I vowed, I would tell everyone: "I am off-duty!" Hey, there's enough to stress about on potential vacations without work: preventing your child from whining on the long travel journey; forgetting to pack the insect repellent; trying to remember how to say, "Where is the bathroom?" in another language before your child pees her pants. We don't need to be dealing with faulty attachments, computer blow-ups, or being tied to the phone.

Jennifer, a thirty-two-year-old graphic designer from Georgia and mom to three kids ages five, three, and eight months, remembers being on vacation during a time when a project was dragging on that she'd expected would be finished by the time she left. She recalls, "I spent the morning hunched over my laptop uploading files to a printer in Germany while my family waited. We were headed to an aquarium and my kids were bursting with excitement. The longer I took, the more they melted down. My husband was doing the best he could, but they needed Mom, and my client needed the edits done now. I remember trying to justify to myself that this one project would more than pay for the week of vacation, but it didn't make it any better. I hate that one of my kids' vacation memories is me stressing over a slow connection and not enjoying every moment being with them."

So if there's any choice in the matter, take the vacation. The reason it exists in the first place is to help us replenish and unwind. It's not healthy to go months on end without this. Stephanie Smith, a clinical psychologist from Erie, Colorado, says that in addition to creating family memories, vacations not only give us a break from the stresses of work and maintaining a household but "also give us perspective on how we might be placing too much importance on nonimportant things."[9] We can't do that if we're bringing our work with us!

Now, I know for a lot of moms, it's utterly unrealistic to take a vacation and not check in at work—at all. A recent survey by *Working Mother* magazine revealed that 75 percent of working moms check in at work one or two times each day while on vacation.[10] Hey, if you have to in order to keep your job, then you have to. However, you can still set limits to safeguard your family time. Carol Evans, president of Working Mothers Media, advises, "It is essential that you limit the time that you are working to no more than thirty minutes a day." If you're traveling with a spouse, she advises, "have the kids go off and spend one-on-one time with him for that thirty minutes." Do not make your kids hang out and wait for you for an hour, which is going to bum everyone out. They're going to feel (rightfully) shortchanged, which is going to spill onto the rest of the day. This is your time to connect with your kids, and unfortunately, you don't get a do-over. So leave the laptop and the BlackBerry safely back in the hotel.

Proceed with Caution If . . .

you find yourself screaming at your kids on days when your routine goes off the rails. Of course you get frustrated that you're not able to get your work done—or that your sick or injured child is yelling "Mommmm!" every twenty seconds for a pillow fluff, back scratch, or saltines. But taking it out on your child is going to make both of you feel a whole lot worse. So when you find yourself about to blow, give yourself a time-out in another room, take a few deep breaths, and remind yourself that your child needs your attention right now more than work does—and that this is a temporary situation. Accept from the get-go that the bulk of your attention is going to be on your child today; it'll be far less frustrating once you resign yourself to this.

On the Flip Side . . .

avoid giving up work altogether on the off days. Sure, it might feel good to say, "Oh, screw it," and just let go of work until your child is back in school. Well, if you can swing that, lovely. But if your work is going to pile higher and higher, leaving you even more stressed just thinking about it, it's not worth it. Find small chunks of time to get just enough done so that you won't be left drowning in work upon your child's return to school. Hire a babysitter to come for a couple of hours, if need be, so you can carve out even an hour of work time (yes, even if it's on the weekend). Just knowing you've made a tiny dent will give you at least some peace of mind.

SHOUT-OUT TO . . .

Eleanor, a thirty-two-year-old attorney and mom to a four-year-old daughter. She says the nature of her corporate culture means staying long hours until the work is done. That said, Eleanor has consistently drawn a line when it comes to her daughter, Morgan, being sick. While she has worried in the past about coworkers thinking she's slacking if she leaves to get her sick daughter at school, Eleanor has made it clear to everyone at the office that she's leaving if Morgan is sick. "When my daughter had a 103-degree fever," she says, "I called my assistant and said I'm leaving and I'll see you when I see you." She added, "I don't think any of the people that I work with could possibly think, 'Oh, you've done the wrong thing by going to get your sick kid,' but it wouldn't matter if they did. It helps me to be clear on this."

Chapter Wrap

- - - - - - - - - - - - - -

Step 1: *Know when to call a sickie a sickie.*

You can save yourself aggravation if you know ahead of time when you can't send your sick child to school.

Step 2: *BYOT (Bring Your Own Toys).*

Stash activities and quiet games at your office for those unexpected times when you have to bring your child to work with you.

Step 3: *Take your pom-poms for a spin.*

Take stock of all that you were able to manage on the challenging, unstructured days, rather than criticizing yourself.

Step 4: *Drop the bar (way) lower.*

Make a list of priority items that need to get done and forget about every other task that isn't on that list.

Step 5: *Expect the unexpected.*

Have a plan in place and medicine on hand before your child gets sick.

Step 6: *Delegate all that you can.*

Have standby troops in place for emergencies when you can't get to your sick child right away.

Step 7: *Take the vacation for real.*

If you're spending the majority of the day checking emails and texting to ease your workload, you're missing the major point of vacation.

CONCLUSION

I hate the phrase "work-life balance." (There, I said it.) It gives off the impression that there is an achievable state of being where we spend the exactly right amount of focus on family and career, life is running smoothly, and all we need to do is maintain the perfect plan we've created, for as long as possible. It's preposterous, and we shouldn't be striving for it. Instead, we should recognize that some days will go easier than other days, and our priorities will often change week to week, sometimes day to day. And no matter how much perspective we gain, we are still likely to send our child to school sometimes when the thermometer warns us not to, feel weepy when we miss our child's milestone because we got entrenched in a work deadline, or suffer in moments when we feel like we're not doing enough for someone. Given that, how can you know if this book is bringing you *success?* There will be no concrete evidence to prove you've achieved a huge life transformation. Unlike with other prescriptive reads, you can't prove this book worked by reaching one specific goal, such as landing a job in a new field, making the perfect crème brulee, or losing those last five (or fifteen) pounds. However, there are ways to know whether we're changing significantly for the better, by using the benchmarks described below.

You are better able to tune in to your feelings and experience them. If you miss an important staff meeting because it's your child's last class breakfast, you recognize your worry that coworkers will be mad—even as you experience the happiness of taking part in your child's community. When your child experiences a lovely milestone that you miss because of work travel, you allow yourself to experience the sorrow and then let go of it. If you end up yelling at your child because she keeps interrupting you during a work call, you can name the frustration you feel at yelling, the embarrassment of seeming out of control on the call, as well as the guilt of snapping at your child. You understand the value of experiencing the myriad feelings rather than burying them, and see that stress diminishes when you let them move through you.

You are relying more on your own intuition. The truth is, we know our children and what motivates them better than anyone else—even experts with a wall full of degrees and numerous awards lining the shelves. There is no expert that can offer a blanket statement about how long it's acceptable for a working mom to leave the country on business, or how many days she should volunteer for the community, or whether she should go to her child's concert or agree to be a keynote speaker at a conference. It depends on *your* comfort level, how you predict your choice will affect your family, whether you are able to line up help, and what the family calendar looks like in any given week. You—along with your family—are typically well equipped to know how to cheer your kid up, when to tell your boss you're staying home with your kid, and when you've had enough of those snarky comments from others about moms who work. The more you are able to tune in to and trust your own values, the less you'll find yourself caring about others' opinions and the more confident you will feel in making the best choices you can for yourself and your family.

You are comfortable asking for help and sometimes lowering the bar. When your child or work needs extra attention and support for whatever reason—and there's not enough of you to go around for work and family devotion—you immediately farm out whatever practical tasks you can. If it means getting through a challenging week, you are prepared to open your wallet and pay for help (or barter if the wallet is bare), and you don't feel guilty about it or worry it won't be good enough. If you're on a major deadline, you're prepared to serve takeout food every night for as long as it takes to get through this period of time, send out your laundry to be washed and folded, and ask a coworker to take on some of your work this week and you'll repay her next month. You'll know you're succeeding when you can delegate without feeling bad about needing extra help, and even applaud yourself for lining up the assistance.

You're spending more time with friends, and less time asking for rain checks. You will know you're on track when you are making a genuine effort to see pals who make you laugh, cheer you on, and dole out supportive hugs when you need them. If you noticed you no longer had close friendships left to revive, you have started looking for women to connect with. You appreciate the sustenance friends bring to your life and the need for adult playdates. You have more energy to do this because you are wasting *less* time with toxic friends or relatives who deplete you emotionally and/or erode your confidence. You see that you don't have to convince these people that your family is just fine. They can think whatever they wish, and it doesn't seep into your basic sense of self.

You know you are creating a healthy model for your children, not just by showing them what it looks like for a woman to parent and partake in work that she finds immensely satisfying, but also by communicating in relationships. If you've been over-apologizing or overexplaining, you're reining in your behavior and keeping discussions more direct and clear. You're also, where age-appropriate, asking your children for their input on how you connect with one another—whether it's staying in touch while you're away on business, choosing which school events or volunteer requests to take part in, or deciding how you can celebrate their achievements or victories if you have to miss the main event. You empathize with your children when they are sad that you can't be there but are still able to hold on to the fact that you're a good, loving mama. You also fully accept that sometimes, more than you like, you're going to screw up the work-parent juggle—because you're not a robot. But when you do get things right—whether it's making more time for a good friend, helping out a coworker who has helped you in the past so you could get home sooner, volunteering at your child's school in spite of an overbooked schedule—you sing your own praises. You celebrate the efforts that you're making, whether or not they're always victorious, and let your children see what that looks like.

NOTES

Introduction

1. Modern Ghana, "Are You a Working Mom? Learn How to Deal with Working Mom Guilt," March 25, 2011, iVillage.com, http://mibn.org/site.php/snew/read/are_you_a_working_mom_learn_1/ gina robison billups.

2. Anne-Marie Slaughter, "Why Women Still Can't Have it All," *Atlantic Monthly,* July/August 2012.

3. Modern Ghana, "Are You a Working Mom?" (see no. 1).

4. Terry Greenburg Star, "Am I the only working mom who doesn't feel guilty about working?" Circle of Moms blog post, December 22, 2008, http://www.circleofmoms.com/working-mums/am-i-the-only-working-mom-who-doesn-t-feel-guilty-about-working-440276#.

5. Stephanie Himel-Nelson, "What About Moms Who Work," The Washington Post online, On Balance blog, January 9, 2007, http://voices.washingtonpost.com/onbalance/2007/01/draft_lawyer_mama.html.

Chapter 1: *The Sorry Loop*

1. Denise Mann, "Three Easy Steps to Breaking Bad Habits," WebMD, November 2007, http://www.webmd.com/balance/features/3-easy-steps-to-breaking-bad-habits.

2. Victoria Samuels, "How to Get Your Child to Listen," SuperNanny.co.uk, April 5, 2007, http://www.supernanny.co.uk/Advice/-/Parenting-Skills/-/Routine-and-Teamwork/How-to-Get-Your-Child-to-Listen.aspx.

3. Ronald L. Pitzer, PhD, "Setting Limits for Responsive Discipline," online parenting resources, University of Minnesota Extension, November 2008, http://www.extension.umn.edu/distribution/familydevelopment/W00011.html.

4. Ronald Alexander, PhD, "The Wise Open Mind," *Psychology Today,* May 15, 2010, http://www.psychologytoday.com/blog/the-wise-open-mind/ 201005/recovering-sorrow-loss-and-heartache.

5. Ibid.

6. Tobi Spino, "The Joys—I Mean Guilt, Wait, No, I Mean Joys—of Motherhood," Urban Suburban Mom, September 22, 2010, http://rivertowns.patch. com/articles/the-joys-i-mean-guilt-wait-no-i-mean-joys-of-motherhood.

7. http://www.focusonthefamily.com/parenting/your_childs_emotions/emotional_development/acknowledging_feelings.aspx.

8. G. Alan Marlatt, PhD, and Deborah S. Romaine, *The Complete Idiot's Guide to Changing Old Habits for Good* (Alpha Books, 2008).

9. Michelle Ghilotti Mandel, "How to Grow from Mistakes and Stop Beating Yourself Up," TinyBuddha.com, April 27, 2011, http://tinybuddha.com/ blog/how-to-grow-from-mistakes-and-stop-beating-yourself-up/.

Chapter 2: *Multitasking Mishaps*

----

1. Suzanne Bates, "Careers and Sexes: Are Men Better than Women at Social Networking?" CNBC, July 26, 2011, http://www.cnbc.com/ id/43894882/Are_Men_Better_than_Women_at_Social_Networking; Marcia Sirota, "What Men and Women Really Want (and How to Get it)," Huffington Post, November 9, 2011, http://www.huffingtonpost.ca/ marcia-sirota/what-men-and-women-really_b_1078012.html; anonymous, "Sex-Life Road Test," Redbook.com, http://www.redbookmag.com/love-sex/ positions-toys-techniques/slrt-minty-delight-clone.

2. Christine Rosen, "The Myth of Multitasking," *The New Atlantis: A Journal of Technology and Society*, no. 20, (Spring 2008): 105-110.

3. Ibid.

4. Krista Milne, "Compartmentalize at Work, a Balance that Works," Examiner.com, March 12, 2010, http://www.examiner.com/article/ compartmentalize-at-work-a-balance-that-works.

5. Cara Gardenswartz, PhD, "Are you a working mom? Learn how to deal with working mom guilt," MyJoyOnline.com, September 24, 2011, http:// lifestyle.myjoyonline.com/pages/relationships/201101/59753.php.

6. Lylah M. Alphonse, "Can Your Kids 'Catch' Your Stress," Yahoo! Shine Parenting blog, September 23, 2011, http://shine.yahoo.com/parenting/can-your-kids-catch-your-stress-2565619.html.

7. Henrik Edberg, "8 Ways to Return to the Present Moment," The Positivity Blog, February 2008, http://www.positivityblog.com/index.php/2008/02/15/8-ways-to-return-to-the-present-moment/.

8. Phillippa Lally, et al, "How Are Habits Formed: Modeling Habit Formation in the Real World," *European Journal of Social Psychology* 40, no. 6 (July 16, 2009): 998-1009.

9. Lynn Thynn, MD, "Staying with the Moment," Living Meditation, Living Insight, Buddha Dharma Education Association, http://www.buddhanet.net/lmed2.htm.

Chapter 3: Unexcused Absences

1. Rachel Lucas-Thompson, Wendy Goldberg, and JoAnn Prause, "Maternal Work Early in the Lives of Children and Its Distal Associations with Achievement and Behavior Problems: A Meta-Analysis," American Psychological Assocation, *Psychological Bulletin,* vol. 136, no. 6 (2010): 915–942.

2. Nichole Smith, "Fumbling My Way Through Raising a Family and a Home Since 1995," The Guilty Parent website, http://www.theguiltyparent.com/category/family-2/.

3. Katherine Reynolds Lewis, "Dealing With Working Moms Guilt, Whether You Love or Hate Your Job," About.com, http://workingmoms.about.com/od/todaysworkingmoms/a/workguilt.htm.

Chapter 4: On the Road Again

1. Edward Chalmers, "Make the Most of Business Trips," Power and Money, Askmen.com, http://www.askmen.com/money/successful_100/118b_success.html.

2. Phaedra Cucina, "Make Mom's Business Trips Easier on Everyone," *Chicago Tribune*, March 8, 2009, http://articles.chicagotribune.com/2009-03-08/features/0903050651_1_kids-car-seats-special.

3. Susan Bartell, *The Top 50 Questions Kids Ask: The Best Answers to the Toughest, Smartest, and Most Awkward Questions Kids Always Ask* (Sourcebooks, March 2010).

4. Jill Frank, "3 Simple Ways to Take the Pain out of Business Travel—for Traveling Moms," Smart Women Travelers, March 7, 2009, http://www.smartwomentravelers.com/2009/07/3-simple-ways-to-take-the-pain-out-of-business-travel-%E2%80%93-for-traveling-moms/.

5. Bartell, *The Top 50 Questions Kids Ask*.

6. Barbara Meltz, "When Mom Has to Travel for Work," Child Caring, Boston.com Moms, January 27, 2010, http://www.boston.com/community/moms/blogs/child_caring/2010/01/whem_mom_has_to.html.

7. Anuradha Koli, "When Mommy Hits the Road: Helping Your Little One to Cope while You Are Away," *Working Mother*'s Growing Up blog, January 2008, http://www.workingmother.com/2008/1/home/when-mommy-hits-road

8. Kim Schneider, "Business traveling moms treasure alone time, new poll shows," Mlive.com, November 12, 2009, http://www.mlive.com/travel/index.ssf/2009/11/business_traveling_moms_treasu.html.

9. Kathleen Barton, *The Balancing Act: Managing Work & Life* (Kathleen Barton Presentations, 2012), http://www.yourlifebalancecoach.com/products.htm.

10. Kenneth N. Condrell, PhD, "Understanding Your Toddler," Parenting Topics blog, Fischer-Price online, http://www.fisher-price.com/en_US/playtime/parenting/articlesandadvice/articledetail.html?article=tcm:169-20570.

11. Tracy Porpora, "7 Tips To Make Business Travel Easier for Working Moms," About.com, Working Moms blog, http://workingmoms.about.com/od/yourinternalmeasure/a/7-Tips-To-Make-Business-Travel-Easier-For-Working-Moms.htm.

12. Bartell, *The Top 50 Questions Kids Ask*.

Chapter 5: The School Drop-and-Dash

1. Benjamin Gissin, "Economics Outside the Box: Looking Beyond the Limits of Cash or Credit," *Barter News,* November/December 2007, http://www.barternews.com/pdf/looking_beyond.pdf.

2. Lori Link, "The Importance of Follow Through," *The Link Letter,* October 2005, http://resource-link.com/LinkLetter_htm/LinkLetter2005_10/page1.html.

3. Robyn Silverman, PhD, "How to Write a Thank-you Note to Teachers: 9 Things to Remember," Dr. Robyn Silverman Blog, June 13, 2008, http://www.drrobynsilverman.com/parenting-tips/how-to-write-a-thank-you-note-to-teachers-9-things-to-remember/.

4. Shann Vander Leek, "Working Women in the 21st Century—The Great Balancing Act," True Balance Life Coaching blog, 2007, http://www.true-balancelifecoaching.com/articles/working_women_in_the_21st_century.php.

Chapter 6: Friendship Hiatus

1. Cyndi Sarnoff-Ross, "The Importance of Friends," DailyStrength.org, April 22, 2009, http://www.dailystrength.org/health_blogs/cyndi/article/the-importance-of-friends

2. Rebecca Tatum, "Top 5 Reasons Parents Need Community," Family Friendly Blount blog, February 3, 2012, http://familyfriendlyblount.com/directories/top-5-reasons-parents-need-community/.

3. Peter McWilliams, "Mistakes, obviously, show us what needs improving. Without mistakes, how would we know what we had to work on?" Think exist.com, http://thinkexist.com/quotation/mistakes-obviously-show-us-what-needs-improving/357162.html.

4. Scott H. Young, "Don't Use Email for Conversations," Get More From Life blogspot, April 1, 2008, http://www.scotthyoung.com/blog/tag/technology/.

5. Mary Grogan, PhD, "Managing Expectations," Change It Column, Mind-food.com, October 5, 2010, http://www.mindfood.com/at-managing-expectations-change-it-blog.seo.

6. Dan Rockwell, "10 Power Tips for Leaders Who Talk Too Much," Leadership Freak blog, February 7, 2012, http://leadershipfreak.wordpress.com/2012/02/07/10-power-tips-for-leaders-who-talk-too-much/.

7. Alan Dunn, "Easy Tips for Hosting a Great Party," Every Day with Rachael Ray blogspot, http://www.rachaelraymag.com/easy-party-ideas/party-tips-ideas/easy-tips-for-hosting-a-great-party.

8. Meagan Francis, "Do You Suffer from I'm-So-Busy-Itis?" TheHappiest Mom.com, July 2, 2009, http://thehappiestmom.com/2009/07/do-you-suffer-from-im-so-busy-itis/.

9. Ann Pietrangelo, "Loneliness Harms Health: Why You Need Friends," Dr. DeanRaffelock.com, http://drdeanraffelock.com/custom_content/c_171018_lonliness_harms_health__why_you_need_fri.html.

10. Mama Bee, "Six Tips to Find New Working Mother Friends," the Mama Bee blog, April 14, 2009, http://themamabee.com/2009/04/14/six-tips-to-find-new-working-mother-friends/.

11. Rachel Wilkerson, "Lesson #114: How to Pick Up Women (Part 1)," The Life and Lessons of Rachel Wilkerson blogspot, January 4, 2012, http://www.rachelwilkerson.com/2012/01/04/how-to-make-adult-women-friends/.

12. Jan Yager, PhD, *365 Daily Affirmations for Friendship* (Hannacroix Creek Books, Inc., March 7, 2012).

Chapter 7: Odd Woman Out at Work

----

1. Taylor Wiles, "Bonding With Coworkers and Productivity in the Workplace," YPNation.com, April 7, 2010, http://www.ypnation.com/blogs/bonding-coworkers-and-productivity-workplace.

2. Ibid.

3. Beth Braccio Herring, "Smart Socializing with Coworkers," Careerbuilder.com, February 5, 2011, http://www.careerbuilder.com/Article/CB-2265-Workplace-Issues-Smart-socializing-with-co-workers/.

4. Ibid.

5. Denise Mann, "Good Relationships With Your Coworkers and a Convivial, Supportive Work Environment May Add Years to Your

Life, New Israeli Research Finds," Health Day column, USAToday. com, August 12, 2011, http://www.usatoday.com/news/health/story/ health/story/2011/08/Getting-along-with-co-workers-may-add-years-to-your-life/49946988/1?csp=34news&utm_source=feedburner&utm_ medium=feed&utm_campaign=Feed:+UsatodaycomHealth-TopStories+%28News+-+Health+-+Top+Stories%29.

6. Ibid.

7. Katrina Katsarelis, "Set Boundaries at the Office to Balance Work, Family," Jobs column, USAToday.com, November 26, 2002, http://www. usatoday.com/money/jobcenter/workplace/lifeworkfamily/2002-11-26-set-boundaries_x.htm.

8. Lizzie Skurnick, "That Should Be A Word," *New York Times Magazine* online, November 27, 2011, http://www.nytimes.com/interactive/2011/11/ 27/magazine/27-OPM.html.

9. Betsy Shaw, "Talking About Our Kids at Work," Babe's Blog, BabyCenter Blog, March 6, 2011, http://blogs.babycenter.com/mom_stories/talking-about-our-kids-at-work/?utm_source=twitterfeed&utm_medium=twitter.

10. Bill Lampton, *The Complete Communicator: Change Your Communication, Change Your Life* (Hillsboro Press, March 1999).

11. Linda Lowen, "Online Communities for Moms—Social Networking Sites for Moms: Connect With Other Mothers Around the Block and Around the World," Women's Issues column, About.com, May 5, 2008, http://womensissues.about.com/od/communityconnection/a/MomOnline-Comm.htm.

Chapter 8: *Heading Toward Burnout*

- -

1. R. Morgan Griffin, "Chronic Pain: Why You Shouldn't Ignore It," WebMD. com, February 26, 2007, http://www.webmd.com/pain-management/ features/chronic-pain-why-you-shouldnt-ignore-it.

2. Jenny Stamos Kovacs, "Blissing Out: 10 Relaxation Techniques to Reduce Stress on the Spot," WebMD.com, October 21, 2011, http:// www.webmd.com/balance/stress-management/features/blissing-out-10-relaxation-techniques-reduce-stress-spot.

3. Tanveer Naseer, "Got A Few Minutes? Why It's Important to Take That Daily Break," Tanveer Naseer, blogspot, December 3, 2009, http://www.tanveernaseer.com/why-its-important-to-take-that-daily-break/.

4. Cara Stein, "The Path to Productivity: Short Hours, More Breaks," WorkAwesome.com, March 25, 2012, http://workawesome.com/productivity/productivity-path-short-hours-more-breaks/.

5. Susan Cullen, "Stress Management," Quantum Learning Solutions blog, April 16, 2011, http://www.quantumlearn.com/blog/bid/52697/Stress-Management.

6. Patrick O'Neill, "Christmas Presence," Extraordinary Conversations blog, December 2011, http://www.extraordinaryconversations.com/newsletter/trans-leader-dec11.php.

7. Lama Surya Das, *BUDDHA STANDARD TIME: Awakening to the Infinite Possibilities of Now* (HarperOne, June 2011).

8. Jan Chozen, "Mindful Eating," in *The Mindfulness Revolution,* ed. Barry Boyce (Shambhala, March 2011).

9. Sarah Napthali, *Buddhism for Mothers of Schoolchildren: Finding Calm in the Chaos of the School Years* (Allen & Unwin, July 1, 2010).

10. O'Neill, "Christmas Presence," (see no. 6).

11. Steve Silberman, "Digital Mindfulness," in *The Mindfulness Revolution*.

12. Timethief, "Blogging and Cell Phone Addiction," One Cool Spot blog posting, September 4, 2011, http://onecoolsitebloggingtips.com/2011/09/04/blogging-and-cell-phone-addiction/.

13. Kovacs, "Blissing Out: 10 Relaxation Techniques to Reduce Stress on the Spot," WebMD.com.

14. Jason DeRusha, "Good Question: Why Do Women Still Do Most Chores?" CBS Minnesota online, August 10, 2011, http://minnesota.cbslocal.com/2011/08/10/good-question-why-do-women-still-do-most-of-the-chores/.

15. Anna D.H. Kudak and Carol J. Bruess, *What Happy Couples Do: Belly Button Fuzz & Bare-Chested Hugs—The Loving Little Rituals of Romance* (Fairview Press, January 2008).

16. Caitlan Friedman and Kimberly Yorio, *The Girls' Guide to Being a Boss (Without Being a Bitch): Valuable Lessons, Smart Suggestions, and True Stories for Succeeding as the Chick-in-Charge* (Broadway, May 2007).

17. "Annual Sleep in America Poll," National Sleep Foundation, March 7, 2011, http://www.sleepfoundation.org/article/press-release/annual-sleep-america-poll-exploring-connections-communications-technology-use.

Chapter 9: Blurred Boundaries at Home

----

1. Francis Horvath, "Work at Home: New Findings from the Current Population Survey," U.S. Department of Labor Women's Bureau, November 1986, http://bls.gov/opub/mlr/1986/11/art6full.pdf.
2. Brian Amble, "Homeworking: A Double-Edged Sword," Management-Issues.com, April 28, 2004, http://www.management-issues.com/2006/8/24/research/homeworking-a-double-edged-sword.asp.
3. Monte Enbysk, "10 Things You Need for a Home Business," Microsoft.com, 2011, http://www.microsoft.com/business/en-us/resources/startups/home-businesses/10-things-you-need-for-a-home-business.aspx?fbid=dLsf_NQtWbr
4. Virginia Woolf, *A Room of One's Own* (Penguin Books, UK; Revised edition, November 2009).
5. Alexis Rodrigo, "20 Productivity Tips for Work-at-Home Moms of Young Children," MyLifeShift.org, January 28, 2008, http://mylifeshift.org/20-productivity-tips-for-work-at-home-moms-of-young-children/.
6. Tammy Harrison, "Be Clear about Your Goals," ChristianMommies.com, April 2003, http://www.christian-mommies.com/special-features/just-for-moms/be-clear-about-your-goals/.
7. Gerry Hartigan, "Know Your Weaknesses and Build Your Strengths," EZineArticles.com, May 31, 2009, http://ezinearticles.com/?Know-Your-Weaknesses-and-Build-Your-Strengths&id=2577389.
8. Rodrigo, "20 Productivity Tips . . ." MyLifeShift.org.
9. Mikelann Valterra, "Make More Money!" *Seattle Woman Magazine* online, 2006, http://www.seattlewomanmagazine.com/articles/jan06-2.htm.
10. Tory Johnson and Robyn Freedman Spizman, *Will Work from Home: Earn the Cash without the Commute* (Berkeley Trade, August 2008).
11. Kate Lister and Tom Harnish, *Undress for Success: The Naked Truth about Making Money at Home* (Wiley, March 2009).

12. Katie Morell, "9 Productivity Tips for Working from Home," Open-Forum.com, January 9, 2012, http://www.openforum.com/articles/9-productivity-tips-for-working-from-home.

13. Christine Webber and David Delvin, "Stressbusting Techniques," Net-Doctor.com, December 7, 2010, http://www.netdoctor.co.uk/diseases/facts/stressbustingtechniques.htm.

14. Linda Wasmer Andrews, "10 Solutions for Work-at-Home Stress: Tips for a stress-free home office," *Psychology Today* online, November 5, 2011, http://www.psychologytoday.com/blog/minding-the-body/201111/10-solutions-work-home-stress.

Chapter 10: *Frenemies and Family Critics*

- -

1. Katherine Bowers, "What Moms Choose: Stay at Home or Work?" *The Working Mother Report 2011*, The Working Mother Research Institute, http://www.workingmother.com/special-reports/what-moms-choose-stay-home-or-work.

2. Rachel Lucas-Thompson, "Maternal Work Early in the Lives of Children" (see chapter 3, no. 1).

3. Susan Newman, PhD, "Go to Work, Mom, the Kids Will Be Fine," *Psychology Today* online, August 19, 2011, http://www.psychologytoday.com/blog/singletons/201108/go-work-mom-the-kids-will-be-fine.

4. Ibid.

5. Mark Tyrell, "Stop Being So Defensive: Why People Get Defensive and 3 Tips for Breaking the Habit," Uncommon Help blog, 2010, http://www.uncommonhelp.me/articles/stop-being-so-defensive/.

6. Alexander Kjerulf, "How Not to Let Annoying People Annoy You," PositiveSharing.com, May 3, 2007, http://positivesharing.com/2007/05/how-not-to-let-annoying-people-annoy-you/.

7. Diane Mapes, "Toxic Friends? 8 in 10 People Endure Poisonous Pals," TodayHealth column, MSNBC.com, August 22, 2011, http://today.msnbc.msn.com/id/44205822/ns/today-today_health/t/toxic-friends-people-endure-poisonous-pals/#.T8-gG9WJd8E.

8. Emilie Wapnick, "Criticism Stings and That's Okay," PuttyLike.com, February 17, 2011, http://puttylike.com/criticism-stings-and-thats-okay/.

9. Jonathan Kandell, "Stand Up for Yourself, Be Assertive!" University of Maryland Counseling Center, http://www.counseling.umd.edu/Selfhelp/sh_asser.htm?t=print.php.

10. John C. Maxwell, "When You Get Kicked in the Rear, You Know You're Out in Front," The John Maxwell Team blog, January 3, 2011, http://johnmaxwellteam.com/blog/rear-kick/.

11. Ibid.

12. Heather Hatfield, "Less Friend, More Foe," Women's Health column, WebMD.com, 2006, http://women.webmd.com/guide/toxic-friends?page=2.

13. Sherrie Bourg Carter, "Dealing with People Who Drain You," *Psychology Today* online, March 3, 2012, http://www.psychologytoday.com/blog/high-octane-women/201203/dealing-people-who-drain-you.

14. Katherine Bowers, "What Moms Choose: Stay at Home or Work?" (see no. 1).

15. Lori Deschene, "10 Ways to Deal with Negative People," TinyBuddha.com, http://tinybuddha.com/blog/how-to-deal-with-negative-people-or-difficult-people/.

Chapter 11: Sick Days and Other Setbacks

- -

1. Kate Fleming, "One-Third of Working Moms Have Sent Sick Child to School or Daycare According to Working Mother Survey," PRWeb, February 2007, http://www.prweb.com/releases/2007/02/prweb505426.htm.

2. "Give it 100 Percent," Topic of the Month column, Juvenile Products Manufacturer's Association online, May 2011, http://www.jpma.org/content/parents/topic-of-the-month?page=13.

3. "Fever Facts," Kidsgrowth.com, http://www.kidsgrowth.com/resources/articledetail.cfm?id=1087.

4. Sarah Baker, "How to Care for a Sick Child and Still Make Deadlines," WAHM.com, http://www.wahm.com/articles/how-to-care-for-a-sick-child-and-still-make-deadlines.html.

5. Vincent Iannelli, MD, "Why Do My Kids Get Sick So Much," About.com Pediatrics blog, http://pediatrics.about.com/library/ask/blask_121901.htm.

6. "S: Sick Days Paid," MomRising.org, http://www.momsrising.org/issues_and_resources/paid-sick-days-all.

7. Ibid.

8. Sabrina O'Mallone, "Superwoman Doesn't Exist," The Mustard Seed Preschool and Childcare Center online, http://www.gotomustardseed.com/superwoman.htm.

9. Marianne Schwab, "Working Moms Vacation Dilemma," Best Travel Deal Tips online, http://www.best-travel-deals-tips.com/working-moms-vacation.html.

10. Ibid.

ACKNOWLEDGMENTS

Let me start by thanking all of the fabulous working moms who shared with me their hopes, worries, confessions, and strategies around juggling career and parenting. I've tested many of your ideas already and appreciate what an enormous difference they've made in my life.

I am grateful to Laney Katz Becker, my agent, who is wise and steadfast, and has been an ongoing mentor to me in learning the business side of publishing. Merrik Bush-Pirkle, my editor and psychic twin, I am so appreciative of your amazing talent, hilarious emails, and always encouraging words. Thank you to Brooke Warner, executive editor at Seal Press, who believed in this book from the get-go and found me my home there, and to my enthusiastic publicist Eva Zimmerman. Thanks to Tabitha Lahr for making my book look pretty on the inside, and to Kate Basart for making it inviting on the outside.

Thank you to the many experts who took the time to answer my endless questions, and offered considerate real-world advice. I know I am a better parent for having connected with you: Susan Bartell, F. Diane Barth, Kathleen Barton, Amy Brinn, Sarah Buckwalter, Kathy Caprino, Sherrie Bourg Carter, Carin Goldstein, Joshua Eagle, Sandi Stewart Epstein, Susanne Gaddis, Cathy Greenberg, Lara Galloway, Kathleen Hall, Beth Braccio Hering, Allegra Inganni, Lynn Kenney, Irene S. Levine, Lizzy Mc, Susan Newman, Barbara Pachter, Aurelia Palubeckas, Carl Pickhardt,

Nichole Smith, Amy Kossoff Smith, Rachel Starck, Nicole Taggart, Roseanne Tobey, Leslie Truex, Meri Wallace, Jan Yager, Julie Zeff and Laurie Zelinger.

I am indebted to my mom, Bobbi Silver, who in addition to being a good friend, modeled for me what it looks like to be fired up to go to work. To Jules Spotts, an expert quoted in this book, my family would not run nearly as well without you. Thanks for ongoing support from the Silver family and the Chasin crew.

Big joyous hugs to my friends (many of whom appear in the pages of this book), who keep me grounded and make me laugh so hard that I sometimes pee my pants a little: Lev Baesh, Caroline Berz, Jenny Berz, Betsy Block, Kathy Bloomfield, Shelley Blue, Jacquie Boas, Susanna Bray, Kerry David, Wendy Diamond, Joshua Eagle, Lindsey Fieldman, Lisa Frattini, Alanna Mallon, Tanya Michaelson, Pam Templer, Robyn Schaefer, and Dana Waring Bateman.

Thank you to the wonderful staff of the Hadassah-Brandeis Institute, where I work as an editor. I feel lucky to be amongst such brilliant women who truly value life balance.

Boldest thanks to my husband, Ezra, and daughter, Risa. You are not only the loves of my life, but the source of top-notch research material.

And, last, a quick thank-you to the makers of Trader Joe's Bay Blend Ultra Dark Roast for helping me find my desk each morning.

ABOUT THE AUTHOR

Michelle Cove is the coauthor of the national bestseller *I'm Not Mad, I Just Hate You!: A New Understanding of Mother-Daughter Conflict* (Viking, 1999), which was profiled on national talk shows, including *The Oprah Winfrey Show* and the *Today Show*. She is also the author of *Seeking Happily Ever After: Navigating the Ups and Downs of Being Single Without Losing Your Mind* (Tarcher, 2010), which is based on her award-winning documentary *Seeking Happily Ever After* (Lionsgate). Currently, Michelle is making the documentary *One and Only,* about one-child families. She is also the editor of *614: the HBI ezine*, an online magazine that explores hot topics for Jewish women. Visit www.michellecove.com for more information.

SELECTED TITLES FROM SEAL PRESS

For more than thirty years, Seal Press has published groundbreaking books. By women. For women.

No Excuses: 9 Ways Women Can Change How We Think about Power, by Gloria Feldt. $18.00, 978-1-58005-388-4. From the boardroom to the bedroom, public office to personal relationships, feminist icon Gloria Feldt offers women the tools they need to walk through the doors of opportunity and achieve parity with men.

Book by Book: The Complete Guide to Creating Mother-Daughter Book Clubs, by Cindy Hudson. $16.95, 978-1-58005-299-3. Everything moms need to know to start a tradition that builds strong bonds and opens new avenues of conversation with their daughters.

The Maternal Is Political: Women Writers at the Intersection of Motherhood and Social Change, edited by Shari MacDonald Strong. $15.95, 978-1-58005-243-6. Exploring the vital connection between motherhood and social change, The Maternal Is Political features thirty powerful literary essays by women striving to make the world a better place for children and families—both their own and other women's.

Bringing in Finn: An Extraordinary Surrogacy Story, by Sara Connell. $24.00, 978-1-58005-410-2. A remarkable, moving story of one woman's hard-fought, often painful, journey to motherhood—and the surrogacy experience that changed her family's life.

Seeing Ezra: A Mother's Story of Autism, Unconditional Love, and the Meaning of Normal, by Kerry Cohen. $16.00, 978-1-58005-433-1. An inspirational chronicle of a mother's struggle to protect her son from a system that seeks to compartmentalize and "fix" his autism, and of her journey toward accepting and valuing him for who he is—just as he is.

Kissing Outside the Lines: A True Story of Love and Race and Happily Ever After, by Diane Farr. $16.00, 978-1-58005-396-9. Actress and columnist Diane Farr's unapologetic, and often hilarious, look at the complexities of interracial/ethnic/religious/what-have-you love.

Find Seal Press Online
www.SealPress.com
www.Facebook.com/SealPress
Twitter: @SealPress